Practice, Power, and Forms of Life

Practice, Power, and Forms of Life

Sartre's Appropriation of Hegel and Marx

TERRY PINKARD

The University of Chicago Press
Chicago and London

The University of Chicago Press, Chicago 60637
The University of Chicago Press, Ltd., London
© 2022 by The University of Chicago
All rights reserved. No part of this book may be used or reproduced in any manner
whatsoever without written permission, except in the case of brief quotations
in critical articles and reviews. For more information, contact the University of
Chicago Press, 1427 E. 60th St., Chicago, IL 60637.
Published 2022
Printed in the United States of America

31 30 29 28 27 26 25 24 23 22   1 2 3 4 5

ISBN-13: 978-0-226-81324-0 (cloth)
ISBN-13: 978-0-226-81547-3 (e-book)
DOI: https://doi.org/10.7208/chicago/9780226815473.001.0001

Library of Congress Cataloging-in-Publication Data

Names: Pinkard, Terry P., author.
Title: Practice, power, and forms of life : Sartre's appropriation of Hegel and Marx /
    Terry Pinkard.
Description: Chicago : University of Chicago Press, 2022. | Includes bibliographical
    references and index.
Identifiers: LCCN 2021021122 | ISBN 9780226813240 (cloth) | ISBN 9780226815473
    (ebook)
Subjects: LCSH: Sartre, Jean-Paul, 1905–1980. | Marx, Karl, 1818–1883. | Hegel, Georg
    Wilhelm Friedrich, 1770–1831.
Classification: LCC B2430.S34 P545 2022 | DDC 194—dc23
LC record available at https://lccn.loc.gov/2021021122

♾ This paper meets the requirements of ANSI/NISO Z39.48-1992
(Permanence of Paper).

To Susan

Contents

Preface

Sartre's *Critique of Dialectical Reason* appeared in 1960 to great fanfare, had great influence on a variety of people and movements—Fanon supposedly lectured to the revolutionaries fighting the colonial powers in Africa on some of the topics of the *Critique*[1]—and then rapidly fell from fashion. In part, this was because the book was seen at the outset as Sartre's attempt to fuse together his earlier existentialism with his later Marxism. As the appeal of existentialism rapidly waned and as Marxism came to be displaced by other social theories at the time, the idea of fusing two dead movements itself also lost much of its attraction. Another blow to Sartre's reputation was Foucault's dismissal of the book as a "magnificent" but also "pathetic" attempt to use the nineteenth century to think about the twentieth.[2] Foucault's offhanded dismissal of the 1960 book looked to be its epitaph before its burial, and 1989 seemed to be the funeral.

Another reason for the decline in interest in the work is Sartre's own fault. By anybody's standard, even for those who regularly deal with difficult texts, the *Critique* is an unduly obscure work. Simone de Beauvoir relates that it was in fact the only manuscript she had ever seen Sartre—who normally was a stickler for correcting, correcting again, and then correcting once more—compose without making virtually any corrections.[3] He wrote the book in a rush helped along by a heavy use of amphetamines—easily available over the counter in France at the time—to push himself each day ever harder and to keep up his pace.[4] Since he was also at the time one of the world's most famous intellectuals, he was therefore able to get away with producing for publication the kind of book that an unknown philosopher in the provinces, hoping against hope to find any audience at all for his or her work, could only hazily dream about.

The idea that the book was the reconciliation or fusion between existentialism and Marxism has lasted, but it is not the best way to see it, nor was it really Sartre's central intent in writing the book. Independent of the so-called fusion of Marxism and existentialism, Sartre had two different although related projects in the *Critique of Dialectical Reason,* and the two themselves were, and by and large still are, conflated with each other. There is the project articulated in *The Problem of Method* (presented more or less as a kind of introduction or preface to the original French edition), which is later and finally pursued in Sartre's great labor of love, his volumes on Flaubert, and in his writings on the history of France and the Russian Revolution (most of which were unpublished in his lifetime).[5] At the time of writing *The Problem of Method* (which was a few years prior to finishing the *Critique*), Sartre perhaps still had in mind the fusion of existentialism and Marxism, and probably the actual process of composing the piece stimulated the turn in Sartre's thought itself. Although it seems clear that he thought the two projects were internally related to each other, they were nonetheless different.

The project outlined in *The Problem of Method* has to do with how we are to pursue a kind of project in history, sociology, psychology, and biography that will help us comprehend the singularity of actors (such as Flaubert) while at the same time locating them as representatives of larger social forces and ideas, and how to do this without either reducing or belittling the singularity of individual subjects to the larger social forces, or reducing the social forces to mere summary rules of the different actors — nicely encapsulated in Sartre's famous line "Valéry is a petit bourgeois intellectual, no doubt about it. But not every petit bourgeois intellectual is Valéry."[6] The *Critique,* on the other hand, is concerned more with a more formal theory of agency and of individual and collective action, carried out in light of Sartre's newly found appreciation for the Hegelian side of the Marxism to which he had become attracted after 1946. The *Critique* is self-consciously a successor to the tradition of German idealism as it had been transformed and challenged by Marx's "materialist" reinterpretation of that line of thought and of Marxism itself as it had been further reworked by (what came to be called) Western Marxism (with the names of Lukács, Bloch, Korsch, and Gramsci as the boldfaced names in the movement). The *Critique*'s project of course underpinned the Flaubert project in a very specific way, but it was nonetheless crucially different from it.[7]

The turn to a more Hegelian version of Marxism was new for Sartre. It is certainly debatable just how deeply steeped Sartre was in Hegelian philosophy in his early work, even in his early masterpiece, *Being and Nothingness,* with its whole array of Hegelian-inspired terminology (most famously, that of the for-itself and the in-itself).[8] By the time of the *Critique*, however, he seems to have more fully studied at least large parts of Hegel's *Phenomenology*, almost certainly by way of Jean Hyppolite's masterful translation of it, and he was almost certainly influenced by Hyppolite's contemporary writings on the topics of Hegel, Marx, and Heidegger. (He certainly read Hyppolite's sterling commentary on Hegel's *Phenomenology*.) One of the interpretive hypotheses I put to work here is that Sartre, by way of Hyppolite's (and to an extent Maurice Merleau-Ponty's) writings, rethought his relation both to Heidegger's thought (particularly the later Heidegger) and more specifically to Hegelianism, all of which in turn led Sartre to rethink, really from the ground up, the positions he had staked out earlier in his career, while still holding fast to many of them.[9] In particular, by way of the later Heidegger's work—especially after Heidegger's 1946 *Letter on Humanism* (published in 1947), which was (and is) a reply to and a trenchant criticism of Sartre's 1945 *Existentialism Is a Humanism* (published in 1946)[10]—Sartre was led to fundamentally rethink some very basic views on meaning and practice, and he brought those to bear, so I will try to show, on his late rapprochement with some of Hegel's ideas while maintaining his distance from what he understood the Hegelian position to be.

Given the controversies that have always surrounded Sartre's writings, it is no easy matter to think about how best to approach Sartre's later thought. There are of course many ways of looking at the history of philosophy. One way is straightforwardly historical: one looks at who read what, who taught whom, who could have known or met whom, and so on. Another way is look at a few ideas and how they move across time and different writers. Sometimes that involves one person reading another, but sometimes it does not. In the case of Hegel and Sartre, it is clear that Sartre read Hegel, reread Hegel, and read people who wrote about Hegel.

Sometimes there is the interpretive strategy of writing the philosophy out of the work and understanding it in terms of how it contributed to a particular worldview at the time or was an expression of a particular political movement. In Sartre's case, the fall from grace of his reputation motivated some to see the *Critique* as best understood in terms of being a kind of political intervention on Sartre's part in a particular episode in French political life at the time it was written.[11] It certainly was that, but seeing it in only these terms radically shortchanges it. Seeing it that way simply reworks the error of concluding that once one has said that Valéry is a petit bourgeois intellectual, one has said all that really needs to be said about Valéry.

Nonetheless, there is a space of ideas that crisscross among Sartre, Heidegger, Hegel, Merleau-Ponty, and sometimes there is overlap.[12] (One could add Wittgenstein to that list of crisscrossing ideas although the influence of either on the other is zero.) A larger history would take into account all the other interlocking ways these ideas get formed, transformed, and redrawn. In this case, one would need to go into German neo-Kantianism, the influence of Schopenhauer at the time, the role Nietzsche played for all these people, and that would be just the start.[13] Instead, I am interested in the role that dialectic played in both Hegel's and Sartre's work and in the way that the concern with dialectic crisscrosses with some but certainly not all of Wittgenstein's ideas about thinking, understanding, and meaning across his works.[14] Behind all of that is the well-documented and immense influence of Heidegger's *Being and Time* on Sartre's early works and how it influenced Sartre's reworking of his early fascination with Husserl and his own take on the later Heidegger, his newfound appreciation for Hegel, his involvement with Marxism, and his conception of the relation between meaning and practice. However, or so I will argue, some of the very basic ideas taken from the later Heidegger, starting with his *Letter on Humanism*, played a very significant role in Sartre's later thought. (Not for nothing did Raymond Aron, Sartre's youthful comrade and middle-aged political opponent, remark that Sartre was "the most Germanic of French philosophers."[15])

At first, however, it is important to set the scene for Sartre's *Critique* by going through some of the ideas and arguments he made earlier in his career that carry over into the *Critique*, even if many of his earlier ideas were discarded or transformed in the ensuing years. In particular, it is worth considering his arguments about what could be called his move from a more monadic view of subjectivity in his early writing to a view of agency as intrinsically reciprocal. It was through this "reciprocity" conception of agency that he integrated some newly rethought Hegelian views with some Marxist views as they appeared in light of this kind of neo-Hegelianism circulating at that time, together with his appropriation and transformation of some of the later Heidegger's views.[16] This integration of Hegel, Marx, and the later Heidegger into Sartre's own original conception led Sartre into a new view by at least 1960 and thereafter.

Sartre did not simply jettison his older views when he got to the *Critique*. He held onto some of them but saw how the case he thought he had made earlier for many of his views about subjectivity had in fact—one might say rather dialectically—transformed themselves into a case for something else. Sartre's earlier thought forms the brief against which the case he makes after 1960 has to be framed.

As I noted, the most common interpretation of the *Critique of Dialectical Reason* is that it is Sartre's attempt to render two of his positions compatible

with each other: his early existentialism, and his assumption of some form
of Marxism in the 1950s. Seeing it that way means seeing it as starting with
two types of commitments as given (both existentialist and Marxist commitments) and then seeing how each can be accounted in a way that renders what
would seem like fundamental incompatibilities to be compatible—such as
agency being understood as freedom, and agency being understood in terms
of vectors of competing social forces.

It is not, however, how Sartre himself describes the project of the *Critique* (as a combination of two otherwise fixed views, whose fixedness will, of
course, be unsettled by the combination). He describes it in a more Kantian-
Hegelian manner: "This is a matter of *formal* intelligibility. By this I mean that
we must understand the bonds between *praxis*, as self-conscious, and all the
complex multiplicities which are organized through it and in which it loses
itself as *praxis* in order to become *praxis-process.*"[17] In turn, that amounts
to the demand for "requiring Marxists to establish their method *a priori*,"[18]
which itself rules out simply accepting Marxism and then seeing if it can be
squared with existentialism (or vice versa). The *Critique* should thus be understood as Sartre understood it, an investigation that is organized formally,
fully in keeping with his intentions about the status of his earlier work, *The
Transcendence of the Ego.*

The point about formality is not a slip of the pen. In the book, Sartre
stresses over and over again the "formality" of his enterprise. The *Critique* is
thus more like the *Phenomenology of Spirit* in its stated aims than it is like any
kind of empirically based philosophy.[19] However, in a way very much like the
Phenomenology, it is rich in historical examples, all of which are insightful
and challenging, all of which are revelatory, but which can also sometimes
obscure the main point of the endeavor, which is to make sense of agency
in general.

There is an easily foreseen objection to the line of interpretation proposed
here: for most of the 1950s until his death, Sartre was a political militant of the
Left, and he saw his work as contributing to the leftist politics he espoused
at the time. Moreover, he certainly saw the *Critique* in that light, and it was
certainly the political context in which he found himself that motivated him
to write the work. Those who follow Sartre in that line of thought might well
be suspicious that what is really being proposed here is a suggestion that we
disregard Sartre's politics and, going against the grain of all of his professed
intentions, see the *Critique* and his other writings orbiting around it as somehow detached philosophical works that stand outside of the politics of his day
or his own professed politics. Now, it is certainly true that Sartre thought of
his work as political in the way I just described. However, it is also true that

Sartre also thought that this kind of pure investigation was needed for the kind of political ends he had in mind but was not constructed instrumentally to achieve those ends (in other words, his book was not an ideology but a work of philosophy).

Another suspicion might be that this takes us away from the wealth of examples Sartre offers in favor of a more pure and austere but therefore less phenomenologically rich account. Sartre's multiple examples are dazzling. He was a gifted writer and a remarkable phenomenologist. However, the status of phenomenological description in the *Critique* is one of the points of contention in interpretations of it. It does not seem to me—but this will have to be shown in the exposition—that attending more carefully to the examples would change this interpretation, although completely ignoring the examples would surely shortchange Sartre's appeal and would likely distort the overall view. (Only Hegel himself rivals Sartre in coming up with the sharp dialectical metaphors and illustrations for what is going on.) Sartre was constructing a formal theory, but he clearly also wanted to show how it could at least illuminate some basic real, urgent, and not just imagined political and social issues.

A third suspicion would be that this is investing too much sociality into Sartre's later thought, a misgiving that will come naturally to those who think that his later thought is by and large continuous with his earlier thought and the basic ideas about agency and sociality are the same in both books. That can only be allayed by laying out the alternative.

As its title indicates, Sartre's book is about dialectical reason. Although Sartre admitted later in an interview that his earlier work (he was speaking of *Being and Nothingness*) was not dialectical at all (something he said he regretted), his conception of dialectic goes back to a long-standing theme in all his work, in particular, to his earlier sharp metaphysical contrast between free agency and the rest of nature.[20] For Sartre, dialectical reasoning only fits the kinds of things that demand a teleological account of themselves. In the terms of *Being and Nothingness*, that would be "being-for-itself" (human reality) and nothing else. In his later work, starting with the *Critique* of 1960 and developing itself in the writings for a volume on ethics and politics, some of which surfaced in his lectures in Italy between 1961 and 1964 and some of which surfaced in the projected but never given lectures on ethics at Cornell in 1965 (and some of which appear in the unfinished second volume of the *Critique*, which only saw posthumous publication in 1985), Sartre broadened the concept of agency to include the concept of life in general in addition to self-consciousness. In doing so, he also began to displace the centrality of the concept of self-consciousness in his work to speak instead of a kind of mutual self-relation of agents. By the time he had formulated the *Critique*, he had come to think of the dialectic in the terms in which Hegel speaks of the move from self-consciousness to spirit in his 1807 work, *Phenomenology of Spirit*, as the move from an "I that is a We, and the We that is an I," which was the place at which dialectical thought was appropriate.

To get there, Sartre rethought his earlier views about agency into a view that made reciprocity among agents essential to agency itself. The "I" and the "We" are formally prior to but have as their content the relations formed in the second person of agents to each other as embedded in historically distinct forms of life. To work that set of ideas out, he had to develop a distinctive concept of human habit and disposition in which the spontaneity of agency cannot be thought outside of the necessities that come to it from its own place in the natural order, the social order, and in history. That in turn led him to a new understanding of how the rationality of revolt is to be comprehended and to the way in which collective actions require us to think of purposes that inform the collective that are not the additive result of individual purposes. Sartre argued that there is a first-person plural apperception ("We") alongside that of the first-person singular apperception ("I") that does not require there to be anything like a separate element to the set of persons that each individually make up the "We." Earlier in his career, he had staked his claims on the impossibility of any fully apperceptive "We." In the *Critique*, he reversed himself on that.

In particular, as already noted, all of this required a reappropriation of some facets of Hegelianism—all the while firmly committing himself to what he understood to be an anti-Hegelian view—together with, so I shall argue, Sartre's new appropriation of the later Heidegger's thought as it appeared in Heidegger's *Letter on Humanism* and his other later writings. In both Hegel and the later Heidegger, he found the idea that the dualism between the active and the passive was not a final, absolute dichotomy, and that there was a way of understanding the relation of practice to individual act that should not be thought in terms of which part produced the other part, or where the "meaning" came from. Although this way of putting things was also to be found in Hegel, Sartre thought it appeared there only in a distorted way. In particular, it was by way of this rethinking of Hegelianism and his appropriation and transformation of the views of the later Heidegger that Sartre then worked his way through his complicated relation to Marxism, and this had to do with Sartre's rethinking of his views on the apperceptive "We." The result was, I argue, not an eclectic or syncretic combination of these views but something new and different. Along the way he developed some themes in common with Wittgenstein, although Wittgenstein played no role at all in his forming those views. I will argue that something very much like the Hegelian and even the Wittgensteinian conception of "forms of life" plays a key role in Sartre's thought.

To see how he got there and what this all means, we have to start more or less at the beginning. The issues he raised for himself in *The Transcendence of the Ego* turned out to be the issues that were driving Sartre in his later work. His later work, to use one of his own terms, was a *dépassement* of his earlier work, a way in which his earlier views were "passed" and thus "overtaken" by his later ones. A very short and highly condensed overview of his earlier work shows how, in a nutshell, the issues that obsessed him involved the complexities of "self-relation in relation to an other."

The first part of this book tries to show, however briefly, that the early work set the terms for the later work even though the later work had to go beyond it. To show that, I have left most (but certainly not all) of the citations from Sartre's texts in the endnotes (sometimes offered as direct answers to the skeptical question "Where does Sartre say *that*?"). This allows for a more narrative exposition of Sartre's thought in the main text while leaving the more scholarly tug and tussle with other scholars for the notes.

1

Spontaneity and Inertia

1. The Background: The Form of the "I"

Sartre begins *The Transcendence of the Ego* (1936) with a statement of his basic and, at the time, surprising thesis—namely, that the ego, the "I" does not "inhabit" consciousness but is "outside, in the world . . . like the ego of another."[1] Sartre's focus from *The Transcendence of the Ego* through *Being and Nothingness* all the way to the *Critique of Dialectical Reason* is on subjectivity, and, even more specifically in the earlier work, on self-consciousness. His guiding idea is that a substantive "I"—or what we might think of the "I" as an object of awareness—as that which underlies consciousness (or "inhabits" it) is itself unintelligible. Why? First, the idea that self-consciousness is a subject making itself the object of its awareness leads to an infinite regress. If self-consciousness consists in the subject being conscious of itself as an object, then the subject that is aware of the subject that is not itself an object is not itself self-conscious unless it has, as it were, another subject (another version of itself) conscious of it, ad infinitum.[2] Or, as Sartre also puts it, "if the *I* is a part of consciousness, there would then be *two I's*: the *I* of the reflective consciousness and the *I* of the reflected consciousness,"[3] thus requiring yet another "I" to identify them.[4] That is Sartre's first step.

However, in the second step, he argues that although that model of self-consciousness is unintelligible, a form of self-relation must be at work in all thought and action for it to be thought and action. This much is established phenomenologically: if one does not know what one is doing, one is not actually doing anything; instead, things are simply happening. What holds the action together as an action and not merely a disconnected series of events is the thought of what the agent is to do, is doing, or has done. The doing is an expression of the thought, not just an event triggered by some kind of internal mental state. However, if this form of self-consciousness, which the

phenomenology of self-consciousness takes as essential to itself, is necessary
to all consciousness, it cannot be a form of consciousness that has the same
logical form as consciousness of an object. Consciousness of an object is, in
Sartre's terms, "positional" or "thetic" consciousness: X is conscious of Y as
something that transcends itself. Consciousness of self, however, would have
to be non-positional (non-thetic). It would have to be aware of itself to count
as consciousness, but it cannot be aware of itself as an object of awareness.[5]

There is thus in Sartre's phrase an "unreflected consciousness," that is,
a consciousness that knows what it is doing but is not necessarily accompa-
nied by a separate reflective act about what it is doing. To bolster this, Sartre
draws on examples taken from absorptive activities—as in "I am trying to
hang a picture" or "I am repairing the rear tire"—to bring out how it is that
you know what you are doing when you are doing it, and this knowledge is
brought out or made explicit when, for example, one is asked what one is doing.[6] This is not a matter of explicit inference, as if being asked the question
"What are you doing?" I infer on the basis of some evidence that I am trying
to hang the picture. (It is neither an inductive nor a deductive inference.) Not
all actions are assertions of some explicit content, but assertions share with all
actions a kind of dependence on knowing what it is that I am doing as I am
doing it.[7] Thus, Sartre endorses the Kantian claim that the "I think" *must be
able* to accompany all my representations, not that it does nor that it actually
must accompany all of them.

Sartre's point is about the form of the activity, which the "I think" expresses, namely, that it is already there as constitutive of human activity in
terms of the self-relation that constitutes the subject as a subject (or the agent
as an agent). The "I think" is not a "making explicit" of something that is
already fully formed but only implicit in the activity. It is something else, on
Sartre's view, namely, a way of showing or exhibiting the meaning of an activity, which he will later refine into a conception of showing and "carrying on"
the background practices that form the horizons of the activity in question.
"Hanging the picture" and "repairing the rear tire" both suppose that I am
part of a practice. It is not that the practice stands apart from a separate "entity" that is the activity that presupposes the practice but that the practice and
the concrete activities that embody it are mutually included in each other.
Each is the actualization of the other rather than being two separate things
that stand in relations of having a presupposition and being a presupposition.

In the early work, Sartre concludes that the "I" is only intelligible as something that is posited by reflection as belonging to non-thetic (non-positional)
consciousness but which is actually external (or "transcendent") to such consciousness. The bare "I" does not imply or contain any mental states, desires,

and so on. They, like tables and rocks, are items in the world, to which I have no more immediate—non-inferential—access than I do to the artifacts, natural objects and social formations of that world. What in fact seems like the "I" of non-thetic consciousness is thus actually nothing. It is something akin to an infinitely contracted point to which we reflectively (and wrongly) ascribe to the "I" that we encounter in reflection.[8] The unreflected, non-thetic "I" is defined only by its form, and the world as I find it, before I reflect on it, has no place in it for such an "I."[9] Thus, if anything, what seems to be the "I" is just another object in the world. What Sartre claims for this is not that we are not self-conscious, but that self-consciousness cannot be fully formulated in terms of the "consciousness of an object" (i.e., in terms of "intentionality" in Sartre's Husserlian formulation). It must be formulated in terms of something else. What Sartre is denying is that self-consciousness can be any kind of intuition of anything like an underlying substrate, a subject-thing.

The unity of the agent that finds expression in the reflectively articulated "I think" (or "I do," etc.) is defined by the form of its unity, not by the unintelligible existence of a different I-substrate that has the properties of the agent (his projects, mental states, fears, deeds, etc.). The expression, "I," in this usage does not refer to anything because there is nothing to which it could refer. It is, as Sartre would later say, a "nothingness," a mere form of unity of an agent that is not meaningless but whose meaning just is this empty form.[10] This unity is the result of what Sartre calls the "monstrous spontaneity" of consciousness, that is, of agency in general. In this "monstrous spontaneity," Sartre notes that "consciousness" projects its own spontaneity into the concept of the ego as if it required for itself a "false representation of itself," namely, as something that looks as if it would satisfy the need for "consciousness" to be its own foundation, to be purely self-instituting (a need that according to Sartre's ontology of agency cannot in principle be satisfied).[11]

The idea of agency that emerges at least in its kernel in *The Transcendence of the Ego* continues to be developed in *Being and Nothingness* and finally more fully emerges in the *Critique of Dialectical Reason* as the conception of agency as self-consciously acting in terms of a conception of its own form (as self-conscious). Indeed, it because of its form that subjectivity is intelligible. In *The Transcendence of the Ego*, however, the "ego" is not intelligible outside of its pure formality, since it is an object produced by the pure spontaneity of consciousness. *Being and Nothingness* expands and corrects that view.[12] In the two early works, the form is that of an individual self-conscious spontaneity that is expressed in terms of freedom in action that has to do with the temporality of individual agency, whereas in the *Critique*, it emerges as also fully social and historical.

Another Sartrean view that emerges more fully in the *Critique* is that the form of agency itself also determines a certain measure of what will count as good for that agent. This was prefigured by Sartre's early work, which culminated in *Being and Nothingness* and which he promised to follow up with an ethics (which never appeared, although his notes for it appeared after his death).[13] The failure to produce an ethics was not an accident, since the earlier work on agency as the expression of a pure spontaneity could not supply any measure other than at best the abstract standard of actualizing one's individual freedom. Although Sartre hoped to generate some kind of ethics from out of such a pure spontaneity, still very abstractly conceived, he found he could not. To do that, he had to revise his conception of agency, so carefully worked out in *Being and Nothingness*, in various ways. (We shall come back to the reasons for this failure.)

Such a self-conscious agent (a being-for-itself, in Sartre's famous, Hegel-inspired term) acts in light of its own form, that is, its own conception of itself. This form is expressed in its actions, and it also serves to explain its actions, since the form involves thetic and non-thetic self-consciousness (one explains why a moth is drawn to flame by appeal to what moths do as a species, and one explains what a human agent does by appeal to the kind he or she is—which, as Sartre conceives it, is because its peculiar self-relation is always a moving target resetting its definition). In the case of being-for-itself, its form is temporal such that, constrained by its past, it projects itself into the future in light of goals that it chooses or that it simply finds itself having.

In *Being and Nothingness*, Sartre himself realized that the only way to explicate that conception further was to turn to the relations agents have to each other. That set the stage for the reconstruction of his theory in the *Critique of Dialectical Reason*.

2. "I" and "We," Singular and Plural

On Sartre's early view, the "I" emerges completely out of reflective consciousness in terms of the reflective subject supposing that its pre-reflective activities must (somehow) be ascribed to some enduring unity as a kind of substance that must always already be there. In *Being and Nothingness*, in which he recasts the self as an activity and therefore as a project, the self is both pre-reflective self-consciousness and reflective self-consciousness at one and the same time, but it remains "nothingness," an empty form whose being is to be free in terms of being undetermined in its future. The end that unites all the other activities and choices made by this self—that of trying to become fully in-itself, passing over from nothingness to being—is not an end that emerges as the final end in a hierarchy of other ends but as constitutive of self-conscious life itself. There may be other ends, which function in deliberation as values, that may be even desirable for their own sake, but each end itself is intelligible only in terms of the way it manifests a lack in being-for-itself, namely, a lack of being-in-itself. Values are projections or promises of the subject's becoming something (in-itself) in the future (for example, someone "who keeps his promises" or who "exhibits filial piety"). They are no more than that, and as such, they are also at odds with the nature of the self-conscious subject.

With that in place, it is unclear what, if any role at all, anything like a "we," a first-person plural, can play in any intelligible sense, and the answer is that it cannot. There are some uses of "we" that are perfectly intelligible, such as the kind of accidental "we" that one finds in statements such as "We have all showed up wearing white shirts"—an empirical description of selves as objects in the world. There is also the sense of "we" as expressing a common project—such as "We are writing a commentary on Merleau-Ponty's philosophy together." There can even be something like a constitutive "we" as in "We, native speakers of English, find your statement to be syntactically incorrect."[14] For Sartre, at that point in his philosophical development, even this third type of "we-subject" does not mark out any deeper sense of shared subjectivity but only manifests the facticity, the in-itself of our subjective lives, the fact that we share a language.[15] Even in that case, the form of judgment at issue remains that of subsuming myself under a concept, into being "one of many" ("a native speaker of English"). Sartre concludes that there cannot be any genuine "we-subject," but at best only various versions of an "us-subject." He takes Hegel (at least in the first part of the *Phenomenology*) to erroneously think he had resolved that in favor of a deeper form of "we-subject," but, on Sartre's reckoning at the time, Hegel's alleged solution really only amounted to a restatement of the problem.

Hegel says in the *Phenomenology* that the result of his discussion of self-consciousness is to be "the experience of what spirit is, this absolute substance which constitutes the unity of its oppositions in their complete freedom and self-sufficiency, namely, in the oppositions of the various self-consciousnesses existing for themselves: The *I* that is *we* and the *we* that is *I*."[16] Sartre agrees that this would be the goal but claims that (like the fundamental project of wanting to be one's own foundation) it is a metaphysical impossibility. For the "I" to really be a "we" would mean that it would give up being an "I," since it would have to merge with the others. Or, if the "we" is really an "I," then the "we" can only be a non-additive unity of many individual "I's." The "self-sufficiency" of the "I" of which Hegel speaks should in fact rule out any genuine, non-additive "we," and in saying that it does not, Hegel (on Sartre's account) is only presuming at the outset the absolute idealism that he is purporting to prove with the discussion of the "I" that is "we," and the "we" that is "I."[17] How to reconcile the "I" to the "We" without absorbing the one into the other—which Sartre takes Hegel to have claimed to have done—simply is the problem, not the solution.

Hegel's argument moves through three steps, the first two of which Sartre is willing to accept. At the first stage, self-conscious life can be modeled on a loose identity of the "I" and the "We," as when I explain or justify an action by appeal to something like the species of which I am a member: I drink that water because that is the kind of thing we mammals do. This type of explanation/justification works for social forms as well: I dress like this because that is the kind of thing we do in this part of the world. Such explanations/justifications make intelligible something mattering to me because it matters to the kind of creature I am. At the second stage, let us imagine, using the familiar Edenic image, there is fruit for the picking, and it matters to me that there is fruit for the picking because that is the kind of thing that matters to the kind of creature I am. If another agent enters the picture to whom it also matters that there is fruit for the picking, it can be the case that the mattering itself now comes to matter to me, and I am called to explain or justify why my mattering takes any priority or no priority at all in its mattering to the other. (This leads in Hegel's narrative to a third stage, soon to be negated and partially preserved, of a struggle for recognition that results in the statuses of mastery and servitude.) In *Being and Nothingness*, Sartre stops there and accuses Hegel, more or less, of pretending to have resolved the problem while in fact he should have stayed at the very entry point of the so-called problem of mastery and servitude. That Hegel thought he could go further rested on his taking the standpoint of "totality," of looking at the world as whole, which would in turn mean he would have to be standing somewhere outside of the whole to contemplate it, and that would be impossible and any statement of it would be nonsense.[18]

Sartre's criticism of Hegel sidesteps the way Hegel develops the conception of plural subjectivity in the rest of the *Phenomenology*, but he expressly rules out any kind of "dialectical solution" in terms of the self-reflexivity of thought itself grasping itself in grasping its "other." (This has to do with Sartre's fundamental ontological separation in *Being and Nothingness* between being and nothingness.[19]) For Hegel, the thought of the self-conscious subject itself as any kind of starting point is, Hegel argues, already itself only seemingly, not really, intelligible. The "I" has no determinacy of its own other than its empty form, and it was the illusion entertained by Fichte (and to a lesser extent, Kant) that in speaking of the "I," one was speaking both of an abstract principle (like thinkability) and of something that was already determinate outside of its relation to other items (of the "I" for whom the thinkable is thinkable). This requires a "dialectical" concept of a self-conscious life as both general and specific, which required a comprehension of the relation of the individual to the general in judgment that was not that of subsumption of the singular under a general predicate, nor the acceptance of the idea that the singular could only, as it were, be pointed at but not described. Rather, it required a different way of understanding the relation between singular and general. It is to that which we must turn to understand how Sartre managed to switch gears in the *Critique of Dialectical Reason.*

3. "I," "You," and the "Other": Dialectical Thought

As Sartre's thought progressed after the completion of the *Critique,* he even came to argue that one of the implications of his new view was that one could not make sense of human practical reason without seeing it as a development of the kind of teleology already at work in life.[20] Animal life in particular furnishes the basic example of self-movement as opposed to the "inert." There is no special metaphysical life force (or *élan vital*) but only the ability of the animal to move itself and do the things it does in manifesting the features of its species. The self-movement of animals (as "organic") originates as the organization of inert matter (the "inorganic"), and Sartre admits quite plainly that he has no a priori account of how that works except to note the different logical form of judgments of "life" as opposed to those having to do with the indifference or externality of inorganic objects to one another. By that he means that from the concept of such things (all the constituents of the "inert" world), we can infer nothing. We have to empirically validate what kinds of connections between such things can be established, and that is the purview of the empirical sciences (paradigmatically, physics, chemistry, and biology), since, as he puts it, "one cannot set a priori limits to science."[21] With living things (organisms), the whole of the organism (say, a beagle) explains the parts it has, but the whole of the organism is what it is because of those parts. In any event, the parts would not be the parts they are except as parts of this whole (say, as of a "beagle" as contrasted with a "tabby cat"). To note an individual organism as an individual of a kind is to operate with a concept of an organism in terms of how it typically develops, what it typically does, and so on.

All such practical reasoning on the Sartrean model is thereby reasoning for a task (a "project"), and his concern from the beginning was whether

there was any way of specifying any tasks that were a priori practically implied by such agency. Sartre does not pose the problem as that of whether
"pure practical reason" unassisted, on its own, without further empirical in-
put, could generate this or that content—the worry that Kant put on the table for debates about the scope of practical reason. For Sartre, it must always
be taken to be the practical reason of a self-conscious life concerned with
its appropriate ends. If nothing else, his early view leaned toward the radical view that there simply was no content that followed from the "nothingness" of the "I." There were only the choices of the "for-itself," all of which
are made against a contingent background (constraints of facticity) and involving a self-consciousness about how no particular a priori content was
licensed by that facticity (except for the self-delusion in "bad faith" that there
are some things one simply "has" to be). What content there was came from
the particularities of that facticity itself. By the time of the *Critique*, Sartre
had changed his mind: "I thought that total indeterminacy was the true basis
of choice. . . . I now realize that neither my own reasonings nor those of the
respectful freethinker were correct."[22]

Sartre speaks alternately of "action" but more often of "*praxis.*" On the
one hand, the word itself seems fairly straightforward, corresponding to the
Western Hegelian-Marxist sense that it is action that is self-determining by
virtue of its being informed by a larger theoretical understanding of what it
is trying to accomplish (in contrast to being caused in some loosely external
sense by social forces).[23] Sartre himself describes *praxis* in various terms. In
his essay of 1947–48, "What Is Literature?," he says of *praxis* that it is "action
in history and on history; that is, as a synthesis of historical relativity and
moral and metaphysical absolute, with this hostile and friendly, terrible and
derisive world which it reveals to us."[24] He later says it is "knowledge and action together, action that engenders its own understanding,"[25] and at another
time he says that "although *praxis* is self-explanatory and transparent to itself,
it is not necessarily expressible in words."[26] At yet another time, he offhand-
edly adds that *praxis* is an "action of the historical agent,"[27] and he says that
it is "the transcendence of all the inertia of the 'material conditions' toward
an objective."[28] *Praxis* "explains itself" as the action that it is by appealing
to the end it is trying to accomplish—an answer to the question "What are
you doing?"[29] Near the end of the book, he gives a full statement, saying he
is "defining *praxis* as an organizing project which transcends material conditions towards an end and inscribes itself, through labor, in inorganic matter
as a rearrangement of the practical field and a reunification of means in the
light of the end."[30]

Sartre's concept of *praxis* has to do with his use of the terms "analytic" and "synthetic" in a different way than they have come to mean in most anglophone writing in philosophy. "Analytic" for Sartre means "additive," whereas "synthetic" means "non-additive," that is, more "holistic." Additive accounts assume that one can determine independently of each other the "units" to be added onto each other, and, on that basis, one constructs the whole by adding up the units in a linearized, step-by-step way. (Typical additive accounts of human agency assume a "desiring, perceiving" part and a "rational, reflective" part that are then added to each other to produce the agent.[31]) A "synthetic," non-additive unity is not constituted by adding up the individual parts, since the parts are what they are only within the whole, and the whole determines what counts as its units. Typically, "analytic" unities for Sartre are the bases for conceptions of goodness or justice when seen in terms as maximizing some good or state of affairs (such as pleasure). "Synthetic" unities are more organic in structure since the individual parts cannot be comprehended outside of the whole to which they belong, and the whole cannot be comprehended outside of the distinct parts that make it up. As Sartre made clear in the late 1940s, this was the problem: How can we have a "synthetic" whole that does not in effect simply swallow its parts?[32] His concept of *praxis* as action informed by one's sense of where one stood in one's own historical context was meant to be the statement of a concept of individual and collective action that was holistic in this sense. Sartre was not denying that there was any possibility of additive accounts of social action (he seemed to think that modern economics was one such type of account), but that they did not replace "synthetic," holistic accounts. In fact, on his account, they surreptitiously rely on such "synthetic," holistic accounts for them even to work on their own additive terms. Additive accounts are the accounts given by thinking subjects for whom non-additive accounts are necessary to think of themselves as subjects. (We will return to the way in which Sartre expands and qualifies this.)

In *Being and Nothingness*, Sartre's main concern was with the reflexive nature of human reality (being-for-itself) as not being constituted out of two kinds of stuff—that of a material thing (the organic body) plus something else (thought, consciousness)—and although the concept of *praxis* was not in use, Sartre's non-additive ("synthetic") commitment was very much present. The subject, the for-itself, simply was the embodied agent. There was an identity there, not two things stuck together. It was not, that is, conceived as an interaction between two independent units (body and mind), and its unity was that of a subject not necessarily thinking of itself but absorbed (or not) in the activities bound up with the problems, possibilities, and opportunities of its practical field. That is, the agent is doing something and is doing it self-consciously but without necessarily reflectively using any concept of a subject that is performing the action. It is simply thinking "hanging the picture," not thinking "I am hanging the picture." Likewise, the thought of what I am doing with my body in the world is, like the pure "I" itself, empty unless it is filled out with the contingencies of what it is that I am doing. If I am washing a plate, I am not so much representing to myself a task to be done (wash the plate) and then causing my body to move. I am simply absorbed in washing the plate. I am being-in-the-world, to use the phrase by Heidegger that Sartre appropriated.

Since in *The Transcendence of the Ego*, the "I" is an object in the world, it already comes potentially with a conception of recognition by the "Other" just as any other object in the world is available to another subject's awareness. In *Being and Nothingness*, on the other hand, there is also a second-person awareness (of "you") that is built into the first person. Sartre offers up his famous example of a man who, out of jealousy, is peeking through a keyhole to see who is talking to his lover when he suddenly thinks he hears somebody on the stairs behind him. He blushes with shame, only to turn around and see that there is nobody there.[33] The "other" whom he thought was coming up the stairs turns out to be only a virtual "other" in whose eyes he is ashamed. Sartre even says that "if this pure consciousness were only a consciousness (of being) shame, the Other's consciousness would still haunt it as an inapprehensible presence and would thereby escape all reduction. This demonstrates sufficiently that it is not in the world that the Other is first to be sought but at the side of consciousness as a consciousness in which and by which consciousness makes itself be what it is."[34] The for-itself is absorbed not in its inner representations but in the object, and for the earlier Sartre, this other agent is not real but a constituent moment of the for-itself in its fundamental project. As Sartre vividly puts it, "The look which the eyes manifest, no matter what kind of eyes they are, is a pure reference to myself."[35]

At this stage, Sartre thought that the second-person standpoint (that of "the look which the eyes manifest") must be a component of self-consciousness, since he rejected what he took to be Hegel's point in Hegel's dialectic of mastery and servitude. In Sartre's view, Hegel's idea was that the other in conferring recognition on me and I in conferring recognition on him both institute the self-consciousness on the part of each: self-consciousness has a component of my being aware that the other is aware of me and also aware that I am aware of him. Sartre interpreted Hegel as saying in effect that by taking—or "recognizing"—the other at least as the kind of creature for whom things have a significance and with that other person taking—that is, "recognizing"—some other as a creature for whom things have a significance, we institute a kind of self-consciousness on each other's part (assuming that recognition is transitive, such that if I recognize A, and A recognizes B, then I also recognize B). Sartre dismisses that, calling it a "mirror game" that only assumes what it is trying to establish.[36] The recognition and its transitivity work only if one of the self-conscious agents already has the authority to bestow such recognition. Without that authority, he cannot confer it, and the mirror game—that supposes that many such self-conscious agents lacking the initial authority could somehow magically create such authority—can only be an empty play. At this point, Sartre still saw the normative demands (including ethical claims) put on individual agents as sufficiently like those of coming from another agent with a right to command already established on his part, except that for Sartre the other is a virtual other, already contained within one's own first-personal point of view.[37]

Sartre therefore concluded that the Hegelian argument (at least at that time as he took to be) could work only if one could assume a kind of "third party" already endowed with the requisite authority hovering over the proceedings—in other words, God, which amounts to a "lie," so Sartre says, but whose shadow hangs over all those who wish to replace God's view with that of the mirror game of pure reciprocal recognition. In Sartre's eyes, Hegel laid out the problem correctly and gave what, given the way he laid it out, seemed like the only real answer.[38] However, or so Sartre thought in *Being and Nothingness*, Hegel simply helped himself to his absolute idealism (in effect, to God), when in fact the only real alternative is to accept the disturbing conception that the first-person point of view already carries the necessary authority within itself even though it is always faced with the impossibility of being its own foundation—faced with, as Sartre puts it, the "necessity of its contingency."[39] This is disturbing, since it seems both to demand an authorization from on high and to deny the possibility of getting it.

In effect, what Sartre finds adequate in Hegel's conception is what Hegel says he is achieving, namely, the unity of various subjects in a constitutive "we" that does not at the same time undermine or negate the "complete freedom and self-sufficiency" of the first-person singular, the "I." If the "I-We" unity is taken under the model of a subsumptive judgment—such that what "we do" is the rule under which I subsume myself ("We typically do X," thus it follows "I typically do X")—then it seems that one confronts a continual oscillation among several different but related conceptions. One such conception is that of insisting on the complete absorption of the "I" into the "We," where the "I" is just a particular organism acting out a social role (that is, merely occupying a position in social space, merely drawing the inferences always already available in the inferential space she occupies, with there being nothing more to it). Heidegger thought of that in terms of *das Man*, "what 'one' is or does," and many others took the idea as a project for sociological research. In those cases, there is little more to the I than the use of "I" as an indexical. Or one can oscillate to the other extreme, denying the subsumption, in which the full self-sufficiency of each self-conscious life is the model. That itself takes different shapes, for example, that of alienation from or revolt against or refusal of the "We," all the way up to trying to stage-manage the social recognition that the "I" wants from the "We." In between are a number of other strategies.

In his early work, Sartre took the side of insisting on the self-sufficiency of the "I." This changes radically in the *Critique*.[40] The relation between the practice and the actor cannot intelligibly be understood as either one or the other, but as something more like that which Hegel took to calling the "concrete universal."[41]

The idea of a "concrete universal" is used to highlight the way that a universal (for example, a language such as English when taken as an abstract structure) cannot be cleanly distinguished from the actual activities of the people whose practices they are, which would be the case if the actions were only conceived as applications of a general rule (in which both action and rule could be identified independently of each other). It would be misleading to think of the practices exclusively on the model of, for example, a game. The practices as practices are not an isolated set of rules under which individuals subsume themselves. Rather, the particular actions on the part of the participants in a practice do not simply instantiate the rules of the practice but rather manifest them. The particular actions of the participants thus manifest the practice behind them, and the action is not an instantiation but rather an actual generality (or "concrete universal"). The craftsman, explaining to the apprentice how to guilloche a dial quickly and correctly, does it (guilloches the dial) and points to what in particular she is doing, saying, "This is how we do it." "This" points to a specific action as manifesting the practice itself, and the action itself ("this") manifests the universal in its particularity. If one asks which comes first, which is prior, the practice or the action, the reply is that neither takes priority, nor should one be seen as producing or causing the other. (Putting one prior to the other is the result of an additive or, in Sartre's terms, "analytic" conception of a practice.) On the non-additive (or, in Sartre's terms, "synthetic") conception, the practice exists only insofar as there are practitioners, and the practitioners manifest their self-consciousness in their individual acts. The content of the practice is not itself determinate apart from the actions that manifest it, and the content of the action is the self-conscious, self-particularizing particular action it is by way of its being the particular way the generality of the practice is manifested. The practice only is the practice it is in its being actualized, and the particular actualization is what it is only as being the self-conscious actualization of the practice.

In Sartre's helpful metaphor for the way the individual articulates the practice and thus actualizes it, the individual subject is said to "incarnate" the practice.[42] In another place, he says that the generalities (or "universals") of a practice are always "individualized universals."[43] The generality of a practice is, moreover, not that of quantificational universality.[44] From "members of practice-x typically do such and such," it does not follow that any given member of the practice does exactly that. The generality of a practice is a generic, not a quantificational universality. That American robins have red throats is not invalidated by the appearance of the American albino robin (which lacks the melanin pigment), nor does the American albino robin cease to be a robin. Zebra finches who fail to vocalize in the general zebra finch manner (perhaps because of an underlying genetic problem) do not cease to be zebra finches. Instead, some members of the families (American robins and Australian zebra finches) may be better and worse exemplars of the genus, or they may just be different exemplars (which is compatible with cases in which being a "worse" exemplar may prove better when the environment around the organism changes). Individual actors may be better or worse exemplars of the practice. To put it in Hegelian terms, such actors who are better exemplars are more adequate to their concept. The issue is whether their concept is adequate to itself, that is, whether in the give-and-take of "living together," it will make sense to those living in terms of it or will undermine itself.

Prying the two apart—the practice and the self-conscious actualization of the practice—is the result of "analytical," additive reason that then has to look for some way of binding the two back together, which it typically does by hypothesizing about which of them must be prior. "Dialectical" reason, on the other hand, looks to the self-conscious actions as undertaken in light of an end to be brought about in a temporal unity in terms of a holistic understanding of action and actor. Those actions, as *praxis*, express the form of the agent as self-conscious, and they manifest the practices of which they are a part. Sartre's own language of totality and totalization is actually better suited to make this point. An agent projects an end and acts on it; the series of actions that make up the progressive realization of the end are all intelligible as parts of a projected totality (the action as succeeding). The action starts with the subject's reckoning of a state of affairs to be brought about by the agent, and the bringing about is the "totalization" of the agent and the world: the idea is that the agent is projecting a change in the surrounding environment through an end not yet achieved into one that is achieved (that it "negates" the present situation). As Sartre puts it, "One can define *praxis* as the systematic reorganization of the surrounding field through an end, that is to say, through a future that reveals itself as a negation to be carried out on the present organization."[45] The action is something underway until its completion, at which point it is a totality, something achieved. In an inert world that resists this, the agent aims to bring about a non-additive, loosely "organic" totality of himself and his surrounding world. For an individual action, the parts of the action are parts of the totality that is the action (so that deciding to cross the street, crossing the street, and having crossed the street is one action with many different parts, all of which without the thought that binds the parts together would be a mere heap of distinct events), and Sartre also holds that each of these actions is itself intelligible as an action within the larger project of the agent's fundamental end. Even the activity of thinking of the world "analytically" (scientifically, rationally) is carried out against the background of subjects acting and thinking teleologically in terms of ends and projects. As Sartre rather laconically puts it, "It is true that most people speak according to the rules of analytical rationality, but this does not mean that their praxis is not conscious of itself."[46]

In *Being and Nothingness*, this fundamental end was the project of the for-itself attempting to make itself into something inert (the in-itself), a project that necessarily fails, since the for-itself cannot become inert, and this implies that the real fundamental project of the for-itself is to be self-founding, a contradictory for-itself-in-itself—it wishes to be a self-founding freedom that is the unfree in-itself. In the *Critique*, on the other hand, the fundamental project emerges as something more along the lines of exercising one's agency in order to fully *be* an agent, which in its most developed form would involve actualizing one's freedom as kind of autonomy conceived not as issuing a self-created maxim and then putting it to work but as a relatively complex action that in its development comes to be grasped by the agent as his own. The agent appropriates his action, so we might put it. The agent confronts his own facticity in acting—including his physical makeup and the institutions and norms of where he finds himself in what Sartre almost always calls his "situation"—and finds before him a "practical field" of action in which his own *praxis* is to be carried out. In finding oneself always already in such a practical field, one finds oneself with a set of determinate possibilities that rule other possibilities out, opportunities, obstacles, and so on that are fixed within this practical field. This practical field is disclosed to us not merely intellectually but also through emotions having to do with what the practical field really is and what the kinds of relations are in the midst of which we find ourselves.[47] In moving within the practical field, we act in terms of what shows up as mattering to us, and we do it because it matters to us. Sartrean worries about inauthenticity (from *Being and Nothingness*) play a role here: to the extent that we move in this practical field in terms of simple exigencies, or "doing as one does," we fail to be what we really are, namely, fail to be the kind of spontaneously free agents we metaphysically are. This failing is not a moral failing but a metaphysical failing, not a failure to do what one ought to do but a failure at being what one truly is.[48] The latter is a matter of authenticity and inauthenticity, not necessarily a matter of moral right or wrong. Appropriating the situation for oneself is thus an issue of taking up how the world has disclosed itself to us in all our facticity and not taking the way out by holding that we are simply caught up in its drift. To become truly free in this situation would require therefore not a kind of unanchored free choice in the "situation," but owning oneself and one's actions in the situation, "taking responsibility," as Sartre puts it. One does enter the situation autonomously, but, as Sartre puts it, autonomy would be "conduct that, recapturing itself without cessation, ends by becoming its own foundation,"[49] and, importantly, such autonomy will not be fully realizable.

That is, to actualize one's capacity as an agent would be to realize one's power not to be pushed around completely by "inert" exterior forces but to be capable of at least resisting those exterior forces. This is a subtle transformation of the conception of agency found in *Being and Nothingness* as aiming to form itself into a totality, only to necessarily fail and thus to always be in a stage of being a detotalized totality, that is, of all of its specific actions failing to form a whole, a totality. The subject is always trying to hold itself together as a work in progress even as the attempted totalization of that work in progress is, because it is a work in progress extended over time, necessarily incomplete.[50] For the "totality" to be actual, the subject must be able to survey it *as* a totality, but since the "totality" that is the aim is in constant transition, the intended totality will be essentially unsurveyable. The acting subject requires, so it seems, a surveyable whole in order for his action to be realized, but such a surveyable whole is impossible to achieve in practice. Only the practical, not the fully theoretical, ability to move rationally within such an unsurveyable totality keeps the acting subject together. What moves this away from the conception found in *Being and Nothingness* is the introduction of a "we-subject" in the *Critique*.

This we-subject raises the bar for Sartre. The subject must be taken in its singularity (as a individualized universal), but the universality (or generality) of what he is doing must also be grasped in its own terms. In his earlier work,

Sartre had ruled out such a unity, since the primary conception of communal subjectivity was at best that of a second-person relation (with "the Other" already virtually contained in the first-person singular usage). As he bluntly put it in *Being and Nothingness*, "The experience of the We-subject cannot be primary."[51] The "We-subject" occurs only in those cases where the use of the "we" indicates something that is constitutive of some feature of one's point of view. Sartre's examples have to do with the public signs in the Paris Metro, such as those indicating the exit.[52] One grasps the meaning immediately and without inference because that is the language "we" speak and the signs that typically indicate to us what "we do." It is not the completely accidental "we" (of discovering, for example, that everybody at the store is wearing sunglasses), nor is it the "we" of a common undertaking (as in "we are making dinner together"). The comprehension of this constitutive "we" is, on Sartre's earlier account, itself already parasitic on the grasp of the second-person "Other," since in understanding such instances of public meaning "I am not using it in the absolute freedom of my personal projects. I am not constituting a tool by means of invention; I do not surpass the pure materiality of the thing toward my possibles."[53]

In the *Critique*, this has changed. As Sartre came to see, the dichotomy between active and passive had dominated his earlier discussion. Thus, the for-itself was either actively doing something, or some process was doing something to it. The later concept of the "individualized universal" in the *Critique* was the expression of a way in which that dichotomy did not hold. In doing something, I as singular express in a singularly actual way the generality of a practice, and the generality of the practice shows itself in the action.[54] Both the practice and the actor are present in a unity without one or the other being primary. Neither is the pure actor nor the purely acted-upon. In Sartre's trope, it is "analytical," additive reason that separates them and gives rise to the thought that either one of the pair is the actor or that both are reciprocal actors of a sort, whereas "dialectical," non-additive reason grasps that this stance is neither that of active or of passive but of some other point of view in which both the practice and the individual actor are appearances in the same medium. This way of understanding the relation between general practice and individual action is the paradigm example of dialectical, non-additive thought. It is Sartre's way of appropriating Hegel's thought of the "self-sufficiency" of the "I" being in a unity with the "We" of its practices so that neither is thinkable genuinely without the other, and of Hegel's thought of the "the existence of the *I* extended into two-ness, which therein remains the same as itself."[55]

The totality that shows itself—most often Sartre speaks of *dévoiler* or of *se présenter*—in the actions of each is that of *praxis* as language, something which itself cannot be built up out of individual acts of speech (as, say, a conventionalist account would make it) but which must be already at work in such acts and which is actual only in the existence of such acts.[56]

To some, this might sound decidedly un-Sartrean, so it is worth citing one of the relevant passages at length:

> But this fundamental totality can only be *praxis* itself in so far as it is directly expressed to others; language as the practical relation of one man to another is *praxis*, and *praxis* is always language (whether truthful or deceptive) because it cannot take place without signifying itself. Languages are the product of History; as such, they all have the exteriority and unity of separation. But language cannot have come to man, since it presupposes itself.[57]

Thus, Sartre concludes that the first-person plural—the we-subject—is equally basic with the first-person singular, and the "Other" is not the virtual other of *Being and Nothingness* but the actual other of any given social ensemble, a real second-person address. In a discussion of the role of third parties in the formation of we-subjects, Sartre also notes that at its basis is the binary relation between two agents forming a we-subject, which

> is not something which can come to men from outside, or which they can establish between themselves by common consent. Regardless of the action of the third party, and however spontaneous the mutual recognition of the two strangers who have just met may seem, it is really only the actualization of a relation which is given as having always existed, as the concrete and historical reality of the couple which has just been formed.[58]

The kind of meaning that shows itself in the actions taken by agents who are expressing the practice is always already there, and it does not require (as Sartre continued to think that the Hegelian system does) for there to be some special, extra reality (in Hegel's case, so Sartre thought, *Geist* as a spiritual-metaphysical organism of sorts) behind or above all of that; nor is it simply a summation of individual behaviors; nor, as he puts it, does it require any pre-established harmony, but something else:[59] "The communal *praxis* actually reveals itself (*la praxis commune se révèle en effet*) through an organized multiplicity of free, individual undertakings (within the limits of functions and powers) and each of these presents itself as exemplary, that is to say, as the same as all."[60] This turns out to be an a priori determination of the form of agency itself, the intelligibility of agency as such.[61]

The topic of *praxis* thus assumes a background more or less of what among the English-speaking Heideggerians has come to be called "attunement," and that is part of what "dialectical" reason (for Sartre) takes as its topic. On this view, the singular action (or *praxis*) is not a separate activity from the background attunement (or practice), nor is it merely the instantiation of some general rule. Rather, it is the manifestation of the practice. The practice and the act are two sides of the same (dialectical) coin, not two things, one of which is stacked on top of each other. Thus, Sartre notes that "dialectical Reason is neither constituting nor constituted reason; it is Reason constituting itself in and through the world, dissolving in itself all constituted Reasons in order to constitute new ones which it transcends and dissolves in turn."[62] The background "attunement" is thus practical reason itself, and so the question is, For agency, what does "reason" require?

4. Being Together: "We"

What reason requires turns on Sartre's explication of the various senses of "we" and on how it is the other side of the dialectical coin from "I," so that the "togetherness" of various self-conscious "I's" takes on different forms.[63] The primary way in which people exhibit togetherness is not merely as groups of bodies distinct from each other—what Sartre generally calls "dispersal"— but in terms of how each individually and how the collective itself thinks of itself. Appropriating a term with an ancient provenance for his own purposes, Sartre speaks of a basic mode of this togetherness as "alterity," in which the togetherness of agents is also a matter of (usually non-thetic, non-reflective) self-consciousness about their own distinctness from others. "Alterity" is the term for the sheer "otherness" of each to the other. In the view articulated in the *Critique*, the agent as self-moving, spontaneous, is confronted with the "inert," and thus because of the fact of scarcity in our world, the others (in "alterity") are each incarnations of the possibility of one's becoming oneself superfluous to the others.[64] Each may be the "extra" one who can be dispensed with. In this way, alterity is the "primary human relation" as a mode of "reciprocity."[65] People can see themselves as a "we" engaged in an identical project even when they are not cooperating in any way, or for that matter, even when they are competing with each other.

As an example, Sartre several times describes people waiting around or waiting in line for a bus. Each is fully aware of what they are doing (waiting for a bus). Each comprehends the other as doing the same thing. This is something that they are doing together, but it is not a common project in that nobody is thinking of the other as a component element of a group effort at waiting for the bus. Nor is it a matter of the purely accidental "we," as in "I noticed we were all wearing red sneakers to the meeting." It is a matter of what "we" are doing, and if each asked what each is doing, each could reply,

"We are waiting for a bus." (Sartre will call this kind of togetherness "seriality.") The collective of people waiting for the bus involves reciprocity, but it is characterizable only in terms of the intentions and horizons of meaning shared among the agents and thus only when "interiority"—the subjective lives of the agents and their projects—is kept in view.

This kind of "we" depends on the background attunement of practical reason itself (on a general "we" as a general rational capacity that is manifested in individual acts that are its individualized universals), but that "we" fragments as the actions play themselves out. For any such action, there is a more determinate "milieu," to which Sartre also attaches a technical meaning: a "milieu" is the background of practices (including those involving various class and other social relations) that manifests itself in "seriality." The "milieu," we might say, is the way in which practical (dialectical) reason is made concrete in a series of practices that may or may not actually cohere with each other, but which as the overall "milieu" are more or less invisible to the participants.[66]

Sartre has two issues in mind. First, there is the matter of preserving the distinctiveness, even the opposition of agents. It would be a mistake to absorb the "I" fully into the "We," but, on the other hand, one should not reduce the "We" into a set of merely distributed "I's." Second, and more important in this context, are the different senses of what it would mean for us to be doing things together, and the way in which that togetherness reshapes itself.

All the forms of togetherness exhibit the background of attunement and the individualized universals that show, or manifest, that attunement in their "milieu." In its more concrete incarnation, this background attunement constitutes the shared form of life of the people whose relations to each other manifest this attunement. This basic togetherness is not even properly speaking a social relation, since it is the basis from which social relations themselves emerge as intelligible, and even though it is only within social relations that this background attunement has any reality.[67]

5. Alienation in Inertia

Sartre's *Critique* begins therefore at the point where *The Transcendence of the Ego* ended, when Sartre said: "The epistemological starting point must always be consciousness as apodictic certainty (of) itself and as consciousness of such and such an object."[68] In the *Critique*, however, Sartre pushes this further into a conception of a self-conscious embodied agent moving within the background of attunement who is capable of spontaneity in action, that is, of doing something new. Such an agent is a natural creature, which means that its logical shape is that of an individual which is to be explained most basically in terms of its form, which means more concretely that of its species. (That this also constitutes what is good and harmful for the creature is another point, to which we will return later.) Like all such creatures, the agent's actions both express and are explained by their form and, in the case of agency, by the agent expressing his form to himself in thinking and acting.

Sartre distinguishes between judgments of exteriority, which he takes to be the form of judgments about nature, that is, about what is not itself self-moving (that is, what is "inert") in contrast to judgments about subjects, who are self-moving.[69] Those judgments of exteriority are about independently identifiable things, such that judgments about their various concatenations are additive in character. Judgments about subjectivity (as self-conscious interiority) which are basically temporal and teleological in character and in which the relation between the elements of the thinking or doing is supposed to be logical in character and not just psychological are synthetic, "non-additive." An action underway (washing the dishes) implies that it is aimed at a conclusion (the dishes are washed). It is not merely the observation that washing the dishes is often followed or is linked together in some appropriate theory with washed dishes. This is all part of what Sartre calls a totalization.

The relation of the agent to its own necessary embodiment—since agency is the form of the embodiment of a self-conscious creature—is thus that of integrating the seemingly inert biophysics of itself and its environment into a whole held together both by a certain type of self-conception in terms of various projects (some more basic and inclusive than others) taking place in the practical field. It is practical reason (the self-moving) making itself real in the world of inertia, and, so Sartre will argue, is itself not ultimately to be understood solely in individualist terms but also in social terms.

Such ends form the horizon of plans and expectations for how life will unfold over time and have moral and non-moral goods embedded in them. Family and schooling, finding a job, getting married or finding a partner, for example, are all part of the horizon of a modern life for many societies. Just as a person may suffer from lack of water, inadequate food, disease, or social ills such as loneliness, the person living out his or her acquired statuses may suffer from lack of respect or recognition, lack of self-confidence, structural disadvantage based on ethnicity or religion, inadequate power to move up the employment ladder, and so forth.

The base level starting point in the *Critique* thereby shares with *Being and Nothingness* the view that the fundamental issue to be elucidated is the way in which agency as spontaneity—as self-moving—faces off against an inert world. In the *Critique*, however, Sartre takes a modified path from that followed in *Being and Nothingness*, and to do so, he introduces some new terms and gives some older ones new life. In particular, he introduces the terms *hexis*, "practico-inert," and "*praxis*-process." *Hexis* is (rather obviously) taken by Sartre from the Greek, and in particular from Aristotle's philosophy, where it plays a large role in the *Nicomachean Ethics*.[70] In that context, it is usually rendered as "disposition," that is, as indicating some basic enduring character traits along with habits such that the virtuous agent is said to act at least partly from acquired habit. This is part of the sense that it has in Sartre's work, where it also indicates sometimes a natural disposition on the part of the agent.

We are embodied agents in a social world, and in that world, we take on habits and absorb the norms of that world around us. That much is not terribly controversial. What Sartre earlier called our "monstrous spontaneity" appears here as the capacity to strike a new beginning, to do something new that is not simply "what they do," and to take up something other than what conventionally matters to people.[71] He calls this a power of negation, and it serves to designate the way in which freedom emerges initially out of such inertia and rather abstractly as a power of resistance to such inertia. Although one can of course self-consciously set about acquiring and securing certain habits, *hexis* on the whole is a natural ongoing response to one's environs. In its negative sense, "spontaneity" indicates the resistance to full absorption in some kind of processual sociality, where there is a "way things are done" (very much like what Heidegger calls "averageness" in *Being and Time*), and to "what usually matters" to us in our concrete social lives, but that resistance on its own does not supply any content to itself. As Sartre put it in an interview in 1969, "This is the limit I would today accord to freedom: the small movement which makes of a totally conditioned social being someone who does not render back completely what his conditioning has given him."[72]

Seeing the agent purely in terms of *hexis* as a set of acquired dispositions and habits lends a kind of credence to additive accounts of action. If one views, say, bodily movements on their own and asks what explains the movement, one looks for a separate event that is to be linked with the bodily movement, and this very ordinarily leads to inquiring which dispositions and character traits were at work in causing those movements. For Sartre's "synthetic" non-additive account of action, however, it is a mistake to think that the bodily movements taken as "exteriority" are the same as the movements involved in the whole of an agent operating in a practical field. To see the bodily movements as the action taken as independently identifiable (as exteriority) is implicitly to see them as representing the highest common factor between a movement seen as an arm raising and my raising my arm (to use

Wittgenstein's well-known example).[73] The familiar naturalistic philosophical picture of social life as a system of rules and our being trained to acquire
certain dispositions to follow them is for Sartre an expression of a certain
form of alienated social life. An agent is alienated in this sense when the constitutive aims of her subjectivity are thwarted by the conditions in which she
must act, and the most fundamental form of alienation on Sartre's account
will therefore be the experience of having one's own spontaneity thwarted or
deformed within the social conditions in which one finds oneself.[74]

Sartre's fundamental picture therefore is that of agents, singular and plural, finding that the unit, as it were, that is open to inquiry is the agent in
all their dimensions in a series of practical fields almost always in the midst
of others. In that light, *hexis* itself has to be understood as, so to speak, the
inert residue of a historically indexed goal-oriented *praxis*.[75] It is distinctive
to Sartre's non-additive conception that he pays attention to matters such as
disposition and habit but locates them within a more holistic, non-additive
conception of individual and collective action in terms of the teleology of
action.

In this regard, a crucial aspect has to do with the way in which spontaneous agency (as initially empty) must transform itself into a form of inertia in
order to function, and thus in addition to *hexis*, Sartre introduces what he
calls the practico-inert. Whereas *hexis* has to do with the dispositions and
habits of individual agents that stabilize into an inert background of that
agent's action, the practico-inert is more overtly social in character, and it
fundamentally involves the element of materiality in action. The totalizing
agent in his "praxis as the systematic reorganization of the surrounding field
through an end"[76] is not simply "trying" in some interior fashion to do something, nor is he simply moving his body. Rather, he is engaged with intentionally changing something about the practical field in which he finds himself—
this is true whether he is merely turning off the faucet or participating in
a revolutionary political event. Whatever the agent is doing, he is working
within a practical field in which many of his possibilities and opportunities
are already practically, not metaphysically, limited by the material conditions
(ranging from climate to the available technology to the conditions of ownership of his society) in which he lives. They are not matters open to choice but
instead form the non-chosen background—the inert background—for the
expression of his own spontaneity. As Sartre succinctly puts it, the practico-
inert is "matter . . . unified by an ensemble of practices."[77]

It is also distinctive to Sartre's view that agents can indeed come to see
themselves and others in such additive terms, that is, to see their actions as
machine-like, as sets of dispositions that drive them and which they simply

must follow. This happens first of all in conditions of alienation when one does not think of oneself so much as an engaged subject but rather as a detached subject—as still a subject but also more basically as one more object in the world, or, in Sartre's language, not as a subject fully in interiority but in exteriority. The latter, so Sartre will argue, is a falsification of one's genuine nature as spontaneity, which he characterizes (with his love of seemingly paradoxical wordplay) as the "the milieu of freedom as transcendable untranscendability (*indépassabilité dépassable*)."[78] This is the milieu, for example, of the person who in his exploitation within an unjust system knows himself in reality to be unfree while understanding himself as a subject of free action, capable of spontaneity but seemingly incapable of expressing it. When agency develops itself in terms of its nature as spontaneous freedom, actions have a temporal and teleological structure, but this can fall apart under certain practical, not metaphysical, conditions. In alienated conditions, perhaps all we can do (or all that we can understand ourselves as doing) is "try" (as an internal mental event), which may or may not eventuate in the full characteristics of an action. In a fully alienated condition, it may well be that all we are doing is moving our bodies (just "making the gestures") or that we are just manipulating some machines to produce certain effects. These are all degenerate versions of action, expressions of a capacity whose ends have twisted out of shape. Alienation in this Sartrean sense is thus the condition of self-consciously thinking of one's constitutive aim (freedom) as inevitably twisted and denied by the "inert" conditions of one's life.

To see an action in terms of pure exteriority is to see it not as something that the agent is so much doing as it is to see him as something he is undergoing. An action is a kind of rational unity—an observable set of events held together by the project (the "thoughts") of the agent and the agent's public world (including other agents).[79] If the world of meaning itself falls apart, what is left are just the events, not the self-conscious teleological structure that makes the events into an action. What is then observable is an action in disintegration—for example, now being merely a set of bodily movements and mental events, a disintegrated version of the real thing.[80] Among other examples of this, Sartre describes the plight of the badly paid "gig" worker (as we would now call him): "He goes and sells himself at the factory every morning . . . by a sort of somber resigned *hexis* which scarcely resembles a praxis. And yet, in fact, it is a *praxis*: habit is directed and organized, the end is posited, the means chosen. . . . In other words, the ineluctable destiny which is crushing him moves through him."[81]

If the inertia of the *hexis* were all there was to agency, we would basically be creatures only of inertia responding to matters in terms of the repertoire of dispositions and habits we have acquired (with perhaps some dispositions to change other dispositions being added to the description). In the abstract, spontaneity is resistance to the inertia of practical life. However, inertia is not merely a matter of the natural aspects of our lives together with the dispositions and the habits we acquire and into which we are trained. Inertia also has to do with acquired social norms in which we find ourselves, as well as the prospects for life offered up by social organization and technology. (A person living in a small agricultural village with only a wooden plow has a different set of opportunities than the same person with a metal plow.) It is to draw attention to this other way in which inertia functions outside of the purely natural or habitual inertia that Sartre introduces his term of art, the "practico-inert." As its name implies, it designates the kind of inertia that is the result of our own collective (and to a much lesser extent, personal) activities. Spontaneity, which can negate such inertia, also leaves behind itself practical structures such as norms, which also function as a kind of inertia, and this inertia of the practico-inert (along with that of nature and *hexis*) is the foundation of alienation. Alienation arises in Sartre's terms as *praxis* finds itself dragged down by inertia—acquired dispositions, the weight of authoritative institutions, widely shared and settled norms, the range of given possibilities offered up by the various regimes of inequality, and the class hierarchies such regimes sustain and which are in turn sustained by them. To be alienated in this sense is not to own some key element of one's agency. One can be alienated from, say, parts of one's emotional life to the extent that it seems to be something imposed on oneself by one's own psychology; or one can be alienated from one's political surroundings in the sense that one cannot see the political rule of some over others having anything to do with one's own agency but only acting as a kind of imposed inertial drag on one's own life.

It is constitutive of *praxis* to seek its own free realization, which in its idealization of itself would be an agency that would be its own foundation, a kind of pure spontaneity making itself fully real in the actual world. However, there is and can be no such pure spontaneity. As Sartre puts it, "Freedom is not the free activity of an autonomous organism but, from its origins, a conquest of alienation."[82] Freedom as spontaneity is always a kind of resistance to the inert, to the "average" in life, not in the sense of necessarily denying the "average" but in terms of whether one can "own" it or remake it and find one's home in it. The practico-inert is thus a form of "passive activity" in that it functions as inertia in which we do things as "one does" and that what matters to us are the values sustained in such activity in which things matter "as they do."[83] This is kept up by people keeping it up, by acting in the inert ways the "average" sociality seems to recommend but actually requires. In *Being and Nothingness*, one response to this kind of problem was to call for a kind of authenticity on the part of the agent. That drops out in the *Critique*, where the focus shifts on how to maintain a kind of free *praxis* in an alienated world burdened with inertia and hierarchies of class that thwart and deform the potentiality of people to exercise their agency. The practico-inert itself becomes what Sartre calls by yet another term of art "*praxis*-process," that is, the inertia of the practico-inert being kept alive, as it were, by the conscious actions of a plurality of individuals simply carrying on according to some social rules in terms of what Sartre occasionally calls "active passivity," not just being at rest in the "inertness" that one is but actively striving to keep matters such as social "pledges" efficacious—that is, an active striving to keep such inertia efficacious.[84]

6. Reciprocity in Spontaneity and Reciprocity as Antagonism

Sartre's starting point in his narration of his theory is that of what he calls the singular practical organism, in this case a self-conscious agent acting for an end (that is, *praxis*), which in turn is equivalent to a totalizing activity. For Sartre, since this beginning has to do with individual *praxis*, it might seem as if he was privileging the singular agent in some way in keeping with his earlier existentialism. (He mentions once that this might be called a "dialectical nominalism."[85]) However, each of these individual *praxis*-actions will manifest something of the totality in terms of which the individual *praxis* makes sense. The existentialist-individualism of his earlier work thus gives way to a concentration on unities of singular and collective action that aim at both preserving the independence of the "I" from complete absorption in its social constitution and at the same time holding fast to the concept that a first-person expression "shows" the common practice, the "we" of which it, as the "I," is the other side of the coin. This could be called Sartre's "social" conception of agency, except, since Sartre has a very particular use for the term "social," it is better to use one of his other descriptions and call it his theory of reciprocal agency (or agency-as-reciprocal).

Such an embodied agent expressing the teleology of its species (as an "I" and a "We") is thus qualified by both need—as expressing the felt lack of something on the part of a practical organism—and transcendence (*dépassement*, "overtaking") as expressing the way in which any action is held together by the goal to be achieved (by what "transcends" any present moment in the action in terms of what is felt to be needed). Even a long term action (such as writing a book or going on a trek) is structured by the end, by its

transcendence, and any action can also change its course while it is underway. Different component actions can show up as various external factors
intervene (the tool breaks, new information having to do with the end comes
to light, etc.). The action thus may not, except in small-scale examples, be
carried out completely according to plan, and in general actions will be explained in terms of other actions.[86] This too belongs to the form of agency.

The plurality of agents is already there in the conception of a single agent
itself, since the actions of a single agent already presuppose the background of
attunement, of a projected totality of human projects. Each agent experiences
certain lacks as needs, as something that each must have in order to continue
being an agent, and needs thus are negations and negations of negations. The
need points toward something that the practical organism lacks—it does not
have, say, water—and the project of getting the water and drinking it is the
negation of the negation, as Sartre says. ("Negation" here only makes sense
in the context of action; there is no negation in nature, in the inert, itself.[87])
Together with the concept of need, there is also the concept of scarcity as
a contingent fact of our world. (There is no purely logical contradiction in
thinking of a world in which every organism gets exactly what it needs.[88])
Self-conscious organisms with needs in a contingent world of scarcity face
a particular set of problems that are intelligible, so Sartre will argue, purely
on their own without reference to particular needs or facts about certain
societies.

Because of the fact of scarcity, there is also the possibility of antagonism
among a plurality of such agents simply because of the plurality and the practically inescapable contingency of scarcity, which for each agent is the "basic
contingency as the necessity which . . . forces him to be exactly what he is."[89]
With that, each member, so it seems, of any kind of collective is possibly
the surplus "one," a superfluous person who at one extreme of this line of
thought can be eliminated or, somewhat less apocalyptically, simply be made
invisible and put to social death. This scarcity "marks each member of the
group both as a possible survivor and as a dispensable surplus member."[90]
Or, as Sartre also puts it, "this constant danger of the annihilation of myself
and of everyone is not something I see only in *Others. I am myself* that danger
in so far as I am Other, and designated by the material reality of the environment as potentially surplus with *Others.*"[91]

This kind of antagonism, so Sartre will argue, is a permanent possibility
of all human agency under conditions of scarcity (and plurality). It never
goes away. It is a feature of the concept of human agency as plural and faced
with scarcity, not merely as a matter of a certain human psychology such
as Thomas Hobbes thought. This kind of semipermanent antagonism is su-

perseded at times in history only when there is a certain kind of reciprocal identification in a group that actualizes the full range of spontaneity (that is, freedom) within itself. However, to understand how that freedom could ever be possible, much less actual, one requires some more articulation about the intelligibility of self-conscious organisms confronting each other under the conditions of plurality and scarcity.

Given scarcity and plurality, agency faces problems of alienation and reification. An agent will be alienated when their spontaneity is checked or channeled in some institutional or habitual way that cannot be comprehended as an expression of their spontaneity but rather as something coming from outside to check or put limitations on their spontaneity. Rather than beginning something new, they will, as it were, merely be repeating themselves or some social practice so that spontaneity ends up neutralized by the necessity of what Sartre calls recurrence, the way in which these kinds of problems having to do with scarcity and threats from others pull us into the inertia of habit and the practico-inert.[92] In those conditions, spontaneity has to rigidify itself, which it does by making the recurrence of "what matters" and "what we do" into the rule by which it lives. This type of alienation is a possibility within all forms of *praxis*, and in the conditions of plurality is the reality of *praxis* for human history. Alienated activity is not simply mechanical activity, done without self-consciousness, as can happen at the limit case of merely habitual behavior. Alienated activity involves self-consciousness—knowing what one is doing and continuing to do it in a limited sense "freely"—but doing it not fully out of freedom but instead out of some kind of social necessity and thus having one's activities directed by something other than oneself. Alienation in this sense is a permanent human possibility and not the merely contingent appearance of some deeper structure of a particular kind of society (although some social groups may be more alienating than others, and some will have specifically alienating features to them).[93]

Alienation accompanies objectification, the self-conscious production of things and the production of oneself, as subject, into something approximating an inert thing.[94] To use a term that Sartre does not, objectification results in "material culture," the way in which certain purposes (that is, meanings) become embodied and embedded in produced things or in a reshaped environment. In studying material culture, for example, the historian works from the thing as objectified back to the purposes (the "*praxis*") which brought it about to learn about the constellation of mentalities at the time.

Objectification becomes alienation when it transforms the results of spontaneity into recurrent patterns of behavior (as when the necessity of certain machines in the productive process forces people into a deadening routine) and in particular when it appears as "exigency"—a Sartrean term for "the future which cannot be transcended," that is, the idea that by virtue of the structures of one's specific social order, one faces the necessity to keep on doing the same thing for some indeterminate amount of time so that one's own spontaneity is now being channeled in non-spontaneous ways, or that one's own spontaneity has become oddly passivized, made into not a mere "inert" but into a "practico-inert." As it institutionalizes and regularizes itself, it becomes *praxis*-process, a set of actions carried out without the agent being fully self-conscious of what he is doing as a totalization, even if each of the individual actions that are a component of the whole action are known by him. Various practices, such as that of the so-called free market, are of this sort. Even though the activities of the individual actors can be self-consciously undertaken without there being any consciousness on their part that they are serving any kind of larger purpose in doing so and even though their separate actions are not in fact guided by that goal, they in fact participate in achieving that goal and may even be aware of participating in it. The result of *praxis*-process is the reification of subjectivity, which is not that of making agents into "things" (as the term seems to signify) but that of rigidifying actions into set processes and into preset scripts for them to enact, rather than their spontaneously acting themselves.[95] This picture of *praxis*-process is that of an agent self-consciously dragging himself along the rails that have been laid out in advance for him instead of simply coasting down the rails propelled by his own *hexis*. He is not being pushed, he is pulling himself, but doing it so that he can approximate being pushed. Such is the force not just of *hexis* and its repetitions but of the practico-inert and the lock our own *praxis* lays down for itself. Spontaneity, being empty on its own, necessarily ossifies itself in giving shape to itself, which it then must again resist.

Since each individual is thus potentially the Other, each of whom makes the other into the potentially superfluous "one extra," the possibility of antagonism lies therefore not in the psychology of people—which is not to deny that there can be antagonistic feelings, beliefs, desires, and so on—but in the structure of plural human activity. Since all individual action is the manifestation of a practice—it is the "individualized universal" and thus neither simply the instance of a general rule nor a purely singular event—the basic structure of the plurality is not binary but ternary, that is, of "threes" not just "twos." It is natural to think of the basic unit of sociality as binary, as the first-person plural "we" conceived as constituted by a pair of second-person addresses so that the "we" is the additive unity of "I" and "You." It is nonetheless more accurate to think in terms of a third party for the sociality to be actual. Although it is true that "the mere act of speaking, the simplest gesture, and the elementary structure of perception . . . imply mutual recognition,"[96] and that this mutual recognition itself unfolds itself against a background of "attunement" for each (what Sartre in a Heideggerian way calls the "the world, as the objective envelope of his work and his ends"[97]), the problem with thinking of sociality as reciprocity in binary form is that there will always be struggles over who sets the terms of authority and thus power in the social bond.[98] That much was argued by Hegel in his treatment of mastery and servitude in the *Phenomenology*. The neutral appeal to reason itself will not work unless one thinks that reason already exists in some pristine form that is available and robust enough to serve as a neutral umpire. Sartre, as we have seen, does not deny such Reason with a capital *R*, but claims that it needs to be interpreted, and that interpretation of what reason requires will always be done against a background of other practices that are also constituted in part by partial, one-sided claims to reason backed up by force.

Dialectical reason, as practical reason, is indeed self-correcting, but it does not come on the scene as already corrected. The background attunement must itself be interpreted, made into an individualized universal, and that comes with a third party who makes the claim to speak with authority and more importantly to act with authority for the binary group. The self-correcting aspect of dialectical reason emerges out of that ternary structure. In Hegel's example, as already noted, that leads to the dialectic of mastery and servitude: the two agents are moments of a whole, but each of them claims to speak for the whole (to speak with authority), and when that authority is challenged (even to the minor point of challenging the claim that you and you alone speak for the whole), and when one of them is willing to stake his life on that claim to authority, the struggle for recognition begins. It will only be put off, so Sartre argues, when there is a third agent who has the authority and power to prevent the struggle from emerging in the first place, but Hegel went awry, so Sartre thinks, in proposing that it therefore required a kind of metaphysical "hyper-organism" called *Geist* to serve as the mediating third that in turn swallows up the antagonistic individuals into itself. (That is at least Sartre's version of the Hegelian system.)

Sartre thinks Hegel also went wrong in not treating matter as the mediating factor among the individuals—that is, in not treating scarcity as the fundamental point of possible antagonism. Instead, Hegel focused rather on the projection of each to put something else above the preservation of life, with one person (the individual who falls into servitude) abandoning what had started as an unconditional commitment on his part once he was faced with either holding to that commitment or dying—that is, the one who falls into servitude manifests by his act that his commitment had never actually been fully unconditional but was only at best a kind of conditional aspiration to manifest such an unconditional commitment.[99] Sartre also makes it clear that the kind of attunement and reciprocity he is proposing is itself, at least at the outset, not weighted in any ethical sense. Southern plantation slavery was a form of deformed reciprocity, and "reciprocity, though completely opposed to alienation and reification, does not save men from them."[100] In the case of the slave societies of the American South, one encounters the inhuman face of reciprocity, which manifests itself in its individual acts as "the contradiction of racism, colonialism and all forms of tyranny: in order to treat a man like a dog, one must first recognize him as a man."[101]

However, this form of reciprocity has within itself the resources for thinking about individual freedom in a different way. If the problem is that of the spontaneity of the actor having their spontaneity frozen into routinized or institutionalized forms, or their freedom frozen by the "third party" exercising domination over them in the form of outright oppression or by means of a dominating ideology, there remains the possibility of a spontaneity that is possible only in the spontaneity of others, in which each serves as the mediating third party to any other two, such that "it is not that I am myself in the Other: it is that in (true) *praxis* there is no *Other*, there are only several *myselves* (*il y a des moi même*)." (This is Sartre's own way of rephrasing the Hegelian concept of being at one with oneself in an other.[102]) That depends on certain types of social action within basic forms of social life, whose intelligibility is to be established as conceptual phases of an ongoing explication of practical (dialectical) reason in a plural human world characterized by scarcity.

Spontaneity's Limits

1. Tragic Counter-Finality

Dialectic draws on a conception of negation and negativity that people who invoke it (Sartre included) often distinguish from the more ordinary sense of negation used in standard post-Fregean logic. In its Sartrean, as in its Hegelian use, the "negativity" of some conception or some form of life has to do not merely with incompatible commitments (which are to be found across the board in all kinds of situations). In those ordinary situations, when faced with a direct contradiction, we are then also faced with the need to clean up the contradiction (or obscure it if deception is our more basic aim). We can drop one of the sides of it, or we can redescribe things so that what had in fact seemed like a contradiction turns out just to be a matter of faulty description. However, like Hegel, Sartre is concerned with the way in which negativity functions across a whole ensemble of commitments—what, departing from Sartre's own usage (and using instead Hegel's and Wittgenstein's term), we could call a form of life that develops contradictions or contrarieties within itself that do not seem to go away by means of redescription nor by attempting to drop one of the sides of the contradiction. In Sartre's conception, it is more of a matter of why certain types of contradictions in *praxis* necessarily reappear over and over again, and that has to do with a form of life, a way of "being together," that is at odds with itself, and this also has to do with what he calls the various forms of the inert.[1]

This is illustrated by the concept of a counter-finality, which is where the more dialectical part of Sartre's dialectic really comes to the forefront. The familiar and popular picture of dialectic coming down from Hegel to Marx is that of some type of process or activity in which something originally in play turns out to transform itself into something other or perhaps to generate something other than itself that undermines it. Sometimes it is used to indicate some kind of historical or economic development that works off the interplay between two opposed elements, each of which continually modifies the other as they play off against each other. Sartre's dialectic belongs to that family, but Sartre (like Hegel and Marx) gives it a more formal shape than the looser and more popular picture would have it.

Although it would be easy to conflate the concept of counter-finality with that of "unintended consequences," this would be a mistake.[2] Sartre is instead focusing on what it would mean to say that actions, especially collective actions, can turn out to have ends that were not in the original plans of action *and* are at odds with the original plans of action, so that an individual, but more especially a collective, can turn out to be doing something at odds with what it set out to do. This is dialectical in that a plan of action (as a totalization) turns out to engender its opposite as a matter of the meanings at work in the action. Or, to put it roughly, in undertaking one thing, we find that we have really undertaken another, that our action means something other than, even opposite to, what we originally set out to do. Unintended consequences play a role in counter-finality, but they are not the same thing.

Unintended consequences are the causal results of actions that were not foreseen, and which perhaps could not have been foreseen by the actors (e.g., in lighting the candles, one did not intend to burn down the house). However, counter-finalities are, after all, finalities, ends being pursued that turn out differently than they were conceived in the original project. Such counter-finalities are not defined by the causal network, but, as Sartre says, "in being realized, human ends define a field of counter-finality around themselves,"[3] which, he adds, is "the deep meaning (*sens profonde*) of the aim pursued,"[4] as well as the "hidden meaning" of a "*praxis without an author,*"[5] and which is a finality "lived as the deep import (*signification profonde*) of the task being performed."[6] A counter-finality is thus part of the normative sphere of meaning, not that of causation. Counter-finalities are finalities, ends not intended, not part of the plan but nonetheless inevitably taken up as ends. Part of what these other meanings of the action are has to do with the way the sphere of the inert (both natural and practico-inert) may or may not harmonize with what it is we take ourselves to be underway in accomplishing. As Sartre notes, because "individual *praxis* [is] the unifying and reorganizing transcendence of existing circumstances towards the practical field,"[7] all action is necessarily linked to the inert (practical and natural).

This is Sartre's tragic conception of dialectic, a line of thought that brings him closer to Hegel than it does to Marx. For Sartre, the tragic moment in this has to do with humans discovering a fate they have brought on themselves by their own free actions as a result of the ends they have set for themselves and as ends for which they are driven to assume responsibility.[8] It is tragic in that it manifests a way in which humans are not in harmony with their world, such that their best actions or even who they are betray them.[9] Agency, as aiming (and failing) at being the full foundation of itself, fails in this because of its intertwining of the inert (both practical and natural) with spontaneity itself. Full autonomy, except in the rarest of cases, is unachievable, and we are thus always fundamentally at odds with our world in that respect.

In Sartre's view, there are two ways to fatally misunderstand this. We can resign ourselves to a view that we are fundamentally always pushed around by forces external to us (by "exteriority," the "inert"), in which case we lose ourselves. Or we can fall into the other trap, thinking that what is at stake must be something like "giving ourselves the law," or "thinking things through rationally and thoroughly and acting on them." That is, we can fall into the twin traps of thinking that we are not really free at all in any important sense; or that we are perfectly free and simply have not tried hard enough.[10]

Sartre is drawing on something very similar to what Hegel called the distinction between action and deed, that is, the distinction between what we intentionally choose to come to pass and what the result of the action actually is (such as the intention to light the candles and the deed of burning down the house). The tragic feature of counter-finality is linked to this and to the idea that there can be "*praxis* without an author." The analogue is that of the ancient Greek conception of *nemesis*, fate, following upon even the best laid plans, which leads them to opposite results from those intended. It is not merely the thought that things turn out differently than we might have thought, but the realization that this different outcome turned out to be included in our ends after all and that we ourselves were responsible for these unanticipated results.[11] Our action leads us to a kind of responsibility for that which we did not intend and which undoes our original sense of our plans. The actions that lead to the counter-finality are not directly intended by anybody—one of Sartre's many examples is that of the air pollution brought on by modern industrialization—but the effect is such that the "deed" is one for which those who instituted the action bear responsibility, and this is "praxis without an author." Something has not merely happened but was something that was done, even though nobody took themselves to be doing that and for which the original actors take responsibility.[12]

One paradigm of this is explicitly discussed by Sartre: Fernand Braudel's account of the discovery of gold and silver mines by the Spanish in what then counted as Peru. The Spanish, like many other Europeans at the time, were covetous of Chinese goods (a fact not mentioned by Sartre), but since Europeans had little to sell that the Chinese wanted, they were forced to pay in silver (which the Chinese did want). The bounteous supply of silver and gold in the New World seemed to promise that at least in the case of trade with China, the sky would be the limit for the Spanish in the purchase of Chinese goods. However, as more gold and silver from the New World streamed into Europe itself and out of Spain for the purchase of other luxury goods (and to support warfare), the value of gold and silver coins diminished because of the inflation brought on by the oversupply, which led the Spanish into even more intense mining of these metals, since they judged the national wealth to be identical to the gold they possessed. This was the way in which the "inert," "exteriority" itself, in the form of the laws governing such economic transactions, had consequences for the lives of those who labored for wages: "The possibility of being added up as discrete amounts, that is to say, the fact of not being together, becomes a kind of bond of interiority for the workers."[13] Life itself began to lived differently under the conditions both imposed by exteriority but which had the meaning they had by virtue of their place in the practical field. This was a way in which an "additive" exteriority acquired a non-additive sense that was not simply sense grafted onto otherwise senseless matter.

The other way in which this works is not discussed by Sartre in the *Critique* but follows the logic of his own tragic plays. The example of Oedipus in Sophocles's tragedy shows us a man who kills his father and marries his mother without knowing or intending either. When confronted by this (and the plague he has brought on Thebes), he gouges out his eyes, becoming one with the blind seer Teiresias, who had initially warned him of such a thing. Oedipus was not guilty in the narrow moral sense (he never intended to marry his mother); nonetheless, he felt he was somehow impure and to blame not for a moral infraction but for who he had turned out to be.[14] He exhibited what Sartre in *Being and Nothingness* analyzed in terms of shame, a disappointment with or even horror of what one is, and not simply guilt at having done something wrong.[15] The example of Oedipus is that of counter-finality as individual, not social, but it is still the kind of tragic counter-finality with which Sartre is concerned. This is why the "deep meaning" of the actions plays such a role in Sartre's conception of counter-finality and therefore of human history itself. In such situations, the experience and the comprehension of the counter-finality among the collective is not just that "something has accidentally gone wrong," but "this is what we have done," and thus "this is who we turned out to be."

2. Practical Identities, Singular and General:
Differing Conceptions of "We"

One of the most basic forms of collective life is seriality—Sartre's own term
for self-conscious togetherness as pursuing a common aim but without any
real sharing of the aim even when those involved see themselves as sharing
the aim. Seriality can be antagonistic or relatively placid. The relation of seriality is not that of a simple heap of people pursuing different aims, nor is it
simply a set of people who share some characteristic, such as when somebody
happens to notice, let us imagine, that he and everyone else on the street cor-
ner is carrying an umbrella and maybe even thinks to himself, "My! We are all
carrying umbrellas." It is not thus simply a distributed, additive "we." Nor is
it necessarily people engaged in any transaction with each other. In seriality,
one is aware of oneself and others as engaged in something together without
being engaged with each other. The person waiting for the bus can think of
herself as sharing this aim with others as she silently stands at the bus stop
or as each unreflectively moves around to avoid any kind of direct encounter with the others. Each thus thinks of himself or herself—not necessarily
reflectively—as doing the same thing together, as being a member of a series.
Thus, in that concatenation, one's own membership in the "we" of seriality is
in principle open-ended. One can imagine a group of people waiting with the
others for a bus each responding at the same time without any further reflection to, say, a text message that asks, "What are you doing?" with the simple
"Waiting for a bus." The people waiting for the bus share an interest and thus
very loosely an identity (those queuing for the bus), and they are, as such,
each abstractly identical to the other. Each has, as Sartre richly describes it,
the "fate as Other *by every Other as Other*" as "identical instances of the same
act."[16] They can even act as a group of sorts, but the "we" is not a fully apperceptive "we." Although each member is conscious of himself as a member,
the series itself is not fully conscious of itself as a series.

Yet, as the example illustrates, this common project, which can be lived
in isolation from the others, can also be lived as so engaged. Although its
commonality does bring the individuals together, it is also what they have in
common (as a series) that drives them apart. Thus, every member of the series is potentially the "extra" person, the superfluous one, the one fit to be ex-
cluded, the one who does not get a seat or a place on the bus once it is full. It
is a monological relation to others that is monological only as being mediated
by the relation to others. Seeing oneself as "a person queuing for the bus"
among others is not necessarily to see oneself purely as an individualistic,

monadic subject (as we might think if we took something like game theory as our starting point) but as an isolated subject engaged in a common project that by its nature requires the isolation of its members for its commonality. Those in the bus queue are not merely a heap of bodies in a similar space but are related to each other via matters of interiority—their own project of catching the bus in order to X—that isolate them from each other.

Seriality is a step in the direction of the "atomization" of society in which one has not merely isolated individuals but instead the figure of the individual so familiar in game theory who is forever calculating what to do in light of his own expected utility, which in turn takes into account his predictions and expectations of what others will do. However, "atomization" and seriality are not the same thing.[17] Atomization is the experience of sharing nothing in common with others, so that all forms of "we" would be merely distributed versions. Serialization is self-consciousness about a common project in which one is nonetheless not engaged with others in terms of a common project. Serialization can, moreover, take positive and negative forms.[18]

Such forms of a "We" can become (what Sartre calls) "gatherings" if the possibility of a unitary, common action is given by the presence of each to each. In times of shortages, for example, people queuing before a shop can quickly coalesce into a protest or riot.[19] There can be indirect "gatherings," such as an isolated set of people listening to the same radio program with each aware that she is doing what others do. In all the examples, the unity of the series comes not from the attitudes of each to the other—none is engaged with the other—but from the objects (taken in a general sense) that bring them together into a common project. The common project of a series is not merely the sum of various commitments undertaken (for example, the sum of individual commitments such as "I shall take the bus" adding up to the same unity as "My! We are all carrying umbrellas"). It is a way in which "we" think of ourselves as engaged in something that is not simply the sum of various unrelated first-person commitments. It is the weakest form of totalization, that is, of encountering the practical field as something like a kind of organic connectedness.

These examples, though, are not Sartre's real focus. His real interest is in how the concept of seriality makes intelligible the modes in which a social identity takes shape, especially those having to do with things like class identity and the free market. People waiting for a bus are not acting in a vacuum. To comprehend that, we need the concepts of bus, public transportation, jobs, time schedules, and for that matter embodiment and matter (to make sense of why, for example, it would take too long to walk the distance that the bus traverses more quickly). In lots of ways, the whole panoply of serialization can come into play: the modes of dress common to people at the time, the common interest as commuters in the bus arriving on time, the concern about possible increases in the fare, and so on. The commuters are, as it were, given a (social) serial identity; it is given to them by way of each of them incorporating it into their own projects. It is of course an abstract identity (not a "rich, differentiated synthesis"[20] of moments of lived reality), which they take on themselves (as spontaneous) in terms of a larger practice (which forms a "milieu") that constitutes a form of life that stands outside of them but only exists in and through their actualizations of that form of life. In that form of life, each exists in "their interchangeability: each of them is effectively produced by the social ensemble as united with his neighbors, in so far as he is strictly identical with them."[21] All of these express the exigencies—the "future which cannot be transcended"[22]—of the social order as they have become themselves subjected to the practico-inert. The spontaneity of the agents crystallizes, that is, into a set of identities that are given to them but exist only as they interiorize them as "interiority lived in the milieu of exteriority," in which "recurrence" is the mode by which the social identity is sustained.[23] In this way, seriality functions to display an illusory sense of togetherness, namely, the illusion of doing something together when in fact no real togetherness is present. (A contemporary Twitter rage might be an example.)

Some social identities, such as class, will be more central than others (certainly for Sartre) and will press more heavily on the subject's own sense of himself, since some kinds of serial collectivities will be seemingly impossible to avoid. Whereas in *Being and Nothingness* Sartre had presented human reality as the attempt by "nothingness" to "be" (that is, for self-conscious agency as the for-itself to be in-itself and thus to be the impossible for-itself-in-itself), in the *Critique* self-conscious agency is depicted in terms of always already "being" something (a member of this or that class, this or that ethnic collection, etc.) and is always at least on the way to finding a way in which its spontaneity could be expressed that would transcend its "being."

Relations of seriality, so he seems to argue, in principle cannot be the modes in which spontaneity can achieve its adequate expression. Seriality creates "general individuals" (as distinct from "common" or "communal" individuals, which Sartre introduces later in the book[24]), that is, agents whose possibilities in life are determined by the serial groupings to which they find themselves, as it were, assigned. One says, "as it were," since it is rare that anybody actually does that kind of assigning, but it nonetheless becomes part of the practico-inert and therefore of "recurrence" within a social formation that is always already structured in its own way. The more basic point, however, has to do with the way in which such seriality "forces the working woman to live a prefabricated destiny as her reality" (and likewise the "working man" or the "working transgender" in lots of different and specific ways).[25] It is "pre-fabricated" for the working person as the life that is imposed on the disadvantaged by virtue of the relations of power (and thus of income, wealth, and education) existing as the practico-inert of that society.

Given these terms, almost any "prefabricated life" would be incompatible with expressing adequately the agent's spontaneity, since in such a life the agent's spontaneous choices would find themselves already channeled into set pathways in life. Nonetheless, such "prefabricated lives" can never exhaust the spontaneity of the actors, whose own "negativity"—their capability of entertaining a different future and possibly acting on that idea—is not eradicable, even if the inertia inherent in the practico-inert puts limitations on the really possible. In particular, such seriality is always constituted by the relations among the subjects as themselves relating to the objects of the material and social world (in conditions of scarcity, where everybody is potentially the "one extra," the superfluous person, the potentially jobless without means of support). These relations are therefore all mediated by the materiality of things involved.[26]

In the kind of class society that Sartre thinks that much of the world (at least around 1960) exhibited, the background attunement will be shown and revealed in the ways in which membership in classes displays "the inertia which infiltrates freedom."[27] Acting in terms of the inertia prescribed by one's class is an "individualized universal," a specific act that is universal in its meaning while being singular as an act, and which in turn produces oneself and others as the "general individuals" that are defined by their social identities (including class). This is not a matter of exercising some special faculty like a causally independent free will but is that of a material self-conscious being exercising the capacity for spontaneity—its negative relation to the self itself, its "totalizing" its life over its temporal series in trying to comprehend its life as a whole (a "totality") in which the parts serve the whole, and the whole is what it is by virtue of the parts. Such "totalizing" beings never succeed in totalizing themselves—they never actually become a "totality" and must remain by virtue of their negativity and the contingency of the world always therefore a "detotalized totality," an intrinsically failed attempt at grasping the world, to use the phrase Thomas Nagel has made famous, from the view from nowhere.[28] The "view from nowhere"—what Sartre calls the "absolute witness"[29]—would be the view of the world as a whole that would require us to have a standpoint somewhere outside the world—the God's eye view, which is consistently denied as a real possibility throughout Sartre's writing.

3. Spontaneity within the Revolt of the Oppressed: The Spontaneous "We"

In Sartre's way of putting it, "everyone makes himself signify by interior-izing, by a free choice, the signification with which material exigencies have produced him as a signified being."[30] Or, to put it in the Kantian terms that have almost become cliché, spontaneity without the recurrence and exigen-cies of life would be empty, but those exigencies without spontaneity would be blind.[31]

However, not all exigencies give spontaneity a content that can survive the kind of being together that reciprocity requires. Freedom as spontaneity occurs in "seriality," but it is bounded by materiality and cannot thereby be the full actualization of freedom as spontaneity. "The inert gathering with its structure of seriality is the basic type of sociality," Sartre notes, and in serial-ity, one's freedom is mediated by relations to inert objects and exigencies.[32] What it makes rational sense to do is bounded on all sides by one's own em-bodiment, the world around oneself, and the plurality of others in that world. Sartre's bus riders almost never have the bus to themselves, and even when they do, they are bounded in their action, if by nothing else, by the nature of the bus itself. One is not free to set one's projects in any way one pleases; both the material and social worlds put limitations on free action. Spontane-ity per se does not set any content to itself.

When the relation of one subject to another is direct, a fully actualized freedom emerges. In Sartre's version of dialectic, the paradigmatic form of the social and of sociality is that of the "inert gathering with its structure of seriality," in which there is a common project within which shared purposes may come about but without any common purpose at first.[33] In this para-digmatic form, the relations between agents are mediated by their relation to material things. Therefore, in this paradigmatic form, freedom cannot be fully actualized if in fact freedom consists in a spontaneity unhooked from exigency.

Sartre distances himself from Hegel in this regard (or at least from what he calls the "transcendental, idealist dialectic").[34] From the Hegelian standpoint, freedom would have to emerge as the way in which basic contradictions (or, perhaps in a more limited sense, basic unlivable tensions) were to be found in forms of sociality that themselves could only make sense if there were to be a development out of them so that freedom would be more fully actualized. As also already noted, Sartre identifies that as following too closely the fully organic metaphor of society, in that (so he thought) it sees social life in terms of something like a hyper-organism developing its own parts (its organs) in order to complete the whole. However, Sartre's point is that the actualization of freedom must itself be the result of a free act or set of acts, not something that quasi-naturally develops out of something else. Freedom is spontaneity, which by definition is a new beginning. How is that supposed to work? How could it even work?

It involves a shift in self-conscious location vis-à-vis others. In seriality, there is a common project, but there is no shared project. Each relates to the other as a rational, self-conscious being in a system mediated either by rules (somewhat similar to that of participants in a game) or by the relation to the same object (such as the bus for which they may all be waiting). If something comes about to motivate it, the gathering can shift from a "collective" (another technical term for Sartre) to what he calls a "group" (which he also uses as a technical term). In a "group," the primary relation is not that of a direct subsumption of an "I" under a "we" but of a form of second-person address through which the "we" is constituted in a new kind of triadic relation.

Sartre uses this to construct something similar from Hegel's idea of mastery and servitude but without making a step toward Hegel's "spirit" or *Geist*. The distinction is the following. In the Hegelian setting of the scene where masters and servants emerge out of a struggle with each other, one imagines the encounter between two self-conscious agents, each of which claims to be doing what he does and justifying what he does by reference to what "we" do (that is, by reference to the "whole"). More specifically, he claims a kind of identity between what "I do" and what "we do" such that "I" need not draw the distinction sharply. To return to the previous example used to illustrate Hegel's encounter: if I encounter fruit ripe for the picking, I can justify my picking it because that is just the kind of thing that "we" (members of the human species) do. The fruit matters to me, and I do what we do in the face of such mattering. If to another agent it also matters that there is fruit ripe for the picking, he has the same explanation and justification. When both realize this, there is a shift of viewpoint from merely "it matters to me because this kind of thing matters to us" to "it matters to me that it matters to me in light of the possible conflict at hand."

At this point, the shared background of meaning (the generality of "what 'we' typically do") is too abstract to provide any real guidance. Typically, we may cooperate and share, but just as typically we may also oppose and fight. In the Hegelian stage setting for this part of the dialectic, both of the agents (to whom this matters) stake an unconditional claim, namely, to demand to have full authority to decide the matter (in his favor) about what "we" shall do, and in the ensuing struggle, one of them gives up the fight in order to live—and thereby shows through his action that the demand was never actually unconditional for him—and becomes the bondsman or slave.

This particular relation of master and servant is deeply irrational—since it requires the master to demand recognition as master from a person who by the master's own terms has no authority to bestow that recognition—and in Hegel's development of the narrative the apparent irrationality of the master-slave relation prompts the development of the concept of a third perspective besides that of the dyad of master and slave. In Hegel's 1807 *Phenomenology of Spirit*, this third perspective is at first that of reason in general (which is then given a richer social and philosophical development), but this conception of reason is still too individualistic to make adequate sense of itself, and, as Hegel narrates it, it too fails in its own self-explication, which in turn develops into the more concrete concept of social self-conscious life, *Geist*, which assumes a variety of historical shapes itself in working out what it would mean for self-conscious life to adequately comprehend itself.

It is in Hegel's move to *Geist* that Sartre draws his line, since Sartre only understood Hegel's *Geist* as a kind of hyper-organism, that is, a kind of idealistically conceived spiritual organism of which individual agents are merely the parts (or "organs") themselves. Yet he also holds that insofar as the relation is conceived along the lines of two self-conscious agents each seeking independence, something like Hegel's "struggle for recognition" is the logical consequence, and the solution has to be "as if" there actually were such a hyper-organism directing the matter without there being in any sense other than "as if" there actually is such an entity.[35] Sartre's own transformation of the Hegelian proposal is to see the third element not as an independent, "hyper-organism" *Geist* but as another individual agent totalizing him- or herself in the practical field that includes the two other agents, and—this is the crucial part—with the other two agents serving in turn as the third element to what becomes the dyad to him or her (as the third). Agent A is the "third" to agents B and C, Agent B is the third to agents A and C, and agent C is the third to agents A and B. Each is independently totalizing the other two, but each is also therefore internalizing his or her own dependence on the activities of the other two.

The triadic relation is conceived as a kind of circularity in motion. In this way, the mediation of agent to agent via the material object drops out, replaced by a direct, spontaneous relation of agent to agent in the triad. In such a "group," which is Sartre's technical term of art for this kind of togetherness, we get an abstract picture of what a full actualization of freedom would be like: it is spontaneity freed from exigency. Moreover, this extends what seems to be Sartre's earlier adaptation of the point of Kant's paralogism about the unity of the "I": if it is a mistake to infer from the identity of the "I" to something material like a "soul-thing," it is equally a mistake to infer from the identity of a "we" to something like a we-hyper-organism. Besides the apperceptive "I" (the first-person singular), there is an apperceptive "we" (the first-person plural) that does not require there to be a separate thing of sorts to be the subject of such a first-person plural apperception.[36] The triadic structure of "totalization" is supposed to avoid that.

Rousseau and Kant both spoke of political and moral associations where each would be both sovereign and subject: each would function as a spontaneous, unconstrained lawgiver as "sovereign," and as "subject" would be constrained by the laws given by himself and others. (Sartre puts a caveat on this idea, describing that kind of individual sovereignty as "quasi-sovereignty," but that caveat requires some more explication of what Sartre takes to be the limits of the intelligibility of common actions.[37]) Each agent authorizes principles or rules—Sartre prefers the term "statuses"—to the others and comprehends the others as authorizing such "rules" to him so that a common action is created. They are not, however, merely authorizing rules. As practical agents, they are creating a common action together, and the agents in a group thereby form an association of full reciprocity (or "mediated reciprocity," as Sartre prefers to say[38]). The action of each is the action of the other in the group.

This leaves open the question as to what actions they are or should be or must be authorizing for themselves. In introducing the idea, Sartre dramatizes the issue with illustrations from the French Revolution of 1789, from the revolution of 1830 establishing the July Monarchy, and from the revolution of 1848 establishing the short-lived Second Republic. The revolutionary group "fuses" into its triadic form out of seriality because each individual in the series suddenly sees him- or herself as threatened by an "Other." In Sartre's original illustration, this has to do with the way in which a section of the people of Paris in 1789 become convinced that the king's armed forces in Versailles (forces composed of some French people and some mercenaries from other countries) were being assembled by the king in order to put down the newly formed revolutionary government. A few weeks before, the Estates General (the assembly of the three estates—commoners, nobility, and ecclesiastics) had dissolved itself into what they called the National Assembly, and in the Tennis Court Oath (in a room where they had met when they believed that the locked doors to their assembly hall had been purposely locked on the king's orders—which they weren't—in order to shut down the Assembly, which the king by that time almost certainly wanted to do in any event), they vowed to give France a constitution. A few weeks later, after people had begun arming themselves to face down a feared military incursion into the city, a crowd gathered in Paris in order to obtain more arms and gunpowder. They marched to the Bastille peacefully to obtain the arms and gunpowder they believed were stored there, and the troops defending the fortress opened fire on them. A full-scale firefight ensued, many people were killed, the Bastille fell, victims' heads were paraded around on pikes, and July 14 entered the lexicon.

Sartre sees this as a series forming itself around a negation served up to them by the soldiers defending the Bastille. Each individual in the gathering felt himself threatened and vowed to resist. Each reasoned (accurately) that as an isolated individual, he could not win and saw the others as means to his end (his own project), but each in seeing the other as means also had to see himself as the means to the other's end. Each thus saw himself and others as both means and ends, in particular as the means by which the fused group's intention now took shape as "We, defenders of the Revolution, fight the defenders of the Bastille" and not as "I, and I, and I . . . fight the defenders of the Bastille." Sartre therefore concludes that in fact the group can only come into being (or "fuse") in light of a threat, most particularly a threat to life itself. He supplements that with a series of vignettes about people confronting the police after demonstrations, falling apart, regrouping, and so on to make his point. He seems to be saying that groups form only under the threat of mortal violence.

However, he partially reverses himself on this in a footnote. He says, "Obviously it is not under a threat of mortal danger that anglers form their association or old ladies set up a system of swopping books," but he claims that other such "groupings" are only "superstructures," that is, "groups which are constituted in the general, permanent regroupment activity of collectives," and "thus I need only concern myself here with the fundamental fact of grouping as the conquest or reconquest of the collective by *praxis*."[39] That is, he seems to assert that the negative feature of a group (as this group, not that one) can only come to it under some kind of existential threat (or something close to it) from something outside it that the group in formation then interiorizes as it proceeds on the rapid path to fusion. The crucial point for Sartre is that it is only in such groups (of shared *praxis*) that we achieve at least the abstract conception of what freedom as actualized would look like. Sartre's sympathies also go with the revolutionaries seizing the moment and gaining their freedom against the real oppression by the king, the nobility, and the church by way of such radical action. It is only near the end of the first volume of the *Critique* that Sartre mentions that the same line of reasoning also applies to the nobility. They too would see themselves as a unified group "negated" by the revolutionary group on the way to fusion. They too would see their pushback against the Revolution as the actualization of their freedom.[40] And in fact many of them did just that.[41]

Sartre's gripping descriptions of the way the gathering comes together to form a revolutionary grouping at the Bastille can give the impression (which Sartre does little to dispel) that his account in fact rests fully on that example (as if he were doing some kind of historical phenomenology of the actors' viewpoints, which Sartre's other activities as novelist and playwright surely suggest). His stated intent, though, is to make the events of the Revolution intelligible, that is, to show how as a matter of dialectical—that is, practical—reason, such groupings have an a priori element to them that follows from what it is to be a being-in-time spontaneously projecting itself into a future, constrained by its past, and absorbed in its current world, and who is guided by an aim of spontaneous expression in reciprocity with others.

Although in its general shape, Sartre's overall interpretation of the French Revolution is generally Marxist—he sees it as the class revolt of the bourgeoisie against the nobility—he actually rejects the orthodox Marxist approach of his own time that by its own lights tended to see the actors as merely swept along by historical forces that they themselves did not or could not necessarily understand. On Sartre's view, that would simply make no sense of the action. Rather, the Revolution was, as it were, a developing story without a script but which in turn developed in intelligible ways that itself in turn transformed the actors themselves by virtue of the counter-finalities that emerged in the course of the struggle. For example, the newly formed National Assembly was not originally in favor of the violent action taken by the citizens against the Bastille, but as revolutionaries, they were also reluctant to condemn it, since it was being done in the name of the Revolution. For many of the members of the Assembly, it was in all other respects a criminal act, but it was also a revolutionary act, which meant that it was deserving of both condemnation and praise, and that not so incipient contradiction changed the context entirely of those people of the Assembly making decisions afterward, at least so much that they would in turn come to rename themselves the Constituent Assembly and change their self-interpretations accordingly. Revolutionary government, and then not so long thereafter, revolutionary justice, developed out of the initial two to three weeks of revolutionary activity in both the Assembly and the streets.[42] Counter-finality (and not merely unintended consequences) emerged rapidly in the course of the Revolution. There was no "law" pushing the Revolution forward to its climax, nor were the results of the Revolution merely the contingent outcome of a set of either laudatory or unfortunate passions on the part of its leaders, nor was it simply

the logical consequence of a Rousseauian idea taken to its logical and unsat-
isfying conclusion. It was the way in which people seeking a certain end and
acting collectively found themselves irretrievably committed to another end
that none of them had willed at first.

Sartre of course sides with the revolutionaries revolting against oppression and not with the nobility who wish to maintain it. However, to entitle
himself to that, he has to do more than give his social ontology with its theory
of freedom. Like Heidegger, he gives an account of the form of agency and its
sociality, but, also like Heidegger at least up to this point in the development
of Sartre's theory, he gives himself no way of distinguishing the most repre-
hensible forms of agency from its far more praiseworthy forms. To draw out
the obvious difference between the revolt of the oppressed and the counterrevolutionary pushback of the privileged required Sartre to develop his fledg-
ling ethics (which he never published, although he gave a couple of public
lectures on it). But before he could do that, he also had to develop what he
argued were the inherent limits built into dialectical (practical) reason not
out of anything like the frailty of the human passions but of the nature of
embodied spontaneous agency itself.

4. Actualized Freedom's Fragility in the Myths of Self-Authorization

On the Sartrean scheme of the *Critique*, freedom can only be fully actualized in a plurality of agents. Since such freedom encompasses what Sartre
would call both the social and the political, it would be misleading to call
this "social freedom," if this is taken as the union of individual freedom as
following one's own ends together with an identification with the rational
institutions of one's society.[43] (That conception of freedom is far too metaphysically optimistic for Sartre's tragic conception of counter-finality.) Nor is
it the freedom of individuals as individually coordinating their actions with
each other (that would still be a "collective" and a form of seriality), nor is it
straightaway a matter of individuals freely willing to "identify" with the social
institutions in which they live. For Sartre, it is a manner of doing something
together such that the doing of one is the doing of the other and the joint
doing-of-one-being-the-doing-of-the-other is essential for the freedom of
each. The emptiness of the "I think" or "I intend" is filled out with content
coming from another agent, and in the group on the way to fusion, it is this
circulating dependence on others that establishes the true independence of
the singular agent.

The "we" of a group on the way to fusion ought to be distinguished from
that of an already fused group, a distinction that is not always completely

clearly drawn in Sartre's text. In an already fused group, practices have been established, and the use of "I" and "We" is there to articulate the established practice such that "voting for the chair of the department" (by filling out a ballot or by raising hands) makes sense as the act of voting for the chair only because the background practice has already been presupposed. For example, games display this: one moves one's bishop in chess, one moves one's checkers in checkers, one moves one's stone in Go, and so on, only because there is already a background practice of checkers, chess, Go, already in place.

In a group on the way to fusion, however, there is no determinate background practice for the actors to plug into, although there have to be other, more general practices for them to share. By virtue of what Sartre at first only imagines as an existential threat, the actors each spontaneously take up the position of the regulating third party, the group forms, and at the point of unification, they experience the "apocalypse," Sartre says, borrowing a term and idea from André Malraux.[44] Moreover, such a spontaneous unification (as a totalization in progress) is the expression of the background attunement that is always already there and shows itself in the discrete acts of those who are manifesting this background meaning in the very act of fusing (vis-à-vis each as third party) into the group.[45] Once the group has fused, it then may spontaneously organize itself into the kinds of differentiations that make up a practice, but while it is fusing, it is pure spontaneity, not yet constrained by any norms peculiar to it except those of the freedom of each, as it were, suddenly making its appearance in the fusing group. It does this by restructuring the kind of dependencies that are present in all the types of serial unities into a set of dependencies that serve to liberate the agent from dependency on the arbitrary will of others and for each to be "sovereign," that is, self-determining with regard to himself. Each as the regulating third party to the others both authorizes the status and is subject to it.

The group on the way to fusion presents a unity of agents who are not, in forming such a group, expressing an already developed practice. In this case and this case only, the "individualized universal" is not the incarnation of a practice but rather forms the free-flowing unity that may then be stabilized into various practices. Nonetheless, it still requires the background of agency in general as thinking, meaning, understanding, and acting (and speaking) in terms of an ongoing totalization. That background cannot imply on its own the more determinate shapes the group will take as it fuses. Once the group has been formed (and is a "group-in-fusion"), the group itself develops (although not fully self-consciously or necessarily in any reflective way) the various standards for what will count as the practice of the group. Dialectical reason can thus be distinguished according to whether it is constituting or constituted dialectical reason, that is, whether it is reason as constituting a practice or reason as working within an already constituted practice that shows itself in the activities (linguistic and otherwise) of the practitioners.[46] (The distinction is relative. Constituted dialectical reason is sustaining and transforming the practice through its "individualized universal" acts, and constituting dialectical reason is always already operating within the bounds of other, already constituted practices, even when it is empowering the pure spontaneity of the group on the way to fusion.)

At the point where the group on the way to fusion comes together (that is, "fuses"), it sets about transforming the practico-inert feature of its members (and therefore itself as a group) by establishing the baselines of what counts as manifesting the practice and continuing it in the same ways. (Sartre speaks of this as "inertia" coming into play.) In the group on the way to fusion, what unites the gathering is the sudden shared awareness of a common objective (the "apocalypse") but no awareness yet of the group as a group. From the outside, one can speak of a group intention in its gathering to, say, storm the Bastille, but from the inside, the group has no intention. Rather, there is, to use Sartre's metaphor, the swirling circle of individuals each seeing themselves as the "regulating third parties" of the group (with each taking the position of a sovereign issuing orders) and as members of the group acting under the orders given by other third parties. There is the group's doing something, but the group is not yet operating as a hyper-organism with an intention of its own. The group comes to have an intention as it forms itself and acts self-consciously as a group.

In such a group on the way to fusion, there is a fundamental discovery uncovered in the experience of equality by all the members, and, in discovering equality, they actualize their freedom as spontaneity together with their rotating dependence on each other (as "third parties) and establish a kind of independence (as absence of subordination) on the part of each. Each therefore finds him- or herself in a society of equals in terms of being "like" (or the same as) the others in the group on the way to fusion, whatever other distinctions there may be among them.[47] The equal status each has in the group on the way to fusion has to do with the sudden recognition of each other as the same in regard to the group's perspective.[48] The unity of such a group on the way to fusion is, as Sartre puts it, a "unity as ubiquity,"[49] that is, a "we" that is not that of an accidental "we" (as in "we are all wearing black sweaters"), nor is it the kind of constitutive "we" that functions as the background of meaning (such as that expressed in "we speakers of English . . ."), nor is it even the "we" of a common project conceived as the coordination of various individual self-conscious agents as in game theory. It is rather that of a genuinely shared content of practical thought, that of, what "we" are doing as a group. Each as the singular incarnation of the general unity encounters each as an equal, and only in such an encounter is genuine freedom lifted out of the "practico-inert" into full spontaneity. Sartre puts it succinctly: "The universal that I realize here is always under the form of singularity. This is what I call incarnation."[50]

In actualizing freedom as spontaneity, the group also produces a motivation on the part of its members to continue itself.[51] The group initially has no aims except to actualize the freedom of its members by providing them with the power created by the plurality of the group. After it has formed, it provides its members with a motivation to keep it, as the actualization of freedom, in existence, and it thus has a reason to construct binding norms for itself and to provide motivation for its members to abide by those norms, which means fashioning itself into a formation of a practico-inert.

As was the case in *The Transcendence of the Ego*, Sartre rejects psychologism in both the cognitive and the practical cases. The kind of norms on which Sartre focuses are thus themselves features of situations. Typically that kind of attention to reasons involves a sensitivity to certain features of situations as calling for a certain type of behavior, and it is the (generally prethetic) self-conscious grasp of the situation that delivers reasons to the agent to act, with all of this being intelligible only when situated within the context of the extended project of an action or a whole life. What will count as a practical reason for the practical organism will therefore be set (as it is for all organisms) by the possibilities open for that form of life, and in the case of self-conscious life, by the changing set of possibilities brought on by its reshaping itself in its history.[52]

The motive to continue the group's existence instead of letting it dissipate into a "collective" in which such spontaneity is once again hemmed in and channeled into other paths thus involves the plural realizations of a rather indeterminate good that can only be achieved and reachieved through the group that has been formed. Although it is easy enough to read this as a kind of semi-empirical or even phenomenological account of groups arising and vanishing in social life, Sartre's point, as he states over and over again, is in fact not to be interpreted as giving any kind of empirical sociological account or historical description of how particular groups in history have formed and restructured themselves. It is to show how the motivation to keep the group together follows from the reasons for the group coming together in the first place (as the group on the way to fusion). Even if the reason for the group on the way to fusion to form was itself accidental—perhaps it happens by virtue of a perceived threat to each that is not really there—the realization of freedom as spontaneity in the group gives its members a reason to continue it to the extent that the reason for forming it was real.

Where to go from there? What kind of norms would keep freedom in place? Sartre's own response has to do with what is sometimes called the paradox of democracy and sometimes more generally called the paradox of autonomy. In the case of the so-called paradox of democracy, Sartre's response concerns the idea that a people authorizing itself, for example, to write a constitution cannot actually describe itself as an authoritative people capable of such an act until after "they" have written the constitution that creates and authorizes them as a people to do just that. (The United States Constitution, with its famous preamble beginning "We, the people . . ." is one of the paradigm cases.) The paradox of autonomy likewise holds that one cannot be subject to any law that one has not authored for oneself and that any law that is not authorized in light of another authoritative law is not binding, since it is lawless.[53]

One way out of this kind of paradox would be to adopt a more realist or Platonist approach to reasons according to which reasons must always already precede reasoning. On that view, "reason" would be a power or capacity to discern certain types of objects (reasons) that are independent of the power. (Seen from that approach, the "paradox" would not be a paradox at all but only a self-contradiction, since only reasons independent of the actor have any binding force.) Or one might think that a reason is simply the kind of thing that the power of reason happens to discover, and that there is nothing more to the concept of "a reason" than that which the power of reasoning delivers. Sartre wants it both ways: what counts as a reason has to do with the possibilities open to a form of life (in this case, self-conscious life), and this form of life involves a "power" (the capacity to reason, to imagine, to draw conclusions from evidence, etc.) that reveals certain things as reasons that cannot be available to non-self-conscious forms of life.

What is always already there is the background of attunement, but, stated like that, it offers no guidance for any further practical reasoning. In a mode similar to the argument Sartre used for the "I" in *The Transcendence of the Ego*, where the "I" was posited as the unity that supposedly (but wrongly supposed) had to be already present in pre-reflective consciousness, now the group posits itself as having already existed, as "the pre-existing foundation for all its transformations," as "a pre-existing agent."[54] The argument relates to that given by the Abbé Sieyès in 1789 in his *What Is the Third Estate?*: if a nation is to have a constitution, then the nation must be prior to all other law-giving including the constitution it gives itself. The nation and the nation alone can set the terms by which a "people" come to organize themselves under laws. "We, the people" can authorize the constitution only because this "we" is supposed to have already been authorized by the authority of all other authorities, the nation. This was Sieyès's rather famous answer to the alleged paradox, but Sartre will have nothing of it.[55] The "nation is not a group,"[56] he points out, and Sieyès's concept of the nation (which would itself blossom out into the nineteenth- and twentieth-century conceptions of nationalism) is just one more version of the kind of myth the group is motivated to tell about itself in order to have its self-determined rulings not seem simply arbitrary. The group must posit itself not as pure spontaneity but as a set of already existent practices that then manifest themselves in the actions of its members. This move is essential if the group is to continue as the reciprocal recognition of its members as members of *this* group: "It presents itself both as having been performed once and for all and as having to be constantly reactualized."[57] It is what Antigone states in the tragedy of the same name as "Not now and yesterday, but forever / It lives, and nobody knows from whence it appeared," when it is actually a feature of the group in which it will always be tempted to place itself. This feature of collective action and self-understanding, so Sartre says, itself "is the origin of humanity."[58]

The means by which this is done is through the metaphor of "the pledge" (or "oath," *le serment*), itself modeled on the actual "pledge" undertaken in the Oath of the Tennis Court in France in 1789 in the Assembly's pledging itself to give France a constitution. However, whatever its origin, the "pledge" remains only a metaphor. Since each member of the group is free and therefore possessing a negativity toward all things merely given to him or her, the group can only maintain itself if its members maintain it, and the freedom of each implies that this cannot be a foregone logical conclusion. Having established themselves as free and equal in the moment of reciprocal spontaneity (the group on the way to fusion), each must, as it were, "pledge" not to leave the group, or, metaphorically also, pledge not to become more than an equal. Each becomes, by virtue of the metaphorical pledge, an equal and therefore also a communal individual. Since they can be bound by the pledge only if they are equals, the myth of the pledge has to be that the result (equality) was already there and at work in the making of the pledge. By virtue of the pledge and becoming "communal," they all come to share a highly abstract identity. The duty to abide by the pledge cannot come from the pledge itself, since otherwise an infinite regress of such pledges would be needed.

The "pledge" in Sartre's theory cannot be a real pledge. It is the unity of the group as the now established background of meaning that is manifested in the individual acts of those who "pledge," or "swear" their lives, their honor, their fortunes, to the group. Although the pledge also looks like a contract or a covenant, it can be neither. It is itself the basis upon which any binding contract or covenant could even be made. Now, it is probably obvious that Sartre's adoption of the language of the Tennis Court Oath has to do with a set of particular events of the French Revolution, but his point is that the group had to fuse itself in the spontaneity of each individual agent (as mediated by the triadic structure) before the actual "pledge" on the part of the participants had any force. Between two people, any pledge as a "contract" must be enforceable if it is to be genuine norm (at least as Sartre sets up the situation), and for this reason, the third party is always required as the regulator or agent of enforcement. When each is the regulating third party for the other, then spontaneity is actualized.

The norms that are then articulated as basic to the group are the "juridical norms" that govern what it means to be a member with that particular shared, communal identity, and, as norms, they must be enforced. With that, the relation of the members of the group to each other is transformed. From the pure reciprocity of the group on the way to fusion, one moves to the mediated reciprocity of the group-in-fusion as developing a juridical power over its members. (This juridical power should not be confused, Sartre insists, with morals. They are a separate issue, although they obviously intertwine with each other at various points.[59]) The relation among the members is no longer direct and immediately reciprocal (as it might be in a relation of love or friendship).[60] It is now mediated reciprocity, with the relations among the agents beginning to assume something more like the structure of a game in which the relations among the members are mediated by the rules under which they are playing (so that one can, for example, metaphorically be "offside" or be ruled as having committed a foul in one's ongoing interactions with the others). The idea of this as a pledge is pure metaphor, since one is given no choice about whether to pledge. The pledge itself is represented, indeed seems to have to be represented, as having always already taken place, so that one is "pledged" at birth. The pledge functions as a kind of Platonic myth that the group is motivated to form about itself in order to bring its "monstrous spontaneity" back to some kind of inertial fixity. The background of reciprocity among agents, although empty on its own, is taken to have already existed in its stable forms long ago. This quasi-mythical status of the pledge as the answer to what otherwise seems to be the insoluble problem of self-authorization makes it all the less stable as a way of resolving the problems in the idea of self-authorizing groups.

5. Violence in the Enforcement of Norms

Sartre's view on the necessity for the enforcement of these collective norms is thus not Hobbesian or social-contractarian. Independently existing individuals cannot contract or pledge the group into existence. It is instead the group that pledges them into membership, and, following the group structure, this form of mediated reciprocity also is triadic in its structure. Each takes up the point of view of a regulating third party who "pledges" never to become Other (that is, never to undermine the status relationships among the members as members of *this* group).[61] It is part of the logic of such social agency that it presses itself toward a full equality among its members, that is, to a state of each functioning equally as the regulating third party of the others. Once again, the illusion of organic unity appears, since it looks as if the group as an independent organism is developing its individual organs (persons, institutions, practices) in order to pursue its own destiny as being the organism it is. That is the functionalist illusion that suggests that the "we" simply swallows all the individual "I's" into itself. However, the "we" is still the other side of the "I" coin. It is only by the "totalizing project" of each singular "I" that a "we" can ever come to have any real content to itself. If the "we" were only the accidental "We's" of a gathering, or the limited collection of people coordinating with each other in pursuit of a project, then such gatherings (in the sphere of the practico-inert) would arise and fall more or less in terms of how each answers to the rational self-interest, fairly narrowly construed, of those in the group.

One of the reasons for the group-in-fusion to constitute itself veridically is at least quasi-Hobbesian. Each member of the juridically constituted group embodies the possibility of defecting from the group, and that is one of the reasons that a Hobbesian subject in considering the terms of a social contract would think that giving the sovereign the power to prevent such defections is indeed a rational choice. However, that the individual is so constituted so that he has that authority in the first place itself already derives from his membership in the group-in-fusion produced originally out of pure spontaneity in the face of a threat. Thus, Sartre is not denying one of the key premises of any Hobbesian-style account, namely, that rational self-interest may, without further sanctions, lead to group dissolution or even civil conflict. What he denies is that the conception of the pre-political, pre-social individual makes enough sense to put it in the starting block of political or social theory. The individual who would have the authority to establish the contract with others must already be the "communal individual" with the contingent identities that he or she has by virtue of being a member of this or that group. Only already "pledged" members can think of defecting from the group. Sartre is fairly clear in his rejection of contractarian theory, even as he holds to certain more or less Hobbesian views about the necessity of repression in the dynamic of the group: "It is impossible to derive juridical power either from individual freedom, which has no power over reciprocal freedom, or from a social contract uniting several entities, or from the constraint imposed on the group by some differentiated organ, or from the customs of a community in so far as they appear to involve a *hexis*. . . . By themselves they cannot explain repressive power as a practical form of the decision in question."[62]

The group-on-the-way-to-fusion operates without norms but actualizes freedom as equality, whereas the group-in-fusion has to establish norms to keep itself together and to preserve freedom and equality. Nothing in particular follows from this about the content of such norms. That is a separate topic. However, with the establishment of norms comes the enforcement of those norms, and therefore with the power of the group as a whole (as capable of action as a group) comes the repressive power of the group to enforce its norms and sustain the power that arises in the plurality of agents forming themselves into a group. "Power" in this sense appears only in a social and political form, that is, in the plurality of agents who, as fused together while maintaining the recognition of plurality, are able to accomplish what it is that they are seeking to accomplish. Power arises from the mythical pledge that the group puts upon its members and not out of the mythical consent of the pre-political individuals of social contract theory. Such a gain in power only arises if the norms can be enforced. The individuals who populate social contract theory already have to be constituted in a form that would give them the authority to form such a contract, and that authority cannot itself be the result of any further contract.[63] Or, to put it in Sartre's terms, the individuals always emerge as enveloped by relations of seriality and various collective forms of self-consciousness that embody various relations of power coming down from the past.

Enforcement of norms of course means the possibility of force, which is one step away from violence. Sartre does not make the Arendtian distinction between force and violence. However, since he does think that at least sometimes revolution is justified, and since it is always illegal, it requires force. Since the violence exerted by those who challenge the current regime is always illegal, the real distinction, for Sartre, is that between legal force (violence) and non-legal force (violence). Sartre rejects the theories of violence as expressions of the "beast within" or wired into us by something like the complications of evolution. That would be a picture of agency as fully formed outside of sociality with some behavioral disposition to violence either contained within itself or added on to it from outside.[64] Even if that were an explanation of "natural violence," it would completely fail as an account of the kind of social and political violence that is always just below the surface. Human violence arises out of the sense of group identity that by necessity becomes a value to the members along with the awareness of the fragility of this group as threatened by other such individuals and groups. Sartre notes that such "violence always presents itself as counterviolence, that is to say, as a retaliation against the violence of the Other," and its origins lie therefore in the "unbearable fact of broken reciprocity."[65] In conditions of scarcity, since each member of the group is potentially a surplus member, there is always the possibility of expulsion by the others (and at the extreme therefore of starvation, murder, hardship, or social death), and this threat of becoming superfluous and expendable can also be exercised by other groups. However, it does not follow from "the idea that the economy of scarcity is violence" that "there must be massacres, imprisonment or any visible use of force, or even any present project of using it"[66]—and thus it does not imply that we will always live in a violent world—but it does mean that the threat of violence as counterviolence is always present, and that the function of establishing norms is to contain this violence so that the power of the group that has been constituted does not vanish or dissipate. That much at least forms the intelligibility of violence. Sartre has often been characterized as (overly) approving of violence in politics, but his so-called approval is rather more Hobbesian in noting its likely occurrence and not the celebration of violence for its own sake or as some kind of aesthetic expression. Sartre's conception was intended as a way of making sense of violence as conceptually linked to the conception of reciprocal agency in terms of social identities and enforcing norms.

Sartre's real focus is on political violence, both in the revolutionary formation of a group and in the post-revolutionary consolidation of the group. Revolutionary violence organizes itself against oppression, and when it succeeds in forming a group, it must then institute its constitutive norms for membership (along with the norms for what is required of members) with the threat of some type of sanction for those whose defection from the group would be enough to mortally weaken it. Revolutionary violence liberates a collection of people, which then has to found itself anew in a group-infusion. On the other hand, non-revolutionary violence has, on Sartre's view, nothing to recommend it since it cannot aim at the actualization of freedom. However, left at that, there is little to distinguish revolutionary from non-revolutionary violence. Each involves an instituting of norms and their enforcement, but (in a manner similar to Hobbes) there is no specific content to those norms provided by the act of liberation and the foundation of the group-in-fusion, although Sartre is clear that the actualization of freedom is what he has in mind for whatever content can in fact be rationally developed at that stage of history.

Sartre does overdramatize this point. What follows is that that the group must enforce sanctions about its norms. It does not follow that the enforcement must be that of the Terror, as if Sartre were trying to make the Terror of the French Revolution (from 1792 to 1794, with the guillotine as its enduring symbol) into a conceptual necessity for all revolutions and founding acts—something he himself explicitly says cannot be done.[67] He does make the point that in making an ethical choice (more about that later), "it means, therefore, that the [ethical] imperative defines man as always capable of preferring this or that conduct to a series of determinations whose limit-case is life."[68] That, however, is far from claiming that enforcement of norms conceptually requires something like the Terror of 1792–94. It does make the point that if there are unconditional commitments, then something like putting one's life as a whole in view will in fact be the limit case.[69] However, this ethical point is not the one Sartre claims to be making at this point in the argument: "This obviously has nothing to do with morals or even with codes," as he says.[70] The need for enforcement follows from the necessity of the group to provide itself with norms, period.

As a realization of spontaneity, the revolutionary group forms an unconditional commitment, and thus the issue for the members is whether that commitment is genuinely unconditional, as it seems, or, as it sometimes turns out, merely partial and therefore not unconditional at all. Sartre's discussion certainly seems to draw on Hegel's discussion of mastery and servitude in the *Phenomenology*. The party who becomes the servant (or slave) made what seemed to be an unconditional commitment to his own independence, but when his life really was stake, he reneged and chose life over independence. For him, the unconditional commitment turned out to be not unconditional at all, and, so Hegel has it, the party who submits to dependence on the other actually learns the valuable lesson about the importance of life itself. In Hegel's version of the argument, neither the master, who sustains his commitment, nor the person in servitude, who opts for life, is, however, capable of rationally upholding either of those stances, and thus the relationship fractures, dissolves, and develops into something else. Sartre objects to the Hegelian version as too abstract, claiming (just as he makes the same thing about the Terror) that it is false to speak in general of mastery and slavery in this way and that one should instead speak of relations of servitude only in connection with the very different historical contexts in which it appears.[71] In Sartre's amended version, the point is that the revolutionary group either holds fast in its commitment, putting the lives of all on the line, or it dissolves, the revolution is over, and people return to an activity of freedom channeled into determinate paths set by inertia.[72] If the Revolution is to be worth it, it must demand a full commitment to protect itself. It is a very different question if that implied the specific development of the Terror under Robespierre. It is also a very different question as to whether anything like the Terror can itself be ethically justified, even if it can be understood as one of the rational outcomes of a certain development.

In the metaphor of the pledge, the group passes from liberation vis-à-vis oppression, which as a matter of worldly practice often involves violence, to a founding moment in which the new problem is that of creating the institutional and practical structures that will achieve the goal of the Revolution, which, in Sartre's terms, ultimately must consist in establishing some kind of ongoing practical freedom as manifesting spontaneity. This need not be the revolutionary group. Any pledged group counts as a new beginning and therefore as a manifestation of spontaneity.[73]

Ethics in Politics

1. Rules, Groups, and Functionalist Ethics

A pledged group becomes what Sartre calls the statutory group. Unlike pure seriality, the statutory group is more self-consciously organized in terms of achieving a set of ends. If the serial group is structured around a "we" involving ends people self-consciously have in common but do not share (such as queuing for a bus or listening to a radio program), then the statutory group involves a more active commitment to some ends that are shared, and thus involves a different "we" that establishes a set of statuses to bind itself. The homogeneity and equality of the "we" in the group on the way to fusion and in the fused group thus give way to heterogeneity as each assumes a function in the group in terms of the various "offices" and social practices that arise in order to keep the group functioning.[1] One obvious issue is how the status of equality among members is, or even can be, maintained in the statutory group.

It is also in this context that an ethics of sorts appears in the group as those values necessary for sustaining the group's activities. If Sartre concluded his argument at this point, there would be no further basis for ethical values other than those that would emerge as necessary for holding this group with these aims together, where "holding together" also has to mean that the overall project of the group, what it has as its aims to be achieved, has to be a matter of common *praxis*, something internal to the agents that have taken concrete shape within the group. Such an ethics would be "the constitution of communal individuals by imperatives and rights based on pledged inertia,"[2] such that we would "call moral the ensemble of imperatives, values and axiological judgments that constitute the communal bond of a class, a social milieu, or an entire society."[3] These moral norms define who one is as a member of a

differentiated group and are thus fact-stating evaluations of what it is to be
that kind of agent in this specific historical and social context.[4]

In this sense, the specific norms of any given group also are manifestations of the relations among the members of the group as it structures itself.
They form the limits of what it makes sense to think about the future possibilities for agents who live in that group. In this way, the particular norms
seem to be manifestations of a more general normativity having to do with
what governs what it means to be living a meaningful human life at least in
the form it has taken in that statutory group. Yet Sartre also claims that such
a functional understanding of ethical norms (or of any other set of norms)
cannot exhaust the sense of these norms.

As general, the norms are manifested in practices, in acts of individualized
universality, but the practices themselves require the actors to do more than
merely follow the rules. Sartre's own examples come mostly from sports and
the theater. The football player becomes a communal individual as he takes
on a specific function on the team (goalie, striker, etc.), all of which have to
do with various necessities (or exigencies in Sartre's terminology) having to
do with his weight, his training, and such. However, how he fulfills this function cannot follow from the function itself (for example, being a striker).
The feints, passes, and such are themselves not part of the rules, nor is the
decision to take the shot rather than passing the ball to a teammate something that follows from the rules. Or so Sartre sums up the example: "The
action is irreducible: one cannot comprehend it unless one knows the rules of
the game, but it can never be reduced to these rules."[5] The individual action
remains a totalization, a development that is not additive but holistic in its
structure, even when the final objectives of the action (score a goal, prevent
the other team from scoring or from getting into a dangerous position to
score, etc.) are themselves prescribed in advance. The course of the action
is a development as a whole toward the objective: "My action develops, on
the basis of a common power, towards a common objective; the fundamental moment which is characteristic of the actualization of the power and the
objectification of the *praxis* is that of free individual practice (*libre pratique
individuelle*)."[6] An opposing sort of example illustrating the same thing is
that of the world of the theater (at least as Sartre knew it in France at the
time), in which there appears from time to time the "great actor" who takes
it on himself to alter the speeches, the directorial guidelines, and so on, "so
that his free *praxis* posits itself for itself an individuality from beyond."[7] In
both cases, there is a common objective that relies on the free action of the
individual agent to make it real, whose action exhibits the universal practice
in an individual act—just as the practice shows itself in the specific act of

the individual. The team player and the "great actor" are both manifesting in their individual ways the practice that shows itself through them, and they are in turn transforming, however slightly, the practice itself.

This much has to do with what we could call the "social ontology" of the scheme. One problem with situating the ethical element in his account has to do with a kind of tension within the theory itself about the status of ethics in this scheme. On the one hand, to the extent that all these ethical norms are the norms that emerge out of group fraternity based on what is needed both to institute such norms and to enforce them, the norms are completely relative to the objectives of the group. On the other hand, Sartre also commits himself to the idea that ethical norms are those that are the norms that a spontaneous agency would necessarily lay down for itself independently of any particular group membership. Pure spontaneity is always in place "to overtake," *dépasser*, all the rules, that is, to switch, as it were, to the passing lane with the accepted rules remaining in place in the other lane but being left behind. Spontaneity, however, cannot "overtake" itself, and thus whatever ends are bound up with being such an agent are the ends appropriate to such spontaneous agency in general.

For there to be norms at all and not mere regularities laid down by rules (and thus part of the practico-inert), such spontaneity must already be at work. Sartre notes that "the true (*véritable*) aspect of the normative appears here. The unconditioned possibility affirming itself actually as my possible future whatever my past may have been."[8] Sartre also speaks of some more determinate ends as fully binding on us—he says, "liberty, equality and fraternity are fully the terms that designate the 'man to come' as our purpose (*fin*)" (even though he also describes that same familiar triad as the values of "ethical liberalism," which in turn made its appearance in the nineteenth century and whose primary use was to justify the ideology of the "free contract" in the emerging capitalist competitive society, which was really based on the justification of the exploitation of the workers).[9] At one point, Sartre proposes his view as a kind of hypothesis to be tested, to see if "ethical reality finds its true foundation in the intention to produce a community of subjects, [although] it always remains masked by the norms that have a determinate content, which prescribe determinate objectives."[10]

The views set forth in both volumes of the *Critique* tie themselves into a bit of a knot to which Sartre only really attends in his work after the *Critique*. In an extended footnote in the *Critique*, he speaks of ethical values as "the contradictory unity of *praxis* (as free transcendence . . .) . . . and of exigency (as the future which cannot be transcended . . .)" such that "value . . . is the alienation of *praxis* itself."[11] Values on that conception must always be at odds with spontaneity (free *praxis*), since they can serve only to put non-self-drawn limitations on spontaneity. Since the only ends that can count for an agent as purely legitimate are those laid down by a free *praxis* (spontaneity), any limitations can only come from that same spontaneity itself, which is alienated to the extent to which its spontaneity is thwarted. Sartre even suggests in that note that it might seem that the best state of affairs would be where "values will disappear . . . , allowing *praxis* in its free development to be rediscovered as the sole ethical relation between people insofar as together they dominate matter."[12] But he walks that back: if there is such a value that cannot be transcended (overtaken, which is *indépassable*), it would be that of setting our own ends, which is also fully empty as a piece of pure practical reason and is already doomed by virtue of the practico-inert facticity of human agency.[13]

In the *Critique*, he calls this a contradiction, and it is: values are limits to our own spontaneity, but the value of setting our own values is unlimited although empty. Sartre's point is to show how the aspects of valuation and action can pull in different directions. Sartre is committed to the view that (a) some norms or principles are internal to rational agency such that the norm specifies what rational agency is. This is Sartre's view about agency as essentially self-conscious agency. (b) If there are such norms, then those norms measure or evaluate singular agents in terms of how well they exemplify their own kind. This has to do with Sartre's conception of agency as the individualized universal, as a singular agent manifesting the general practice through his individual action as an exemplar and not just the instance of the background practice. If in the *Critique*, Sartre thinks that the only unconditionally valid end has to be that of our freely setting our own ends, then the Sartrean conception at least at the outset sees all other ends as merely provisional. Put that way, that much still sounds like the "existentialism" of *Existentialism Is a Humanism*.

However, even in the *Critique* and in his later unpublished work on ethics, Sartre broadens the conception of what norms are internal to the kind of activity (of "totalization") that constitutes agency. In his 1964 Rome lecture, he reiterates a claim implicit in the *Critique* that life itself is the "absolute foundation of ethical norms,"[14] not in the sense that all ethical norms are simply linked to natural needs or are modifications of natural needs, nor (certainly not) in the sense that "life" always takes first place in conflicts with all other ends, but in the sense that the kind of facts that come with any judgment about the life of the species also involve evaluations of what it is like for that life to go well or badly. Judgments about living things are general statements that do not involve the "all" of quantification—a three-legged cat is no counterexample to the proposition that "cats are four-legged." Such statements about species and about "life" have "generic universality," not necessarily quantificational universality.[15] The facts about the species also determine evaluations as to whether the life of the individual in the species is going well or badly. Judgments such as "Reef-building corals cannot tolerate water temperatures below 64° Fahrenheit (18° Celsius)" say something also about what the conditions are for corals to flourish, as does the judgment "People need kindness from others." Self-conscious organisms (the "practical organism," in Sartre's phrase) have other needs than just those of animal life and social existence. They also need the conditions under which their own spontaneity can exercise itself, but, stated in that general way, not much of any content follows directly from that.

Left at that, the actual normative ethics of the *Critique* is thus very thin to the point of hollowness. As matters are laid out in the *Critique*, one would be left with a functionalist view of ethics as expressing the ethos of a society or even a class, and the rather general (but mostly empty) norm of "spontaneity." Ethics would be a matter of setting up the formal features that appear in specific conditions under which agency (as a totalizing activity) can be exercised within specific modes of production, specific histories, specific geographic areas, and so on. Most of these norms will be those of institutions or of mores as the kinds of inertial shaping of character that are required to keep the given social order functioning. Now, in the actual world, the norms at work indeed shape the possibilities open to the people living in that historical and social milieu and thereby provide those agents with the actual reasons they can have to act and thereby give a concrete shape to their lives. It is this determination of the possible shape of a whole life as "incarnated spontaneity" that defines the ethical as opposed to the more narrowly institutional norms.[16] As such, these ethical norms—indexed to a specific historical and social form of life—form the limitations of ethical comprehension for the members of that form of life.[17] Those limitations, however, seemed to be themselves limited, at least at that point in the argument, only by empty spontaneity and whatever the demands of social exigency require.

2. Active, Passive, or Neither?

Part of the target of Sartre's *Critique* and the works that followed it have to do with the issue of agency in history, and he was always unrelenting in his criticism of dogmatic Marxism for having no real place for such agency. Sartre's main point is that all such emphasis on large social forces as explaining and moving the historical timeline ultimately fail in light of the spontaneity that makes up agency, but that such a conclusion need not drive one back into an individualist or atomistic explanation of collective action. The faulty assumption driving the endless dialectical to and fro between the two views has to do with what is misleadingly suggested by such structural explanations in the first place: What is the active position (expressed as active voice), and what is in the passive position (expressed in the passive voice)? What is producing, and what is produced? It thus seems like ultimately either the practitioner as individual must be the "producer" of the practice, or, if not, then the practice or "structure" must be the "producer" of the practitioner. Either the social forces produce (in some ultimate sense) the actions, or the social forces themselves are in some way not really forces but only the additive reflection of the shape of a large set of individual actions. This runs parallel with the worry about whether the "we" as the first-person plural is no more than an additive result of many first-person singular "I's" or whether the first-person singular is merely the indexical used to characterize the practical organism as a singular entity for which the only content (whether of thought or action) is that specified in the practices that make up "we."[18] On the Sartrean view (as on the related Hegelian and Wittgensteinian views), the individual acts are not caused by the practice, but rather the larger background of meaning—the "practices"—show or exhibit themselves in the individual acts, and the individual manifests these practices in the free acts in which he exhibits them and gives them a determinate shape.[19] Neither produces the other. As Sartre explains it, the temptation to both a kind of subjective idealism (which he had already rejected in *The Transcendence of the Ego*) in terms of which objects in the world are taken to be (in some way or another) constructions of out of subjective experience, and a kind of objectivism that denies subjectivity any place, stems in both cases from the problems that flow out of accepting those assumptions about producer and product.

This assumption was at least implicitly criticized by Heidegger in *Being and Time*, and after Heidegger's self-proclaimed "turn" in his later philosophy, it becomes a bit of a mantra in Heidegger's later work, something to which he attributes the entire history of metaphysics as the misbegotten attempt to find the meaning of being in the discovery or postulation of "a" being that is "more real" than other beings and that grounds or "produces" them. (The use of ironic quotation marks here is not accidental, since Heidegger thinks all of these terms—"produce," "more real"—ultimately do not have much if any real sense to themselves.)

Sartre's early existentialism as expressed in its canonical statement in *Being and Nothingness* took the early "humanist" translations of Heidegger into French as one of its touchstones, but although the evidence for this is admittedly limited, Sartre's *Critique* seems to show that he had been absorbing and rethinking Heidegger's philosophy in the new terms that came after the French response to Heidegger's 1946 *Letter on Humanism*, which was itself intended in part as a rebuke of Sartre's own attempt at an appropriation of Heidegger.[20] For Heidegger, Sartre's early conception of agency was only one more iteration of the search for a being that "produces" all meaning (in Sartre's case, Heidegger apparently thought that would be being-for-itself). However, in his reappropriation of Heidegger, although Sartre does not follow the later Heidegger down the path to *Gelassenheit* (composure),[21] he does use the Heideggerian rejection of the idea that Heidegger sees as hobbling all traditional metaphysics, namely, the idea that some more real being has to (somehow) produce the other beings, in order to fashion his own (Sartre's) theory of collective action, which in turn structures his relations to Marxist theory and which leads him to depart in very fundamental ways from Marxism—something he later acknowledged.[22]

As Sartre puts it in the second, unfinished volume of the *Critique*, "The fact remains that they"—namely, those who eliminate or downplay agency in favor of social forces, as well as those who see the whole only in terms of individual actions adding up—all "see the whole complex of processes as being within totalization (whether they call it that or something else); and that the formula 'being is acting or being-acted upon' ('*être, c'est agir ou être-agi*') is the principle of a pragmatic idealism, in the same way that the other formula, 'being is perceiving or being perceived,' grounds intellectualistic idealism."[23] This is not so much Sartre's existentialism fused together with Marxism as a shift in the perspective of the earlier Sartre (as existentialist) to a different, more reciprocity-oriented perspective and to the perspective more or less in which a practice is said to show itself in the specific actions (the singularized universals) of concrete actors, who in turn exhibit the practice in their actions. The meaning that the action shows is the exhibition of the practice behind it, and the practice just is the meaning of the singular acts. Sartre's use of the term *ensemble* to characterize these unities of meaning (of practice and practitioner) is supposed to convey that point.[24]

This way of reappropriating the later Heidegger is in fact part of Sartre's move away from his earlier position to his later "reciprocity" views on the relations between the "I" and the "We." The relation between "I" and "We" goes both ways, but neither side should be seen as co-producing the other.[25] Switching to a picture of "co-production" does not alter that logic. However, such "co-production"—what Hegel called *Wechselwirkung*, "reciprocal interaction"—is not really "production" at all. It is only the name for a problem that is irresolvable when stated in terms of producer and product

and which in fact is actually the manifestation of a different logic from that
of active and passive into that of practices showing themselves in the acts
that manifest them. The "totalities" in question do not mark one "pole" that
interacts with the other "pole" of singular agency. Both are what they are in
the way that one manifests itself in the other or the way in which one exhibits
the other in itself.[26]

3. Humanism and Humanisms

After the kind of frenzied celebrity status into which he had been thrown after the success of *Being and Nothingness* (along with his plays, his novels, and
his engaged journalism), Sartre attempted to draw out of his earlier thought
a systematic conception of ethics. This came to partial fruition in his 1945
work, the popular lecture *Existentialism Is a Humanism* (which, curiously, is
the only work Sartre ever publicly regretted having published, yet which still
remains as the one book by him most people have read).[27] As its title suggests,
Sartre's post-*Critique* ethics takes its cue from the idea of humanism. Some
background to this is thus in order. The inclusion of "humanism" into the
answer to the question "What is existentialism?" implicated Sartre in a con-
tested debate with various hotly disputed intricacies that had been going on
in French thought since the 1930s. This is not the place to go into the details
of that debate—others have done an excellent job of it[28]—but the central issues had to do with the aftermath of the catastrophe of the First World War
and what it had supposedly revealed about modern European life. In this
hothouse, there was a particularly intense argument about whether "bourgeois humanism" was dead, dying, corrupt, or simply false, and this was connected with an issue coming out of the development of German idealism,
which had reached its high point in Nietzsche's works, namely, the issue of
whether "nihilism" was Europe's destiny. To put to use yet another turn of
phrase Thomas Nagel made famous, nihilism is the view that nothing matters
and therefore it does not matter that nothing matters. In that context, in the
1920s and 1930s, André Malraux's version of the idea that in a pointless world,
only full commitment to a cause such as social justice might look as if it was
perhaps the only redemptive strategy, so that the committed, engaged figure
was, even if doomed to failure, the only viable answer to the worry.[29] Latch-
ing onto this, Catholic thinkers such as Jacques Maritain argued that only
a Christian-humanistic answer could stand up to the crisis, and the com-
munists put forth yet their own version of socialist humanism as a superior
alternative. Sartre was among the young philosophers who felt uneasy about
the dominant humanist neo-Kantianism propounded by the leading philos-

ophers in France—paradigmatically, by the neo-Kantian Léon Brunschvicg. The view was that this form of academic neo-Kantianism, with its emphasis on the investigation of the formal conditions of knowledge and its advocacy for the Kantian idea of universalization in ethics, was simply too abstract and too distanced from the issues actually affecting people. Nonetheless, this kind of neo-Kantianism functioned in many ways as the official philosophy of the Third Republic, which, after the collapse of the republic in the Second World War, made this kind of neo-Kantianism look even more out of place to that younger generation.

In announcing his 1946 lecture, Sartre was therefore stepping into a maelstrom already more than fifteen years in the making. The lecture was a huge success, but it swiftly drew criticism, and the book emerging from the lecture immediately became one of the provocations for Heidegger's writing his 1946 *Letter on Humanism*, which in turn did so much to displace existentialist thought in France in the 1950s and 1960s.[30] In *Existentialism Is a Humanism*, Sartre tried to offer up a conception of ethical judgment as similar to aesthetic judgment. Taking up the example of a man who is trying to make an important choice about his life (to marry but have no children, to marry and have children, or to stay unmarried, etc.), Sartre argued that the real choice there had to do with the broader conception of choosing who one is to be: "A man who commits himself, and who realizes that he is not only the individual that chooses to be, but also a legislator choosing at the same time what humanity as a whole should be, cannot help but be aware of his own full and profound responsibility."[31] Sartre combined that with the view of the logic of ethical judgments as closely resembling the logic of aesthetic judgments, noting, "Let us say that moral choice is like constructing a work of art. . . . What art and morality have in common is creation and invention. We cannot decide a priori what ought to be done."[32] Although he also claimed that in making that comparison, existentialists "were not espousing an aesthetic morality,"[33] he pretty well left it at that and said little more about it.[34]

In *Existentialism Is a Humanism*, Sartre moved away from the "soft" antihumanism of *Being and Nothingness* (nicely encapsulated in the famous line "Man is a useless passion"[35]) into the more full-blown "humanist" claim that humanism consists in self-legislation and thus the existential search for one's own liberation.[36] He had also hinted in a mysterious footnote to *Being and Nothingness* that "these considerations do not exclude the possibility of an ethics of deliverance and salvation. But this can be achieved only after a radical conversion which we can not discuss here."[37] In *Being and Nothingness*, he did not explicitly follow up on that

The only genuinely universal rational demand is that of being "a legislator choosing at the same time what humanity as a whole should be," but without assuming a set of more determinate values, this neither ruled in anything particularly nor ruled out anything particularly. Thus, in the marriage example, one has a determinate social value, but one has to decide beforehand as to what version of that value one is committing oneself, and to choose to marry and have children, "I am nonetheless committing not only myself, but all of humanity, to the practice of monogamy."[38] One is taking a certain value— something having a status independent (and thus "outside") of one's own volition, which is to be found in one's own practical environs—and then universalizing it: Everyone should (or should not, etc.) marry and stay married.

Sartre quickly realized that this case—and especially the more famous one where he discusses the choice faced by the young man about whether to take care of his mother or to join the Free French resistance—turned out to be exhibit A in the case against existentialism's claim to being practical philosophy, since it could provide no guidance to action ultimately except the empty injunction to "choose"—all that, despite Sartre's argument to the contrary, which rested on the idea that "moral choice is like constructing a work of art,"[39] which was supposed to mean that the choice thereby has whatever the inbuilt limits that accompany anything like creating a work of art. Worse, it also went entirely against the grain of Sartre's growing and public opposition to the racism and colonialism practiced by the French state, particularly in Algeria. The idea that there might be "two diametrically opposed moralities . . . yet equivalent in as much as the ultimate aim in both cases is freedom"[40]—which might have seemed appropriate to the debate in 1946 over socialism versus free markets—seemed to make less and less sense in the context of Sartre's engaged and fiery criticisms of the wrongness on the part of the French government and a large section of the French public in the Algerian conflict. There were not two ideas of freedom at work there: there was a side struggling for freedom and another struggling for ongoing domination.

Equipped with the conceptual framework of Being and Nothingness, Sartre tried to work out between 1946 and 1948 what an "existentialist" and "humanist" ethics would look like that would meet those and other objections.[41] After 1948, he seemed to have abandoned the project, sensing that it was a dead end. He put aside the copious notebooks he kept on the subject, and they were only published after his death.

The 1960 Critique gave him the basis for rethinking his failed moral project, although it made no appearance in that book except for some hints about it in a long footnote.[42] Sometime around 1964 he took up the project of working this out and starting once again to write an ethics.

4. System versus Subjective Life

In his earlier conception of the kinds of choices faced by ethical agents, Sartre had stressed the freedom (as spontaneity) of the agent, the agent's facticity (what he called the "situation"), and the agent's orientation within that facticity. The freedom of the agent was exercised in light of that facticity, although the facticity itself did not determine what the agent does, even if the facts actually rationally compel him in one direction rather than another given whatever other projects he has. (This of course runs up against the familiar caricature of Sartre's position that sees him as holding that one's choices are completely unconstrained by any fact in the world.[43]) In effect, Sartre had argued in *Existentialism Is a Humanism* for a kind of "constitutivist" conception of ethics. A "constitutivist" conception argues that the unconditional bindingness of certain norms (such as, for example, those of justice) is to be derived from the nature of agency (and therefore the nature of action) itself. Its basic thesis is the following: because agents are such and such, they are obligated (or bound to) to act in terms of certain norms. Such norms are internal to agency itself and in that sense constitute what it is to be an agent. In *Existentialism Is a Humanism*, Sartre had rather confidently asserted that "when I affirm that freedom, under any concrete circumstance, can have no other aim than itself, and once a man realizes . . . that it is he who imposes values, he can will but one thing: Freedom as the foundation of all values."[44] This followed from the conception of agency taken in *Being and Nothingness* that "what we call freedom is impossible to distinguish from the being of 'human reality'. Man does not exist first in order to be free *subsequently*; there is no difference between the being of man and his *being-free*."[45]

In his later attempt at fashioning an ethics that would fit into the *Critique*'s framework, Sartre begins with the element that holds *Being and Nothingness* together with the *Critique*, namely, the idea that there is a large gap between the inert world (about which *Being and Nothingness* says that "nature" is a prime example[46]) and the self-moving world of agency (of spontaneity). What changes in the interim is (among other things) the role that the idea of a "we-subject"—a first-person plural apperception—plays in shaping action. The idea of there being a sense to our actions begins in the way that individual actors manifest practices, and that the practices "show themselves" in the irreducibly individual acts of those in the practice who "manifest" the practices in their individual actions. The idea that we might build up binding ethical norms out of individual actors making their own radically free choices (which is one of the reasons that the first attempt at constructing an ethics fell apart) is set aside in favor of the reciprocity-oriented view of agency. Sartre

illustrates this with a simple example of two men at work (presumably on a
building site) who are passing bricks to each other as needed. (The scene is
strikingly similar to Wittgenstein's beginning the *Philosophical Investigations*
with two men at a building site passing slabs to each other.[47]) The intelligibility of the activity depends on their already participating in a practice (or
in an *entreprise*, as Sartre puts it), not in each somehow signaling the other
and in turn interpreting the other's signals. In the example, Sartre rejects the
monadic conception of a practice (that is, as something like a game—with
two independent agents linked to each other by a system of independent
rules) in favor of the idea of a non-reflective but still self-conscious reciprocal participation in a practice (involving, as Sartre puts it in his own terms,
a non-positional consciousness of freedom,[48] an awareness of what I am doing without any separate reflective act accompanying it). The passing of the
bricks is not "you and I" but "we" doing something together as a "we," not as
an additive sum of "I's."

It would seem, however, that mere participation in a common enterprise
would not be enough. Sartre himself rather forcefully points out that the
mere fact that something is intersubjectively shared gives it no more binding
power than that of an individual, as it were, binding himself.[49] Just as "I" can
remove the bindingness of something I have arbitrarily imposed on myself
(such as "Eat an apple a day"), that "we" have bound ourselves to something
does not make it any more binding on us simply by virtue of our having supposedly bound ourselves. It is something like this dilemma, so Sartre thinks,
that leads us to come into the grip of seeing ethical demands as imperatives,
which involves the dialectic between "system" and subjectivity (or "system"
and *praxis*). The subjectivity involved is that of a self-conscious agent aware
of itself in its own finitude and thus provoked into thinking outside its own
finitude (contingently existent, constrained by its past, mostly absorbed in its
present, while projecting itself into a relatively indeterminate but nonetheless finite future). The system is that of all the institutions, laws, and concomitant social forces that make up the situation of the agent—in short, the
practico-inert and *hexis* (the acquired dispositions and natural drives) of the
agent. The individual agent is always the point, as it were, where all those
practico-inert vectors come together, but the individual is never merely that
point. Living in time, the individual is always existent in the limitations of
what makes sense to him in terms of his world, and the limitations of what
can make sense to a person at whatever point in time indicate exactly what
the individual cannot himself see at that point. What makes sense has to do
with our being-in-the-world, and what sense we can make thus has to do
with what is "in" the world. However, as totalizing we are led to think that we

must get a view of the limited whole of the world as it is *as* a whole, a totality, and that is impossible. It seems to require the agent to step outside of himself and see himself as a totality, which itself seems to call for the viewpoint of the "absolute witness," the view from nowhere, and that seems to strain at making sense within the limits set by acknowledged finitude. Thus, for any individual to comprehend his life, he would have to see himself in terms of such a totality, but there is no such standpoint outside of the world-as-totality itself, and thus there is no sensible way for individuals to speak with any full determinacy about the sense of their lives. The push to assume the view from nowhere is always present, and thus the temptation to assume that one can actually incarnate that view is always present. It is a temptation that, although always there, cannot be satisfied and is difficult (maybe impossible) to state in any clear fashion. As Sartre put it later in his career, for the person who conceives of their life as located in history, the sense that life itself has its context in something unavailable to anybody, "for the non-believer that I am, what this means is that the real relation of man to his being can only be lived, in History, as a transhistorical relationship,"[50] but, as he notes, that requires a view of history as a whole and thus outside of history, and "we must abandon any idea of humanity historializing itself in the development of a single temporalization which began with 'the first men' and which will finish with 'the last'. . . . Humanity treated as one Man: this is the illusion of the constituted dialectic."[51]

One always begins in a "situation" (to use Sartre's quasi-technical term) that puts restraints on what one can do and how one can think about what one is doing. The "system" sends history off into what seems like a predictable direction, but natural contingency and human spontaneity make that into less rigid a direction than it might seem at first. Since there can be no pure spontaneity outside of a "situation" (with the group in fusion being as close as one can come), one always begins with values that are external to the spontaneity in question—external in the sense that they do not follow from the structure of spontaneity itself but are encountered and made into the practico-inert life of the agents in specific historical circumstances.[52]

As such, since all such past structures of the practico-inert have been hierarchical, class-dominated societies, the idea that morality would consist of a set of imperatives suggests itself as illustrating the way in which in the concrete world social and political superiors could bind the wills of inferiors. That much is a contingency about moral life. In any event, our own social world is enveloped in imperatives: No smoking. Post no bills on this wall. Doctor's orders: Take three a day before meals. The imperatival form imposes what looks like an obligation or semi-obligation, and its basic material shape involves that of a superior to an inferior, where the superior possesses the authority to order the inferior and thereby put him under an obligation (usually backed by a threat). However, not all of ethics—or, for that matter, normativity in general—is imperatival in structure, and these have to do with those cases involving the reciprocity of agency in its basic modes, which are to be found in the mores and ethos of a social order and involve what Sartre variously calls the "ethical objects," "norms without obligations," namely, "values, goods, examples, and ideals."[53] (One of his examples is that of sincerity, for which there is no imperative, even though the ideal of sincerity has an affinity to the imperative, "Always tell the truth."[54])

These kinds of imperatives are the internalized expressions of the social order, which, as Sartre notes, is "the simultaneous constitution of the Other in me and outside of me."[55] My will is guided by some norm (or imperative) that is not the product of my will but is nonetheless taken up by me as my will. It is not possible for the agent to create the norms and values it follows, since if it is me doing the binding, it is me who can also unbind myself. The agent's power of acting requires something other than itself to bind it even if it itself must actively bind itself to this "other than itself" even if this is only a matter of either "active passivity" or "passive activity." None of them is unconditional in character, and this kind of social-functionalist conception of morality, although capturing the way in which the moral life is always a conditioned and embedded part of a larger social whole, cannot bring to account any idea of an unconditional ethical bindingness.

Of course, why would one think that unconditional bindingness is even required at all? This has to do with the attempt by a self-conscious agent to comprehend his life as a totality—an attempt that is impossible to fulfill. The agent lives as a "totalization in course," not as a completed totality, and the idea that we could grasp life in its totality requires us to assume a position outside of the world itself—the "view from nowhere," the standpoint of the "absolute witness." To orient himself in this darkness, the agent needs something tangible, which Sartre usually calls an "image" of what it is to be human. The Sartrean image in its outlines, as we have constructed it, understands the form of our agency as self-conscious, bound to both discursive and non-discursive meaning, and developmental in character. (It is developmental in that we are necessarily subject to education, cultural formation, and socialization for our development to proceed; this is a constitutive feature of our form of life.) This form is general: a possibly infinite number of actors and speakers can fall under it, and they fall under it by (spontaneously) bringing themselves under it by manifesting the structures of the practices in their own individual-yet-general actions. To shift back into a more purely Sartrean way of putting it, the spontaneous agent finds himself always already embedded in a non-chosen practico-inert, manifested in institutional obligations and expectations, by way of a certain *hexis*. One is always already participating in a form of social, communal, and political life that one has not constructed for oneself but which is always already there for one. If life itself and its needs are the basis for ethics (although not fully determinative of it[56]), then it is with the issue of whether to put one's own life on the line for some other end that the idea of the unconditional comes into view. Whether one is justified in doing so cannot be determined without grasping the totality of the world, something that cannot itself be done. The very idea of putting one's life on the line requires, as Sartre puts it, a conception of the "pure future"—a term he borrows from de Beauvoir—that we ourselves cannot fully have in our possession.

"Norms" thus emerge as the orientations for individuals living in the darkness of an ongoing totalization that never accomplishes the "totality" it seeks. Those norms typically take three forms, two of which have emerged as dialectically necessary in the interplay between individual spontaneity and seriality: institutions (especially the law) and mores (non-codified, diffuse, and manifesting themselves as imperatives without any sanction).[57] These constitute the social bonds of various groups whose force has to do with the force of the psychology of group membership itself. The third type of norm—what Sartre designates with the general term "value"—is the basis of genuine ethical life, and it has to do with the general idea of the unconditional as manifesting itself where, at the limit, life is at stake.[58] The emptiness of pure spontaneity acquires its ethical content by reference to these substantive values.

5. Self-Knowledge in the System

Sartre models his ethics primarily on an "axiological ethics," an approach that played a large role in his education as a philosopher. "Axiology" in this sense is the study of what is ultimately worthwhile and not just the study of "value" in general. (One will indeed look in vain for a Sartrean discussion of the golden triangle of contemporary Anglophone ethical theory, that is, virtue theory versus deontology versus consequentialism.[59]) What emerges in the combination of spontaneity and value are the sets of axiological judgments that substantively orient what would otherwise be directionless spontaneity. Although spontaneity itself and the conditions of its exercise assume that spontaneity is itself a value of the first rank, no other substantive values emerge from mere spontaneity itself, but must come from the practico-inert environments of the agent and the kind of *hexis* at work in those environments. Described like that, "value" is just "the practico-inert imposing itself on a freedom,"[60] and those kinds of values that fill in the exercise of spontaneity will be—must be—a function of the specific historical situation in which agents simply find themselves. As Sartre says in a passage already cited, in that context, "we call moral the ensemble of imperatives, values and axiological judgments that constitute the communal bond of a class, a social milieu, or an entire society."[61] These are made concrete as imperatives, orders coming from outside of me and directed to me.

This means that (except for the "unconditional" values) all these "values" are facts. They are facts about how we are to get on with our lives, of our "doing the same" according to them as we move through time and age. Formulated as imperatives, they are, Sartre says, "facts of repetition,"[62] and thus ultimately facts of the "system" that makes up the institutional and practical shape of any given practico-inert and the dispositions that sustain and reproduce it. These facts have to be interiorized in order to be effective, at least in the sense that the agent has to integrate them into his practical field for them to function, for example, as motivations to act. In that context, Sartre dispenses with the concept of "the will" (except occasionally merely as a *façon de parler*), preferring instead to speak of various powers on the part of the agent that lead to thoughts, actions, plans, and so on. He says, "Never speak of the will (*volonté*) that is a determination of consciousness. There are willings (*vouloirs*) corresponding perfectly to powers (*pouvoirs*),"[63] since, as he once put it, in an interview in 1969, "I have replaced my earlier notion of consciousness (although I still use the word a lot), with what I call le vécu— lived experience."[64] The idea of the "lived experience" is a new way of putting the idea already in more or less full shape in *The Transcendence of the Ego* that we must distinguish a representation of ourselves *as* doing something from a representation *of* doing something (in absorption). It is one thing to represent "hanging the picture" and another to represent myself hanging the picture. I am doing it in the second instance, but I am absorbed in the activity without representing "hanging the picture" as having a subject. This is even further from the representation I might form, "I, J-P S, am hanging a picture," and yet even further from representing this as "J-P S is hanging a picture." We may indeed speak of willings or wantings—such as "I want to dine at La Coupole"—but that is also different from, for example, "I, J-P S, want to be the person who dines at La Coupole." In thinking, "I want to dine at La Coupole," I focus not on me (on the "I") but on how I will get there, how I will pay, whether I should wait until I can go there with somebody else, and so on. In other words, I focus on the totalizing activity, on the action in progress of completion, on what I am doing. If, on the other hand, I focus on "I want to be the person who . . ." I focus most likely on something different. In focusing on what to do, I am absorbed in what I am then doing (checking the map, looking at schedules, etc.), whereas in focusing on "being the person who dines at La Coupole," I am more disengaged, and in the example just given, even alienated from the object itself, but both are modes of self-knowledge.[65] One is a self-knowledge that is subjectless in the way Sartre described in *The Transcendence of the Ego*: the absorption of the subject in his actions and thoughts in which I am aware of what I am doing without forming any representation of my doing it. The other is a form of self-knowledge in which I have knowledge of myself doing it perhaps without ever formulating it in terms of "the person who does that" (as when Sartre says in one of his examples, "In my inertia as witness I realize myself as a petty bourgeois intellectual," even though that characterization only comes to me in reflection[66]). For Sartre, the second form of self-knowledge rests on the interiority of the other form of knowledge of what I am doing. (This is also the basis of one form of self-deception: the simultaneous presence of "I am lying" and "I am not the kind of person who lies," prompting the agent with those two thoughts to dismiss the first proposition as necessarily false given the truth of the second, even when it is clear that the activity is underway or has been done. Or it is, as Sartre's example illustrates, one actualizing a status for oneself without reflectively being aware of it and perhaps even in a position to deny it, particularly if one holds that it is true that "I am not a petty bourgeois intellectual.")

For Sartre, the ethical concern has to do with the relation between the kind of subjectless self-awareness and self-knowledge that is bound up with what he calls our "monstrous spontaneity," and the more reflective kind of self-knowledge in which we form the concepts of what exactly we are doing when we perform those subjectless actions. The major issues for him turn on the distinction between spontaneity and system. On its own, spontaneity has no direction, so it requires the full institutional, communal setup of the practico-inert to have any idea where to go. It consists in the ability to begin something new, but it cannot simply by being spontaneous have any specific conception of what its spontaneity should express. It is nonetheless this capacity for spontaneity that puts the agent into the position of moving beyond—as *dépassement*—the kind of conditioning that spontaneity itself needs if it is to be capable of accomplishing anything really at all. Spontaneity may be a "small movement," but it is a movement that changes the organism from merely self-moving life into self-conscious agency.

6. Ethos

Agents always find themselves in a "situation" in which they are called upon to do, forbear, put off, plan for all kinds of outcomes, and any society has a complex set of rules and other norms to secure the kind of compliance that holds that society together. That much of the story falls under the heading "*hexis*/practico-inert" and lends itself to a kind of additive, causal theory of action familiar to Anglophone philosophers. However, each singular agent has to self-consciously take these elements of the *hexis*/practico-inert ensemble and integrate them into his or her own practical field and the teleology inherent to that field. He or she must, that is, spontaneously "totalize" this, put it into a overall project, and that consists in making something of oneself in terms of some picture of what life would be the best given the conditions in which one finds oneself. This forms a picture, however vague, of what it would mean to lead a truly human life.[67] This much remains of Sartre's humanism.

However, there is no one sense of what it would mean to lead a truly human life. In fact, in the realm of practice, the picture of "the human" that dominates comes from those who dominate. To be sure, there are some ethical principles (having do with lying, promising, and such) that seem to transcend many epochs, but these are rather easily accounted for in terms of securing cooperation, of how certain conventions get established, and so on. (Game theory along with various sociologies does a good job of that; or one can look to Hobbes and Hume for paradigm instances of how such explanations might go.) What they have trouble with, as Sartre has noted, is securing the sense of bindingness that any of these norms have. Sartre's own proposal has to do with the idea of totalization and how it seems to involve a kind of epistemic and metaphysical impossibility. Nonetheless, it is in viewing life as a totality with contingent birth on one end and necessary mortality on the other that we get a sense of the unconditioned. It is at that point that the dispositions of the agent acquire any genuine ethical significance—what is worth doing, no matter what—and the various acquired dispositions (for example, to truth telling) become more than merely facts of a sort about oneself and one's society but also moral facts about the agents who are the unity of spontaneity and exigency.

Thus, at any stage of history there is what Sartre calls the ethical paradox.

The paradox (so to speak) has to do with what seem to be contradictory results when we reflect on what is necessary to think of a moral agent. From the standpoint embedded in the practico-inert, the ethical agent is essentially a set of psychological and physical dispositions to do one thing as opposed to another, which in turn is cemented by various practices of praise and blame and so on. However, the ethical agent is also capable of exercising spontaneity and of taking a view of what binds him as transcending even life itself. Even though "life—as it is given by need as that which is to be reproduced—is the absolute foundation of the ethical norm,"[68] the totalizing agent (who as self-conscious is capable of trying to grasp the world as a whole) is also capable of putting even life itself into play, and therefore asking which particular dispositions and responses are worth life itself, and the agent accomplishes this in the act of spontaneity, a kind of "no," a negation, to all that is given. Agents are fully part of the natural world who nonetheless have the spontaneous capacity to act in terms of values that are the "surpassing (*dépassement*) of all factual states," but which on their own bring no orienting content with themselves, merely the "no."[69]

The paradox comes about in that one becomes who one genuinely is only by ceasing to be who one is.[70] One's ethical stance comes from one's acculturation, one's training, the various conceptual tools one has acquired, and so on. That is who one is. Yet the "monstrous spontaneity" at the heart of subjectivity—of self-consciousness—means that one can always negate who one is in that sense, and the question becomes, If not that (who one is), then what (who one is to be or what one has become)? As already noted, spontaneity on its own, apart from the material conditions in which it works, cannot provide any answer.

The paradox, such as it is, is made practical (in another of Sartre's terms of art) in an ethos, the point at which the various elements of the practico-inert (the socialization, habits, institutions, and practices that envelop the agent) are taken up by the agent as expressive of his own spontaneity, and not merely as forces that push him around.[71] It is in holding oneself to these norms in light of an awareness of an ongoing totalization in time—that this is what I am to do, perhaps even over and over (for example, tell the truth)—that one moves from inertia to ethos, and to taking responsibility for who one is and what one does. One resists one's own inertia—this is an agent's "negativity"—and that of the enveloping practico-inert. To remain in inertia is an ontological failing, namely, to be what we are, that is, beings that manifest spontaneity in manifesting the practices that in turn manifest themselves in us.

An ethos is thus a kind of social fact in which the given structures and virtues become integrated into the life of an agent who takes them to be unconditional—that which makes life worth it—and not merely acquired dispositions. Although it might be easy to think of this as some version of the distinction between the abstract and the concrete—with moral principles up there and behavior that sometimes does and sometimes does not comply somewhere down here—that is not Sartre's point. The ethos is the subjective appropriation of one's practico-inert status, so that it becomes not merely conformity to a norm (by virtue, for example, of a mere habit) but a deeper sense of how one is to live one's life so that one is self-directing. One passes from the kind of averageness, as Heidegger calls it, of doing as "they" do, on to owning what it is that one does.[72] Sartre puts it this way: "In this way, in everyday life, ethical experience is the immediate. This does not necessarily mean the most superficial—nor, of course, the most profound—determination. . . . What matters . . . is that the citizen lives in the milieu of the normative. And by this we do not mean that he is subject to the norms as a constraint, but rather that he regains responsibility for them, as a whole, and becomes an ethical agent, not only by using the freedom they give him (an unconditional possibility) to conform his conduct to them, but also by demanding that the other members of the group conform their own."[73] Reversing his often cited existentialist view (voiced in *Being and Nothingness*) that "existence precedes essence," Sartre notes that "socially: essence precedes existence."[74] Viewed from the outside, as it were, there may be no real observable difference between a practico-inert order lived as inertia and one lived as ethos, but viewed from the standpoint of subjectivity, there is a great difference.[75] It is only from the standpoint of ethos and not merely that of the practico-inert that we see how participation in a practice—such as Sartre's two bricklayers mentioned earlier—also provides a bindingness to the practice.

7. Ethos, Inequality, History

Sartre's conception of ethos might sound like his own version of Hegel's conception of *Sittlichkeit*—translated as a term of art as "ethical life," but which might be better rendered as "moral ethos"—and in many ways, it surely is. However, in one major and decisive way it is not. In his 1820 work, *Elements of the Philosophy of Right*, Hegel argues that such a "moral ethos" emerges as the capstone of a systematic combination of the Lockean rights to life, liberty, and property, the post-Christian moral scheme of treating people with dignity and acting only in terms of universal reasons about which one could exercise one's own insight, both of which are in turn actualized within a modern "moral ethos" consisting of the bourgeois family, a civil society with a market embedded in it (and not vice versa), and a constitutional monarchy that holds it all together.[76] Despite all the tensions within such a scheme, the result according to the Hegelian system is harmonious and supposedly therefore stable and capable (as understood within the proper philosophical account) of being the object of a more reflective rational approval on the part of the participants in that moral ethos. On Hegel's account, even though there can be the appearance of great division, the whole (rights, morality, moral ethos) harmoniously coheres.

This is not the case with Sartre's conception of ethos. There is, first of all, no reason to think that an ethos is going to be rational. The values that we have emerge out of a series of historical contingencies as responses and adaptations (as Sartre calls them) to changing material and intellectual circumstances. Values emerging from such contingencies may or not may not rationally cohere with each other. There is, moreover, good reason to think and very good historical evidence to show that such values change as the material and intellectual circumstances themselves change and that they often do clash with each other, not to produce a harmony but instead to clang in great dissonance. Values, which flesh out what would otherwise be the empty axiological practical judgments of spontaneity, emerge out of the way in which individuals have to adapt their conceptions of what ultimately matters in living a whole life from infancy to death, and they have to make sense to those who live by them. Such practical sense-making is always historically indexed. As such, the values of a period will also embody the hierarchies of the period, give them the cover of legitimacy, and thus serve to mask what is otherwise the rather blunt assertion of power.

Second, there is no particular reason to think that the values that hold a capitalist society together will be especially harmonious or rational. A system that has developed out of a series of historical contingencies that involves a continually adapting system of wage labor (instead of bonded labor), private ownership of the means of production, and by and large freedom from centralized authority in decisions about investment of capital (with the elite nonetheless relying on state power to protect and enable those decisions about capital investment) is not a system that will necessarily produce a coherent set of values—even if in the terms of neoclassical economic theory, it will produce a kind of equilibrium—and especially since the system has to rely on the exploitation of wage labor and on the reproduction of certain elites to function at all. If in fact capitalism requires these kinds of hierarchies to function, and these hierarchies are usually what sustains a certain ethos, it is the self-conscious spontaneity on the part of those at the bottom that typically threatens to undo it. Moreover, given the account of agency developed in the *Critique*, there is no reason to think that a kind of completely stable Sartrean ethos (or a harmonious Hegelian *Sittlichkeit*) could ever be in place outside of a short period of time. The idea of such a harmony might function as a kind of ideal but only of the most abstract type—in other words, as some form of abstract utopia in which counter-finality disappears.

In Sartre's account, what appears are the historical forms of social and political life that are contingent upon various material conditions and various conceptions of how to respond to those conditions. The stabilization of institutions in all these historical circumstances creates what Thomas Piketty has recently called "inequality regimes," in which various hierarchies of subordination have to come up with ways of legitimating themselves. (In Piketty's words, "An inequality regime will be defined as a set of discourses and institutional arrangements intended to justify and structure the economic, social, and political inequalities of a given society."[77]) All inequality regimes run up against the way in which subjects come to experience themselves as equals. Paradigmatically, for Sartre this arises out of the experiences of groups in fusion in which each singularly takes responsibility for the group while at the same time comprehending both his utter dependence on the group functioning as a "we" (a self-conscious first-person plural apperception) and thus his dependence on all others. This is both an experience of freedom (as "seriality" vanishes) and of equality (the "one for all and all for one" of the group in fusion). Out of that comes the more fundamental and usually not fully conceptualized experiences of freedom and equality as two deeply linked manifestations of the experience of these groups and therefore as the full actualization of agency.[78] In the Sartrean account, the sense of equality is not, for example, an innate disposition that simply requires the right form of expression. Rather, it is what emerges most fully in the development of the rotating dependence of each on each other in formations such as the group in fusion.

The "practice" account that animates the *Critique* functions in Sartre's sketches for his ethics. One might be tempted to think of the relation between the subject and values as that of the subject on one side of a divide entertaining possible values on the other side of the divide—a version of the picture of the thinker entertaining independent thoughts before asserting one or the other—but the relation between value and agent is something else. The practice shows itself in the subject's activities, and does not first exist and then is related to the language, but rather the subject is always already manifesting the practice, which shows itself in his activity, while the practice is in turn sensitive to how we manifest it. Thus, the values that show themselves in our activities are sensitive to how we manifest them in those activities. Neither one is producing the other, and it is misleading to abstract the values from the practice as if they constituted a freestanding set of rules for behavior and feeling.

What holds all these ethical practices loosely together is that they all amount to a picture of "the human" as it is supposed to develop in terms of its nature. This developmental picture of "the human" is general in the same way that "fish eggs are supposed to develop into fish" is general even though most fish eggs do not develop into fish. (They get eaten, fail to fall into the conditions necessary for development, etc.) It is thus not a statistical statement about human development. What animates any distinct historical ethos is its picture of "the human," which in point of fact will always necessarily involve, if not the complete domination, then at least the hegemony, of the ruling group (the "favorized classes," as Sartre puts it). Although this has been taken (and, at the time Sartre was writing, was in fact taken) by many to show that any appeal to "humanism" is really just an ideological disguise for treating the hierarchies of contemporary capitalism (and its concomitant racism and sexism) as natural or as at least inevitable given "human nature" and is thus best discarded altogether, Sartre holds that in fact all that has been shown is his *après*-Marxist point that the late capitalist form of humanism is to be discarded and not the kind of developmental humanism he is championing. As he puts it, "There is not *one* humanism, there are *humanisms*. By this one must mean the practical unification of the ethico-juridical ensemble appropriate to a determinate social system, inasmuch as the whole ensemble is established and maintained according to the classes it favors."[79] He adds: "Man as a practical determination is always a limitation," and thus "each revolutionary stance inasmuch as it is historical is anti-humanism. Not a universal anti-humanism but *this* very anti-humanism. Put otherwise, the anti-humanism of *this* very humanism."[80] For Sartre, the revolt against the "bourgeois humanism" that privileges white male European property-owning humanity as a prop for a colonial and class-based hierarchy is "this very anti-humanism" he had in mind in the 1960s and 1970s.

This may perhaps also sound vaguely Hegelian, where it might seem that Sartre employs "ethos" more or less to stand in for what Hegel called a "shape of spirit"—a *Gestalt des Geistes*—and thus, as Hegel did, to see history as a succession of such shapes of spirit. However, on Sartre's account, each of these ethoses have to do with the way in which the political hierarchies in a given social order are legitimated and thus serve as ideologies. The different way that given social orders legitimate and enforce their hierarchies, moreover, always runs up against the ways in which the defavorized resist and

learn to move about to their own limited advantage within the terms of the
hierarchy without necessarily explicitly challenging it (since challenging can
oftentimes be fatal).[81] The imposition of a hierarchically charged humanism
has never proceeded seamlessly and, given Sartre's conception of individual
and social agency, could never genuinely be expected to function that way. In
the Hegelian "shape of spirit," the basic terms of what counts as the "absolute" shapes everything else, and thus there is always a deep unity to a "shape
of spirit." That is not to be expected in a Sartrean ethos. Not even the "humanism" of an ethos shapes everything within it, nor is there necessarily only
one humanism to an ethos. Because of human spontaneity, "system" and
subjectivity never perfectly coincide. Nor is there any sense that history is
following a direct path. (As Sartre makes a note to himself in his manuscript,
"Sense of history: image always veering off course, always premature, always
limited, always starting again."[82]) The only non-ideological humanism would
therefore be one that would be non-hierarchical (and therefore democratic)
in orientation (and no such ethos has yet concretely existed).

In light of that, Sartre puts forward his own proposal for what he calls
"integral man" (or "integral humanity," as more recent commentators have
called it in order to give Sartre's language the inclusive feel Sartre intended it
to have). The term itself has a non-Sartrean history to it. It surfaces in a book
on Marx that Sartre read and from which he quotes in the Critique: Maximilien Rubel's Karl Marx: Essai de biographie intellectuelle (1957), in which
Rubel argued that Marx was in essence an ethicist in all of his writings (as
well as being an anarchist), and Rubel characterizes that by what he calls the
"integral individual."[83]

More likely, and maybe even oddly, this also appears in the "humanism"
debates of the 1930s in Jacques Maritain's 1936 book defending a Thomist
approach to contemporary problems, Humanisme intégral.[84] (Sartre does
not discuss Maritain as far as I can tell.) Maritain's conception of "integral
humanity" has to do with the Christian ideal of reconciling the alienation
of man from God, whereas Sartre's conception is that of overcoming human alienation through the construction of a more egalitarian social order.[85]
There is little point in going into a deep comparison of the two, but much of
Maritain's way of putting the problem is echoed in Sartre's much later text,
except for the obvious difference that Sartre's version is thoroughly secular,
whereas Maritain's is Christian.[86] Nonetheless, if we extrapolate a bit from
Sartre's own stated views, Sartre would be arguing that Maritain posed the
correct question but gave not merely the wrong but a metaphysically impossible answer. In the terms of Being and Nothingness, God would be the metaphysically impossible unity of the in-itself and the for-itself. Put in the terms

that structure the *Critique* and the succeeding work on ethics, Maritain (like all Christians) has to claim that there is a human way of grasping the "totality" (the world as a whole) that is in principle not available to finite humans. Maritain, that is, would have to appeal to the "absolute witness," the point of view from nowhere, the seductive idea that we can meaningfully speak of the world as a whole by assuming a position outside the world as a whole, a position nobody can take and which therefore has to rely on a conception of "faith" that is beyond rational redemption. For Sartre, the best finite humans can do is not to make assertions about the "totality" but to understand action as an ongoing "totalization," itself always necessarily breaking down into a "detotalized totality" in that the final end that is being pursued (the Christian life for Maritain, the meaning of history for Sartre) is unavailable and thus the actions undertaken in light of that final end themselves fall apart into bits that do not hang together as part of a teleological whole. Sartre's view is, moreover, not that the world is somehow constructed by us (that would amount to the idealism he spent his career disavowing) but that we cannot make sense of the standpoint of the "absolute witness" even though it is seductive enough for us to want, even want deeply, to make sense of it and therefore to believe we really have made sense of it. The self-reflection involved is always that of the human standpoint, which is always a "totalization" in progress, never a "totality." In terms of his ethics, Sartre remains very Sartrean: we need something (grasp of the "totality") that we cannot have. We must take the point of view of man, not the point of view of God, when it is almost always the point of view of God that we want.

Although Sartre speaks of the unconditional end promoted by his ethics as that of "integral humanity" and as a "plenitude," he never specifies it because, as he puts it in his own terms, it simply cannot be specified. As he says, "This plenitude is not defined because it is not even conceivable."[87] As unconceivable, it cannot therefore play any direct role in practical reasoning except perhaps as holding out the orienting ideal of a classless society even if that itself cannot now be specified any further.[88] (We shall come back to this point shortly.)

It might look as if Sartre could therefore be categorized as a bit of a value pluralist in that he thinks that any given social order will be a mixture of various values—orientations for how one is to live one's life—not all of which will necessarily be consistent or even emotionally coherent with each other.[89] However, Sartre is not advancing the idea merely that there are different and competing values at work. The value attached to being a property owner in "bourgeois liberalism" is indeed one among many values at work in that scheme, and it is not clearly compatible with a number of other values at work in the same scheme. However, it is a value only within that scheme. Values in the Sartrean sense are always in motion, changing and intimately linked to the material conditions in which they are formed. They vanish when the material conditions and the ways agents individually and collectively think about themselves change and vanish, they shift when the material conditions shift, and the material conditions (and all of what Sartre calls the "system" of the practico-inert) change when life in those systems becomes unlivable, when people can no longer be the people who orient themselves by those values. At best these different kinds of very general value-claims— legal, institutional, pertaining to mores, ethical, and so on—can be balanced in terms of a general developmental conception of how best to lead one's life (i.e., in terms of a "humanism"), which in turn requires some conception of how one's own life or the life of a community fits into a larger conception of where things are going in history, ought to be going, and so on. There is, however, except under the most utopian conditions, no reason to think that there is a wide set of values that can be put in any systematic order that is typical of much modern ethical and political theory.

Ultimately, this has to do with various class structures and patterns of domination and subordination characteristic of virtually all societies up until now. The constitutive aim of what Sartre calls ethics, however, is to produce a community of subjects who are free and equal even though at any given point in history the actually existing morality of a community will always have congealed this ethical objective into a series of determinate norms that in effect usually conceals or even distorts the aim.[90] The aim of axiological ethics in Sartre's day was to discover an a priori way of ordering the "values" into some scheme of better or worse, or into a scheme of prima-facie values to be balanced more or less intuitively according to their weight. Instead, he proposes a theory of *praxis* anchored to a kind of historicism.

The contingent material conditions of one's times and one's place, of where and to whom one is born, are contingent but generate in most circumstances a destiny that can also become a fatality (or even a kind of counter-finality). Thus, for Sartre, history ultimately has tragedy written into it. Sartrean tragedy was based on human freedom and the traps that pure contingency and counter-finality can lead such freedom to lay down for itself. By the time of the *Critique* and afterward, it was based on the way in which freedom is exercised to create a destiny and even to create an unwanted fatality. One stakes everything on some view of the "totality," and there is no way to see whether in fact the "totality" measures up to anything at all.[91] This is not a matter of our being subject to natural forces beyond our control (which is certainly true of us) but of our freely producing a kind of inertia that leads us into consequences we find horrible and for which we have to take responsibility, since it is we who did it.[92] Sartre summarizes this in his dictum that "history is the rigorous combat of the practico-inert and *praxis*, each of the two terms triumphing in its turn, since, in objectifying itself in inorganic materiality, *praxis* is absorbed by the practico-inert that conditions it and alienates it."[93]

8. What Follows Marxism?

Sartre certainly started on the project of writing the *Critique* as offering a kind of philosophical formulation of Marxism that he thought was otherwise lacking. By the time he finished it, it was not clear how Marxist it was, and he later admitted that, all in all, his views from the *Critique* onward had never been really Marxist. As he put it in an interview in 1975, "Marxist is a word that I used a bit lightly then. At that time I considered the *Critique* to be Marxist; I was convinced of it. But I have changed my mind since then. Today I think that, in certain areas, the *Critique* is close to Marxism, but is *not* a Marxist work. . . . Now I do not consider it at all a Marxist philosophy."[94] Sartre also admitted in that same interview that all he had really taken over from Marxism were the concepts of class and surplus value (i.e., the key idea of class struggle as essential to understanding history, and unbridled exploitation as central to capitalism itself).[95] Seen in that light, his earlier assertion—that Marxism "remains, therefore, the philosophy of our time. We cannot go beyond it because we have not gone beyond the circumstances which engendered it"[96]—had to mean that what in Marxism in our times could not be surpassed, could not be *dépassé*, was the idea that class society as it had taken shape in late capitalism could be or become in any real sense an actualization of freedom and that everything had to proceed therefore from the inegalitarianism, the ruthless exploitation, and the deformation of subjectivity inherent in capitalism.

Like most other "Western Marxists," one of Sartre's chief concerns was with the way he thought capitalism deforms subjectivity, preventing it from actualizing itself in a proper way.[97] In particular, Sartre thinks that capitalism as a "system" presents a particularly potent form of reification. In *The Problem of Method*, which he wrote and finished some time shortly before undertaking the final work on the *Critique*, he articulated this in the terms of the French-Heideggerian concepts he had used earlier in his career. In that work, he argued that a genuine Marxist theory can comprehend the historical movement as it is, as "alienated existence" and as a "reified human-reality (*réalité-humaine chosifiée*)."[98] The process of exploitation, by which those who control the basic means of production take the surplus value produced by the laborer for their own uses (primarily to increase their own capital), is recategorized as not merely exploitation of the worker's labor power but as a falsification of the worker, turning a free being into a thing of sorts.[99] To put it in the language of Sartre's earlier work, the *réalité-humaine* (*Dasein*) is transformed into the *réalité-des-choses* (*Vorhandenheit*). Sartre holds the view strongly enough even at times to slip away from the orthodox Marxist insistence that the worker does not sell himself per se (and thus become indentured or a slave) but only sells his "labor power" (which makes the exploitation all the more insidious, since it makes the whole system rest on the illusion of ethically unfraught, unencumbered free choices by both employer and employee). Ignoring that, Sartre sometimes slides into the idea that the worker does in fact sell himself and thereby makes himself (and not just his labor power) into a commodity, something whose only value is in terms of a contingent market price.[100] What goes wrong in reification is thus not that the reified agent is following the wrong moral or ethical rules but rather that he is trapped into a false life by virtue of the system of meanings of which he is one of the practitioners. The reified individual takes a purely exterior, objective view of himself as somebody forced into a prefabricated life, which is an outlook that rests on a peculiar type of "active passivity," a concerted effort grounded in spontaneity to make oneself into the non-spontaneous creature one takes oneself to be.[101] Reified, one actively starts to work at being like a thing passively obeying laws external to itself. One actively works, that is, at being something one cannot be, namely, something that does not actively work at it.

On his own terms, Sartre had hardened his opposition to the orthodox Leninist Marxism of his own time and moved in the direction of a more egalitarian aim of the suppression of all "systems" (including that of Soviet-style socialism) that alienate and try to smother spontaneity.[102] He thus dismisses the very idea of the "dictatorship of the proletariat" as not merely optimistic in its outlook[103] but actually "absurd" in its very claims,[104] which, in terms of his theory of collectives and groups, certainly follows from his views. Likewise, with regard to the young Marx's celebrated idea of the typical person in communism who can "hunt in the morning, fish in the afternoon, rear cattle in the evening, criticize after dinner," Sartre likewise dismisses it as at best a "myth."[105] Even as in 1964 when he was still describing support for the USSR as resting on its being the "singular incarnation of socialism,"[106] he said, after his final decisive break with his on-again, off-again support of the Soviet Union, in the second volume of the *Critique*, that the real conditions of the "actually existing socialism" under Stalin "meant that in certain historical circumstances it could be a synonym of Hell."[107]

Sartre draws from Marxism a rejection of the idea that the problem with those in positions of power and authority is psychological, namely, that they are apt to confuse their own orders with moral obligation and to be arrogant about their own cognitive powers and their authority itself—not that Sartre denies that this is all too often the case. Sartre's point is that a class society will have such subordination written deeply into its structure, and the inequality regime to which it gives expression will also serve to justify that subordination or to make it seem at least unavoidable. It is not just that those on the top of the power ladder are making cognitive errors about their own authority and capacities and can perhaps be brought around to a better, more humane view through some kind of, as it were, educational reform. The "system" in Sartre's sense itself needs changing.

What Marxism itself had trouble doing in light of that had to do with how parts of the "system" subordinate and limit others' freedom in ways that only fit badly into the grid of class membership if they fit at all. Examples, from a list of things that were important to Sartre are, race, gender, sexual orientation, and generalized ideals of subordination (for which people more recently have adapted the term "caste").[108] Thus, in his later unpublished writings on ethics, Sartre begins referring more generally to the "defavorized" classes, indicating that conceptions of social justice have to shift in favor of the "least favored" groups.[109] In that way, Sartre reoriented his Marxist-influenced theory into a more general account aimed at disclosing all the different ways in which oppression and alienation operate in social and political life.[110] Rather than the Marxist class struggle per se, the development of political history would be that of the continual eruption of spontaneity into a rigidified order (most often expressed by those who are oppressed by that order), and the overall arc of that story is one of freedom and equality as the inference to be drawn from the conception of the background meaning in which the basic "we" that is consistent with the way in which a self-sufficient "I" shows itself.[111] Class struggle will be an important part of that story, but it cannot be the whole story.

Sartre argues at another place that the purposes of an order of full mutuality might in fact be seen as the realization of the (originally bourgeois) goals of the 1789 revolution—as when Sartre says, "Liberty, Equality, Fraternity are indeed the terms that designate the man to come as our end."[112] In 1789, however, these terms were limited to an interpretation of private property such that although they seemed to abolish feudal servitude in order to make way for free and equal citizenship, in fact they ended up legitimating the further exploitation and oppression of some by others in the capitalism that was on its way and in fact led to the reintroduction of slavery in a short while as a means of maintaining control over, among other things, the lucrative trade from the sugar plantations.[113] Counter-finality resurfaced in the Revolution itself.

9. Liberty, Equality, Fraternity, Colonialism, Racism

Crucially, Sartre also claims in several places that even in its standard "bourgeois" interpretation, "liberty, equality, and fraternity" could not possibly consistently justify or legitimate the "super-exploitation" of the indigenous peoples practiced by European colonialism. Colonialism as practiced in the heyday of European imperialism in the nineteenth and twentieth centuries is and always was simply beyond the pale of justifiability. Racism, on Sartre's account, is the nonsense ideology that emerged in the impossible attempt to make the super-exploitation of the colonized by the colonialists seem like something innocuous or destined in the "civilizing mission" to work to the good of the colonized. The "thoughts" involved in racism and colonialism are fabricated in a fact-free, illogical dreamworld that is put forth as if it were the real world but is really just an illusory story that hides the brutality of the real world the colonists have created. Sartre puts this rather strongly:

> The essence of racism, in effect, is that it is not a system of thoughts which might be false or pernicious. . . . *It is not a thought at all.* (*Ce n'est en aucune façon une pensée.*) It cannot even be formulated. . . . In reality, racism is the colonial interest lived as a link of all the colonialists of the colony through the serial flight of alterity. . . . These determinations of discourse are very familiar: "The native is lazy, dishonest, and dirty; he doesn't work unless he is forced to; he's an eternal child quite incapable of controlling himself; in any case, he lives on nothing, he never thinks of the next day; the native is properly understood only by the colonialist, etc." These phrases were never the translation of a real, concrete thought; they were not even the object of thought. Furthermore, they have not by themselves any meaning, at least in so far as they claim to express knowledge about the colonized. They arose with the establishment of the colonial system and have never been anything more than this system itself producing itself as a determination of the language of the colonists in the milieu of alterity.[114]

Sartre's point is not that racist talk is "nonsense" as a syntactical or grammatical feature of the sentences in racist discourse. Rather, it is nonsense as an illusion on the part of the speakers in racist discourse that they have any clear way of what they are saying in their use of the words. The concept of race, so Sartre argued, was that of an invisible quasi-organism of which members of the race were more or less just its organs, and as such it was pretty much an

empirically vacuous term.[115] "Race" is a metaphysical holistic concept without any real meaning, but which, in terms of its proxy—skin color—has a
lot of social meaning, and serves thus a purely ideological role of seeming to
express colonial rule in terms of concepts and practices that are impervious
to empirical criticism and beyond real metaphysical justification.

Sartre made this point earlier in his career in his short book, written originally in 1944 and published in part in 1945 and in whole in 1946, *Anti-Semite
and Jew* (which was actually narrower than its title suggested, since its real
focus was on the underlying basis of French anti-Semitism at the time).[116]
However, by the time of the *Critique*, Sartre had incorporated some of his
earlier points about anti-Semitism and racism into his critique of colonialism but had modified them in the interim. In *Anti-Semite and Jew* Sartre
argued for, among other things, two claims. First, the way in which racism
becomes practical has to do with a kind of what we may call a "metaphysical
politics" (although that was not Sartre's own term), that is, a politics, as it
were, of looking for the real but non-observable feature of actions carried out
by members of a "race"; second, based on his views about freedom, situated-
ness, and bad faith as articulated in *Being and Nothingness*, he explained why
people are motivated by such a metaphysical politics.

In *Anti-Semite and Jew*, this metaphysical politics is said to not look at
facts about Jewish people but to base itself instead on an idea of both the
metaphysical essence of Jewishness (as a race) and the metaphysical essence
of a "real" France (which, like that of "the Jew," would only accidentally, if
at all, correspond to anything in contemporary French law or actual institutions). On that basis, all kinds of behaviors and motives are ascribed to Jews
because of what Sartre calls their "metaphysical essence,"[117] many traits of
which are mutually contradictory and for which no contradictory empirical
evidence could in principle be found. Thus, whenever some fact is cited as
disproving the anti-Semites' characterizations (such as the supposedly trai-
torous metaphysical essence of the Jews contrasting with the real empirical
presence of Jewish volunteers for the French army in the First World War),
the fact is dismissed either as not being a fact at all—how could it be a fact
if it contradicted the metaphysical essence of a people?—or, if it was a fact,
as not really manifesting the true, non-French essence of the Jews. Even if
somebody contests the asserted fact that "Jews typically do this and that bad
thing" with actual evidence, the anti-Semite will meet them with the counter-
assertion that the particulars do not matter, since even if it were true in this
or that case that any one of them or even all of them acted virtuously, the
deeper meaning, the "metaphysical essence," of the matter is otherwise, that
is, their "essence" is to do otherwise. The anti-Semite and the racist both

hold to a view about what is really going on at the deeper, non-empirically available level, and they therefore cannot be persuaded by any display of empirical facts that it is in fact not going on. The problem is not with metaphysics per se but with the kind of metaphysics of race—with its basis in a crude Manichean conception of the world—and the metaphysical politics to which it gives rise. The racialized individual is thus only a *personnage fantôme* (phantom character), a figment whose sole function is ideological, and thus a figment, as it were, perfectly real in a racialized social world.

At the time of the writing of *Anti-Semite and Jew*, Sartre attributed the motive for this to the anti-Semite wanting to be "like a stone," that is, as an attempt by the "for-itself" to attempt in bad faith to become "in-itself."[118] The anti-Semite could thereby say to himself that he is "really" French ("metaphysically" French, "in itself" a Frenchman like a stone is granite in its nature) because of simply what he is, whereas the Jew can never "really be" ("metaphysically") French no matter what he is. By the time of the *Critique*, Sartre put this account of the motivations for racism partially to one side (although he kept the image of the racist turning his thoughts to stone) and superseded it with his mature view that the kind of metaphysical politics that is the linchpin of racism was the nonsense actually needed by a particular system of colonial exploitation that required something like the spurious metaphysical concept of race in order to give itself the dreamy legitimation story that would ideologically transform the various practices of super-exploitation that are the cornerstones of colonial practice into illusory semblances of perfectly ordinary enterprises. On the surface, the racist, colonial discourse makes what seem to be factual claims, which are actually contradicted by the facts, but are held in place by the system of pseudofacts that make up the colonial racist system. Racism is thus not, as Sartre says, a psychological defense mechanism of any sort—not, that is, a realization of the brutality of the system coupled with a need to provide some kind of self-justification of its brutality that would soften the psychological blow to themselves for the colonialists. Rather, racism is part and parcel of the colonial and the slaveholding system. It is the nonsense that functions as the glue holding the colonial imaginary together. What the colonialists share is the view that the exploitative colonial enterprise itself "must" be legitimate even when it flies in the face of the very values that the colonialist claims to assert about liberty, equality, and fraternity. Racism poses to the serial collective an illusory sense of unity (or "totality") to itself, that it is a complete and finished totality always under threat from a phantom character. The different versions of metaphysical politics grow out of seriality, which lends itself to presentation of itself as an illusory unity or totalization of a collective that, although a mode of "being together," is nonetheless not really shared.[119]

The use of "race" by the colonialist is thus used in the context of something like Heidegger's concept of "idle chatter" (*das Gerede*), in which one is just saying what the "others" (or what *das Man*, "one," "they") says. (Sartre calls his version of Heidegger's "idle chatter" "Other-Thought," *Pensée-Autre*.) It has to do with the origins of the discourse as a way of pretending to justify the patently and obviously unjustifiable (the super-exploitation of the colonized)—a super-exploitation that, even with its complement of racist chatter, is completely unjustifiable even on the colonialist-capitalists' own terms—so that the discourse sounds "as if" one was making sense, say, in a kind of factually grounded discussion of the difference between the colonizers and the colonized, when in fact it is at best "idle chatter," whose function is to allow this kind of metaphysical politics of the "deeper nature" (what the "natives really are" in their metaphysical essence) to obstruct any real thought about the super-exploitation of the indigenous. It is not a senseless babbling but a mouthing of phrases whose only meaning is that it is just what the anonymous "they" say and which cannot be submitted to any kind of real justificatory test on the part of the speaker.

Sartre thus tends to see the colonialism of the nineteenth and twentieth century as an off-loading both of surplus capital and of the people who had been made superfluous by such capital onto foreign lands where new capital could in turn be generated, an outcome therefore of modern capitalism itself and the extreme serialization accompanying it that overtakes political life.[120] This form of political life was in turn held in place by the virulent racism and colonialist mentality that were invented as the nonsense that pretended to legitimate the system of exploitation, and not, for example, primarily as a psychological defense mechanism for the colonialists to feel better about what they were doing. Racism simply was the key constituent of the legitimation story that underlay colonialism, not a kind of psychological by-product. This means both that the kind of racism and colonialism that came to be essential to "bourgeois" society could not be eliminated from it without fundamentally altering the class nature of the society, and that that kind of change to a non-hierarchical order would still have to be accomplished.[121]

10. Morals on Holiday

Any political order is a form of togetherness, a "we," in which the independence of individual agents (as the practitioners, those in whose singular acts the generality of the practice shows itself) is an irreducible part and in which there are differences in the power that people exercise. There is an easily generated illusion that the practice can reach the status of a "totality" as a set of determinate rules fixed independently of the singular acts of agents and under which the agents are merely subsumed. But there are and can be no such totalities. There are only "detotalized totalities," that is, ongoing totalizations that do not reach the comprehension of the whole at which they aim. Instead of totality, there are only forms of life that show themselves in practices in different ways and develop and change as the practitioners develop and change. The illusion of achieved "totality" is what leads the Stalinists and even some of the liberals to think that it is possible to achieve a kind of once-and-for-all social order that sets the rules under which individuals are appraised as instances—the illusion that a form of life can be given something like a complete legal statement in some kind of mythical statutory document, under which individual cases can all be simply subsumed. There are therefore reasons located within the status of agency itself to think that there can be no social and political order in which the basic conflicts will be finally and irrevocably eradicated. Even if the classless society were to come to pass, the inertia generated by the practico-inert and exigency would clash with spontaneity to generate yet another breakdown, and yet again it too would be "overtaken" (*dépassé*) by another.

The individual in a practice is not the instantiation (except in some very game-like examples) of a universal but is better conceived as the irreducible exemplar of the generality of the practice. The exemplar of a practice exhibits the practice not in terms of quantificational generality such that if the "universal" is taken in a more formal sense, then one single counterexample would invalidate it (so that the one black swan shows the falsity of the claim that all swans are white). The generality of the practice resembles that generality that also fits living things as a kind of norm for the kind of thing it is.

Sartre introduces the idea of exemplary individuals in ethical conduct, where the idea certainly seems to be inspired at least by Kant's conception of the exemplary judgments in the realm of the beautiful. The Kantian exemplary judgment applies to what Kant calls "dependent beauty": the beauty of something that is beautiful not only in its form but in being a good exemplar of the kind it is supposed to be (as an artwork—for example, a genre painting—is supposed to do, or equally as being the animal or plant a given organism is). A good horse is an exemplar of the species that exhibits what the species is supposed to be (so that a lame horse is not a fully adequate exemplar of its species insofar as it cannot fully flourish as a horse). In the case of works of art, some artists, so Kant argued, embodied "genius" in that they made works that did not follow the rules (for example, of classical construction or proportion) but which were nonetheless beautiful (and for which there were aesthetic judgments to the effect that X is beautiful, and if one had "taste," one ought to find it beautiful, where the "ought" did not express anything like "falling under a rule"). The artistic genius creates the model that others can only follow in the sense that the exemplar of the beautiful produced by the "genius" is for the non-geniuses merely to be imitated and thus turned into a rule.

Sartre was certainly not the first to want to use such a conception of exemplarity in ethics. For example, the early post-Kantian Romantics of the 1790s in Jena even toyed with the idea of there being "moral geniuses," although this was something Kant himself would have ruled out as absurd.[122] In Sartre's terms, the exemplary ethical actor belongs, as he puts it, to a different normative reality than the usual conduct carried out in the terms that govern the everydayness of social life. The exemplary actor engages in a "singular, dated course of action" that "proves that the unconditional possibility [of the exemplary action] is not destined to remain eternally possible" but really becomes actual in her conduct. Likewise, the conduct of such exemplary individuals "cannot be imitated for the reason that they incarnate ethics in history and that they only have any value as such an example if they retain all their singularity."[123] As an example of the failure of people trying to imitate such singular exemplarity in changed circumstances, Sartre offers the "revolutionaries of [17]89 [who] wished to imitate Plutarch's heroes because they were aspiring to realize the universal man such as he had already existed in antiquity."[124] Such imitations fail because they thereby show "they cannot find the solution to their own problems," and thus the revolutionaries trying to imitate the heroes of antiquity were in effect "aiming more or less obscurely at bringing the Revolution to a halt."[125] In fact, the "ethical" person can, in going beyond the morality of his or her day, be the "exemplar . . . who is different in that he shows that the norm is possible without preliminary conditions. . . . One cannot imitate the exemplary person . . . for the reason that his conduct is at the same time *unconditional* and *singular*."[126]

Such exemplary conduct is a single act or course of action that shows the ethical norm as it really ought to be actualized in a situation where simply following the rules would not be the best exemplar of genuine ethical conduct. It is also the fate of such exemplary conduct to become merely an example, a new rule to be followed, which in turn transforms such exemplary conduct into habit and disposition—a *hexis* in Sartre's terms—that rigidifies itself into "more of the same" (into what Sartre calls "recurrence"). Nonetheless, "in the will of the exemplary person who posits an ideal, I recognize my own will. . . . In fact, I am only rediscovering my own morality, that is, the norms of my group; but I recognize it to the extent that one leads me to go beyond it (*dépasser*) in order to unify it. And I only go beyond it by virtue of my participation in the will of the other, to whom I have recognized the right to go beyond it."[127] However, what such a conception of exemplary conduct shows is that there is a conception of the "ethical" that goes beyond that of mores (as what is required to be "one of us" indexed to a very specific historical context): "The only common aspect to all the ethical norms is that they present themselves as *unconditional possibilities*,"[128] where the "unconditional possibility" is "the negation of destiny at least on the plane where, if it is possible, one can say that the agent escapes history."[129] The unconditionality of these demands for which life is the limit case is not just that they follow from some conception of what reason alone demands—in which case disembodied angels would also have unconditional commitments—but that they come on the scene as possibilities to an agent aware of his or her own finitude, of being thrown into the world at one end of the temporal sequence and of facing the inevitable end of their being at the other. This makes the commitments into genuine commitments, matters that (in the limit case) can be greater than life itself but which, abstracted out of the context of life and its vanishing, could have no real grip at all.

One of Sartre's inspirations in the study of Marx was, as mentioned, Maximilien Rubel's argument that Marx was at his core always an ethicist. In light of that, Sartre notes that Marxism had in the wake of the Bolshevik revolution nonetheless come to more or less eschew all ethics in its belief that history would simply take care of the matter. This general view, that Marxism did not need an ethics, that ethics would simply take care of itself once the revolution had succeeded, amounts, Sartre claimed, to "sending morality on holiday,"[130] since "morals" and "ethics" ended up on that scheme being conceived of only as epiphenomena of the underlying material base and not as matters of their own importance. The problems of Stalinism, however, had only made the error of putting morality on holiday all more important. The condemnation of Stalin's deeds made later by the Communist Party at the 20th Congress in 1956 (after Stalin's death in 1953), were, so Sartre claimed, "not merely an appreciation of a strategic or tactical error but an axiological judgment" (i.e., an ethical judgment in Sartre's terms).[131] History was not just an inexorable process of vast social forces working its way to a satisfactory end on its own. It always involved spontaneity, of individuals making their own way through it in conditions that they have never chosen for themselves. At the crucial moments, people have to choose, and it is always somewhat contingent what path gets taken at that point, which in turn limits or broadens the conditions others in the future will have for their own choices. Historical agents cannot eschew responsibility and leave everything up to capital *H* History.

11. Power, Practice, Practico-Inert

History is both contingent in terms of what happens and also subject to the logic of the ideas in which individuals and collectives think of themselves and the world and chart their actions accordingly. At every given point in history, the past obviously limits what can be done in the present, but it does not determine it. People make their history in light of the ideas available to them, which are in turn limited by the material conditions surrounding them. As a way of illustrating that point, Sartre was thus more than casually interested in the development of the French state as a kind of middle point in history between the ancien régime, consisting of the ternary orders of aristocrats, ecclesiastics, and commoners, the bourgeois order that replaced it, and the (supposedly) classless society that would emerge after the state had (supposedly) withered away.

The state comes into being because of the demand for security and order, and the modern French state emerged once the older regime of three orders held together by a monarch began to lose its own capacity to perform that function (so that the monarchical "state" had to give way to the bourgeois state). Sartre noted simply that the background for such a demand is first that there must already be a mode of "being together" at work for any such demand to take place intelligibly. There must be "human multiplicities united *by a container or by a soil*" (i.e., borders), and "the ensembles in which sovereignty, in some form or other, manifests itself in its full development and power are *societies*," collectives (but not necessarily "groups" in his limited sense) that already have a structure to them.[132] As he further put it in his unpublished ethics, such a power, which is a feature of collectives, of people acting together, is always already present in such ensembles, so that even when one sovereign collapses and is replaced by another the power of the new structure of domination simply steps into and fills the power deficit created by the downfall of the original. As Sartre puts it, when new rule and subjection are "imposed by force, this force itself is already power. . . . It is thus domination and is, for all that, consensual. It is for the vanquished always different and yet the same, they find in it once more the bondage of the will or their power destroyed. . . . The [new] military king is simply another than the military king they had chosen."[133] The basic function of ideologies in these cases is to legitimate the rule established and in particular to legitimate whatever inequalities of status and goods are put into play. Moreover, a legitimate order need not be a just order—just orders can pass illegitimate laws and illegitimate orders can pass (although they rarely do) just laws—but the ruling order must be seen as, if not just, at least legitimate in meeting what Bernard Williams called the "basic legitimacy demand."[134]

Sartre saw the French Revolution as a kind of laboratory for seeing how such ideas in fact played out in history, and he prepared some notes on this sometime between 1951 and 1953, although he never worked them up for publication.[135] Although these notes consist largely of citations from other books Sartre was reading at the time, some of the major themes of his mature works nonetheless emerge in them in more concrete detail than in the *Critique*.[136]

The Revolution was crucial for framing his thought because of two features. First, it presented the prime example of the passage from one form of life to another: from the officially rigid ternary world of the Middle Ages organized into the three distinct "orders" of nobility, ecclesiastics, and commoners suddenly shifting to the post-revolutionary world of supposedly officially equal citizens. Second, and because of that, the French Revolution was thereby intrinsically linked to what was supposed to be its successor, the Bolshevik revolution of 1917. Like its predecessor, the 1917 revolution was supposed to initiate a passage from one form of life to another.

Thus, Sartre saw the debates in the Estates General meeting of 1789 bringing to conscious reflection two different conceptions of the nation: a hierarchical conception of the three orders held together by the king and a conception of the nation as an ensemble of equals. As Sartre saw it, virtually nobody came to the Estates General with the idea in mind of fostering a revolution, and many of the key players who participated in bringing on the revolution did not intend to be doing so, at least at first. In the beginning, the nobility argued that they were in danger of losing their freedom. For the nobility, freedom was conceived in terms of the legally recognized possibility of exercising specified powers that flowed from the essence of nobility itself. Noble freedom was therefore not generalizable (for example, its claim to carry out seignorial justice that was to continue to be restricted to itself). Instead, such freedom was particular and belonged exclusively to itself. In the aristocracy's conception of freedom, "it is free when it has the license to exercise these specified powers."[137] Moreover, its exercise of them, such as the oath to the king, could itself not be compelled but had to be "freely" given.

In Sartre's reconstruction, at first, the Third Estate saw its enemy not in the king but in the aristocracy itself, and thus the Third Estate did not at first press for freedom per se but rather for equality with the aristocracy.[138] The Third Estate was after all accustomed to absolutism, it was suspicious if not hostile to the aristocracy, and it wished to confront the monarch on equal terms with the aristocracy and the ecclesiastics. Sartre notes that this was itself the kind of freedom that is perfectly consistent with despotism, citing Hegel's conception of the "unhappy consciousness" as equality in bondage to a transcendent god, or, in this case, to the king as "transcendent" to the three orders.[139]

What threw all of this into turmoil was the logic of this "third party" (the king) to the three orders themselves and what role the "nation" (as embodied in the state) played in the ideology that was taking shape. The nation, as Sieyès conceived it, was the constituting power of legislation. However, the nation itself was only the sum total of its inhabitants, a heap, as it were, not a "subject" that could have those powers. Yet as this kind of constitutive power, "the free Nation, with neither form nor constraint, defines itself by its creative spontaneity which provides it with an image of itself in the object: the Constitution."[140] Whether it is the king or the nation that is the mediating force between the people and the constitution is not clear on this logic, and by 1793, the course of events seemed to imply rather strongly it was not the king. In the logic of events, the nation eventually absorbed the king into itself and thereby also removed the sacralization of the king and instead sacralized itself—in the sense that it made itself the absolute, the object of an unconditional duty or power, the manifestation of the "supreme being."[141] That sacralization of the nation forms the basis for what Sartre called in 1953 the "apocalypse," the term for when this shaky foundation all comes crashing down and one confronts "the menace of a perpetual upheaval."[142] With that, the "state" in more or less its contemporary form appears as providing the kind of stabilization the "nation" needs.[143]

The state is thus an institution that incarnates what would otherwise be only an empty idea (the "nation") as the purported unity of a society ("human multiplicities united *by a container or by a soil*"). If the nation is the idea, as it were, that the society forms of itself, the state is the institution that (supposedly) manifests the idea in concrete form.[144] The state "totalizes" the society, unifies it, but it cannot on its own wipe away the existing contradictions of that society. It is not simply a class apparatus, as the dogmatic Marxists insisted, working in the interests of the dominant class (although by virtue of its origins, it is that too). It also the unifying element of a society in its serialized, practico-inert form. It is a mode of being-together that perpetually fails in its attempt to be the "totalizing" unity of differing and often antagonistic interests. As such, it remains wedded to a hierarchically organized society that it cannot but help to reproduce. Such a state may be dedicated to the proposi-

tions proclaiming freedom, equality, and fraternity (or solidarity), but only a
non-hierarchical society based on freedom and equality could actualize those
propositions. It might well be that "Liberty, Equality, Fraternity are indeed
the terms that designate the man to come as our end,"[145] but for that to come
about, the state would first have to wither away.

Dénouement

Since the 1970s and the publication of John Rawls's magisterial *A Theory of Justice*, anglophone political philosophy became more or less obsessed with theories of distributive justice, of who gets what share of what burdens and benefits on the basis of which principles would be at work in a just order.[1] Sartre (who wrote of course long before the Rawlsian paradigm appeared) pays scant attention to such issues, not because he does not think they are important, but because he mostly agrees with the point that Marx made in his *Critique of the Gotha Program*, namely, that the issues of distribution are always already framed in terms of the system of production, and (going beyond Marx himself) in terms of the form of life at work at the time, and then even more specifically in terms of the inequality regime then at work in the background practices.[2] Sartre is more concerned with the ways in which reciprocity is incarnated or deformed, and with the kinds of political and social movements that work to actualize some form of democratic equality (what Sartre calls "popular democracy"). He thereby focuses not on distributive justice per se but on power, who has it, what sustains it, what kind of moral psychology underpins it, and what kinds of social movements might change it, and on whether there is any kind of logic to the exercise of power and the change of power.

Sartre himself focused both on the formal aspects of dialectical reason as totalizations involving non-additive wholes operating in a world of exteriority (that is, in the domain of composite wholes) and the kind of logic that underpins that as such non-additive totalizations fall apart into additive composites under the conditions of exteriority and the conflicts of social life. However, besides developing that more formal side, at the same time

Sartre focused mostly on various forms of oppression — ethnic oppression, the oppression coming out of the private property regime of capitalism (with its necessity for exploitation), and to a lesser extent, sexual oppression (specifically of gays and of women, although it would be a bit obtuse to see him as a paragon supporter of feminism, despite his association with de Beauvoir and his encouragement of her writing *The Second Sex*).[3] The systems of oppression on which he focused were not seen in terms of his applying his formal theory to specific cases but as manifestations of the more formal dialectical logic he was developing.[4] In looking at the issues connected to these themes, Sartre did not think that the famous distinction drawn by Isaiah Berlin between negative liberty (absence of obstacles) and positive liberty (self-mastery) exhausted the way we should think of the actualization of freedom.[5] The exploited worker or the super-exploited colonial subject was not free, but did not necessarily suffer from anybody actually stopping them, nor did the exploited worker or super-exploited colonial necessarily lack self-mastery. What they lacked was any effective freedom, since what confronted them was "the reality [as] simply the set of his impossibilities (the impossibility of living humanly or, perhaps more radically, of living at all)," all of which could be summed up as their "material conditions" and could be explicated in terms of their spontaneity, *hexis*, and the practico-inert all playing a role in their oppression.[6]

In the terse footnote in *Being and Nothingness* where Sartre spoke of a way of understanding existentialist philosophy as offering an alternative "ethics of deliverance and salvation," he also said this ethics would require a "radical conversion," the nature of which he left blank.[7] In that light, it would be best to understand the famous but ill-fated public lecture of 1946, later published as *Existentialism Is a Humanism*, as a sketch for what that alternative might look like. Salvation would not come from any form of theism (Sartre was always consistent about that) but from a "humanism" that took our freedom as its own end and came to its conclusion at that point.[8] Sartre quickly concluded that this was a nonstarter. After 1948, "salvation" seemed to drop out of the Sartrean vocabulary altogether, and in those studies for the ethics in 1947– 48 and in the extensive notes he made in 1951–53 on the nature of the French Revolution, he shifted his focus instead to the "sacred" as indicating the kinds of social spaces in which the "unconditional" manifests itself in terms of the values and axiological judgments that take the whole of a subject's life into account. Ethical judgments and principles take on the aspect of unconditionality when they are viewed as necessary for a meaningful life — when "life is put on the table," to use one of Sartre's favorite phrases from that period. So to speak, Sartre at that point began work on a project that could have been called "Marxism Is a Humanism" to replace the failed *Existentialism Is a Humanism*, only to find that once again that project too had not worked out.

Had Marxism been able to produce a satisfactory account of the whole of history as culminating in the classless society of small councils in realized communism, then there would have been a "totality" that would place all the partial totalizations in the correct light. But Marxism, as it necessarily turned out, could not do that, at least according to the conceptual matrix for which Sartre had argued. History as conceived in Marxism, so it seemed, did not seem to be able to step into the role that "humanism" was originally supposed to play in the Sartrean ethics, and Sartre also had to come to the conclusion, surely reluctantly, that the *Critique* "is *not* a Marxist work."[9]

In moving away from the language of "salvation" and toward that of "the sacred," Sartre also began to formulate a conception of the philosophy of history (which he also never fully worked out) in terms of understanding basic types of historical change via changes in what a form of life took to be "sacred," that is, unconditional. (Sartre's version has clear echoes of Hegel's idea that history should be seen in terms of the progressive exposition of the absolute.) What Sartre originally took to be the promise of Marxism was that of a conception of history as mapping a course heading to the achievement of the political and social structure of a classless society—that is, a non-hierarchical order of equality in a masterless world, or, in short, of democratic equality. What the *Critique* and the planned "ethics" ended with was the Marxist idea of history as leading to a classless, emancipated society but without any guarantee that that was indeed where it was going. Instead, one had to place one's bets, to use one of Sartre's frequent turns of phrase, on that idea and then look to philosophy to rationally underwrite the hopes that such a result would be possible, which also meant understanding how tragic counter-finality could intervene to dampen those hopes.[10] As Sartre put it in an interview in 1966, "It is always a question of thinking for or against history. If one admits, as I do, that the historical movement is a perpetual totalization, that each person is at every moment totalizer and totalized, philosophy represents the effort of the totalized person to seize again the meaning of the totalization. No science can replace it, for every science applies itself to a domain of man already carved out."[11] If the argument of the *Critique* is correct, and there is a feature of agency that leads it to demand freedom and equality, then something like the achievement of the classless social and political order functions as a kind of background norm of historical movement that is expressed in real history as a succession of various inequality regimes in various differing historical and material circumstances. It is not a story, at least necessarily, of progress, nor is it one that has a purpose fated to be achieved.

What Sartre did not theorize to his own satisfaction was how there was any plausibly concrete future orientation for him to use, given the underpinnings of the *Critique* and the new "Ethics," along with his own view that there could not be any freedom not already tied down by the practico-inert—except at anomalous moments such as the group in fusion—that is not caught up in its own alienation and tragic counter-finalities. Sartre flirted with political anarchism as one way to go, and on some occasions late in his life, he also took to describing himself as a "libertarian socialist," a term sometimes in use since at least the 1960s to stand in for a kind of Marxist anarchism.[12] Mostly, he simply called himself an anti-hierarchical socialist, although that term itself was at the time also used for some kind of anarchism. Sartre thought that the basis of any genuine participatory democracy had to live off the picture of fully reciprocal freedom that appears most vividly in the "group in fusion" but which is then shaped and institutionalized in various ways that also continually threaten to freeze it and thereby distort it. Although this forms the "anarchistic core" of Sartre's conception of emancipated agency, nonetheless as the "core" it does not or at least need not form the whole picture of what shape emancipated agency would take.[13]

What he did not have and what he gave up on was much of a sense of how to fashion a movement to go from hierarchical capitalism to democratic equality once he abandoned any idea that a Marxist "party" (much less a Leninist party) could play that role. Any such party embodies in Sartre's conception "a contradiction which is inherent in the very function of the party. . . . The latter comes into being to liberate the working class from seriality . . . [but] this seriality of the masses finds expression in the party's institutional character."[14] As he rather pessimistically concluded, "While I recognize the need of an organization, I must confess that I don't see how the problems which confront any stabilized structure could be resolved."[15] His earlier toying with the idea of the state's withering away came to be dismissed as "the pious myth that it would wither away of its own accord."[16]

On the other hand, as he expressed it elsewhere, this simply meant that the struggle over democratic equality had to proceed on other lines and follow other leads. On the Sartrean conception, freedom requires equality, which is why Sartre speaks of the plurality of actors organizing themselves "against a system that reduces us to powerlessness" and thus forms an "anti-hierarchic movement" in itself.[17] Sartre's conception is thus not directly focused on coming up with anything like a set of "master rules" for the equitable distribution of goods but with a kind of reciprocity-based conception of equality and only then looking more pragmatically at what forms of distribution of which goods are required for people to function as equals. Thus, he is led to look to the social movements and practice-oriented underpinnings that are necessary both to move to such a community and to sustain it.[18]

This scheme of looking to dialectic as a way of thinking of political emancipation has echoes in other approaches. For example, while Sartre's conception of system versus subjective life has some similarities to the distinction drawn by the Frankfurt school of critical theory between system and lifeworld, there are some crucial differences. In that line of thought, the lifeworld is the everyday world of meaning and expression as contrasted with something else, the "system," the purely instrumental world of the economy and of certain purely administrative institutions. The lifeworld is the source of values, whereas the "system" is valueless and is only a locus of strategic and instrumental reasoning, not an axiology of the ultimate sort. Jürgen Habermas, for example, argued that the "system"—norm-free capitalism, more or less—was "colonizing" the lifeworld, leading people to use the tools of strategic thinking rather than those of communicative expression and thus tending to obliterate the otherwise crucial elements of substantive values that hold the lifeworld together.[19] Axel Honneth uses "lifeworld" to speak of the kinds of everyday meanings that are the conditions of the more strategic and instrumental reasoning that is typical in the workings of the capitalist economy.[20] However, Sartre's conception of "subjective life versus the system" is of a more logical nature, having to do with the non-additive conception of subjective interiority and the additive conception of the natural world and the partly additive conception of the practico-inert, both of which are components of Sartre's key terms, "totalization" and "detotalization." The relation among all the terms forms the basic logic of Sartre's conception of dialectical reason.

In that sense, the more Hegelian-Wittgensteinian term "form of life" is better suited to Sartre's theory than that of the more Husserlian-phenomenological "lifeworld"—*Lebensform* instead of *Lebenswelt*.[21] The very idea of the "lifeworld" was originally intended to designate the appropriate environment for an organism, the one in which it, so to speak, has its home, in which it can flourish. A "form of life" puts the stress on the logical *form* involved: in Sartre's case, the possibilities of the shapes that various exteriorizations (in practices, *hexis*, traditions, etc. of the practico-inert) can take. For example, an "institution" gives a different shape to the relation between interiority and exteriority than does the "group in fusion." The idea of a "form of life" incorporates the aspects of the "lifeworld" within itself, but it does not and cannot take any particular "lifeworld" as simply given and beyond critique or as the natural locus of special values. In particular, Sartre thought that the capitalist lifeworld was one of thorough alienation. He notes that "capitalism satisfies certain primary needs, and also satisfies certain needs which it has artificially created: for instance the need of a car. It is this situation which has caused me to revise my 'theory of needs,' since these needs are no longer, in a situation of advanced capitalism, in systematic opposition to the system. On the contrary, they partly become, under the control of that system, an instrument of integration of the proletariat into certain processes engendered and directed by profit."[22] Sartre would surely not have been surprised by the way in which the "gig" economy metastasized in the twenty-first century, so that the way in which even one's own "free time" would come to be seen not really as "free" but rather as simply one more resource present at hand, and thus not something any rational capitalist would want to waste. (He had after all already described a version of the gig economy in the 1960 *Critique*.[23]) This kind of commodification of all aspects of life is not something unnatural, not, that is, a part of a real "lifeworld" that is being distorted into falsity. It is becoming the real lifeworld itself as agents in passive activity make it part of their practical field. The point of negativity in such a system is not that of "lifeworld" values versus the strategic reasoning of the "system" but rather that of spontaneity in response to the alienation embedded in it and in response to the system of oppression in all its forms for those who find themselves serving the interests of the system.

Nor does Sartre share some of the recent emphasis on "recognition" as the master concept of critical theory. For him, the master concepts remain those of freedom as reciprocity, an openness to novelty, and an attempt to unite against oppression in all its forms: Iris Marion Young's five faces of domination, marginalization, violence, exploitation, and humiliation.[24] As before, the key idea is that of alienation as a thwarting of the constitutive aims of subjectivity, which involve that of freedom. He does not deny any role to recognition, but he does not give it the status of the master concept of social theory. If anything the master concept is that of the dialectic between practice and practitioner, held together by changing first-person singular and plural apperceptions, in light of a background of inertia continually upended by spontaneity, in which neither the universal (the practice) nor the singular (the practitioner) has priority.

In following out those ideas, Sartre ended up with an unfinished version of a kind of somewhat naturalized left-Hegelianism—Sartre himself would probably say a "materialist" version of dialectic—shorn of many of Hegel's own commitments. The general picture is that of nature as the realm of exteriority (and thus only factual, synthetic a posteriori judgments are to be made about it) with natural beings that "totalize" their lives and thus have an "interiority" that does permit synthetic a priori judgments to be made about them. Sartre himself is more or less agnostic on the matter of whether and how these two pictures (nature and agency) are to be or can be combined.[25] Some of Sartre's compatriots even noted the affinity of Sartre's views to Dewey's pragmatism.[26] At the end, Sartre even found himself committed to some vaguely liberal ideals even though he himself only expressed revulsion at any mention of "liberalism" (by which he seems to have meant laissez-faire liberal capitalism).[27] "Liberal," he told de Beauvoir late in his life, "is a ignoble word."[28] Nonetheless, he incorporated quite self-consciously the core of some very generally liberal commitments—having to do with equality, the unavoidability of social conflict, and a suspicion of all forms of institutionalized power—by transforming those classical liberal commitments by way of Marxist conceptions of power, of class and class struggle, in order to comprehend the ways in which contemporary political and social life necessarily fall short of the 1789 ideals of liberty, equality, and fraternity.[29] He noted that the kind of intellectual after which he patterned himself had to be "a guardian of democracy: he challenges the abstract character of the rights conferred by bourgeois 'democracy,' not because he wishes to suppress them, but because he seeks to complete them with the concrete rights of socialist democracy—while preserving, in either form of democracy, the functional truth of freedom."[30] He intended this not as an external moral critique of modern institutions but as an internal critique of modernity's basic problems and tensions, and, like Hegel, he did not wish merely to "cancel" but to "cancel and preserve."

The liberal Revolution of 1789 replaced the obsolete society of orders with the ideal of liberty, equality, and fraternity, and Sartre, in agreement with Marx, held that the replacement turned out to be instead itself a hierarchical society of class oppression, which then increasingly added newer forms of oppression centered around race, gender, and other ways of "defavorizing" various parts of the population. On Sartre's view, that did not have to happen. There were always alternative futures open. His new ethics based on the *Critique* was never finished, but it illustrated the sense in which Sartre took the ideals of the Revolution to have been thwarted by the capitalist system that grew out of it. What was still to be done was not to work out a completely new ethics to replace the older one but to see how concretely the constitutive aims of agency might in the future not be thwarted by the material and ideological conditions of the present but actualized in a system that takes the reciprocity of agency and freedom seriously within a practice of concrete democratic equality. Seen in that light, Foucault's quip about Sartre's "pathetic" use of the nineteenth century to probe the problems of the twentieth might have a lot more truth to it after all—even for the twenty-first century—but, following the route of a kind of Sartrean counter-finality, not quite in the way the quip was originally intended.

Acknowledgments

Several people encouraged me and helped me along in the writing of this book. Christopher Yeomans read an earlier draft and offered valuable comments on it. Thomas Khurana was a big help early in the project. Along the way, Quentin Fisher made a number of suggestions about where he saw the work going and what the philosophical troubles were going to be. Dick Howard read an early version of the manuscript and returned it with loads of helpful criticism and questions. He also got me started on this topic many (well, many, many) years ago now, and his own work over the years has been a keen guide to me as I decided to write up something on that aspect of Sartre's work. The anonymous reviewers for the press came back with very helpful suggestions and pointers to places in the manuscript that needed more work, and the copyeditor, Marian Rogers, also gave invaluable advice.

Notes

Preface

1. Cohen-Solal and MacAfee 1987, 431.

2. Gary Gutting suggests "touching" would be the better (although far less common) rendering of Foucault's *pathétique* (2011, 68).

3. Cited in Aronson 2010, 2.

4. Sartre admitted that the *Critique* suffered stylistically as a result: "I wanted to write as simply as possible in French, and I did not always do this, as, for example, in the *Critique de la raison dialectique* (which was due to the amphetamines I was taking)" (Schilpp 1981, 11).

5. A good account and critical evaluation (mostly positive) of his writings on the French Revolution is to be found in Wahnich 2017.

6. Sartre 1963, 56. In the English translation of the *Critique*, the title of Sartre's work *Questions de Méthode* (*Search for a Method*) is translated as *The Problem of Method*.

7. This contrasts sharply with the way of reading the *Critique* in terms of the "progressive/regressive" method of *The Problem of Method*. Doing so would eviscerate the Sartrean promise of a formal critique, since the "progressive/regressive" method is self-consciously oriented toward empirical investigations, such as (obviously) the biography of a particular nineteenth-century French bourgeois novelist. This is the basic mistake I see in Catalano 1986. In fact, *The Problem of Method* should have been put at the end of the *Critique*, rather than as its opening preface of sorts, but Sartre decided against that since, as he put it, "I was afraid that this mountain of notes might seem to have brought forth a mouse" (Sartre 1976a, 821; 1960, 9). Unfortunately, by putting it at the beginning, he gave the impression that it was the mouse that made the mountain. Some Sartre scholars want to preserve the idea that the progressive/regressive method is at work in the *Critique*, but even Thomas Flynn, one of the leading contemporary interpreters of Sartre, supports the idea that *The Problem of Method* is of the same cloth as the *Critique*, although Flynn also concedes that "in many ways, the progressive-regressive method is better exemplified by the Flaubert study than by the *Critique*" (2014, 310). I would say that it is not really exemplified much at all in the *Critique*, although Sartre does mention it from time to time. Flynn concludes nonetheless that the method is at work, but he offers to my mind an unconvincing argument. Although he grants that the progressive/regressive method plays a larger role in the biography of Flaubert, he says that nonetheless Sartre's "mention of the regres-

sive and progressive natures of the argument in volumes I and II respectively . . . should settle
the matter regarding the progressive/regressive nature of the *Critique* as well" (2014, 335n2). The
fact that Sartre mentions it cannot settle that question. The progressive/regressive method is
oriented toward understanding the empirical and how it exhibits the universal. The biography
of Flaubert, for example, could not be about Flaubert unless it was empirical in large part. It
therefore cannot be an a priori matter, which, as Sartre insists over and over again, is the concern of the *Critique*. That there are things discussed in the *Critique* that are not a priori (such
as events of July 1789) is not an argument that the purpose of the *Critique* is not itself oriented
toward a pure intelligibility of action any more than the empirical examples in Kant's *Critique of
Pure Reason* show that it is not a critique of pure reason. There are many passages to cite in this
regard, but here is one: "Of course, this is a matter of formal intelligibility. By this I mean that we
must understand the bonds between *praxis*, as self-conscious, and all the complex multiplicities
which are organized through it and in which it loses itself as *praxis* in order to become *praxis*-
process. However—and I shall have occasion to repeat this still more emphatically—it is no
part of my intention to determine the concrete history of these incarnations of *praxis*" (Sartre
1976a, 65; 1960, 153). Thus, even if he does discuss the "concrete history of these incarnations of
praxis" in the book, Sartre seems to be making it clear that such embodiments of what he claims
to be discovering in the book are not its main point. Flynn's other argument is also to my mind
unconvincing: "Even the biographical studies that enter into the latter can be classified as brief
existential psychoanalyses" (2014, 310). The fact that Sartre has some biographical asides as illustrations of the more formal points he is developing is not an argument that the progressive/
regressive method is actually any kind of driving principle for the development of the *Critique*.
Flynn says he is making this argument against Klaus Hartmann's claim (1966) that the two books
are distinct. However, Hartmann (to my mind also wrongly) thinks that the more empirical
Problem of Method simply taints the purity of the *Critique*, which he sees as a kind of dialectical
development along the lines of Hegel's *Encyclopedia* rather than along the lines of the "science of
the experience of consciousness" of Hegel's *Phenomenology*.

    8. In the interview in Schilpp 1981, Sartre says rather unequivocally in response to a question
about whether he read Hegel at the École Normale (in his student years), "No, I knew of him
through some seminars and lectures, but I didn't study him until much later, around 1945" (9).
In the same interview, he also states that he "discovered the dialectic" only after 1945. (Alas, it
should be noted that all of Sartre's interviews from 1975 onward, including that in the Schilpp
volume, must be taken with a grain of salt.)

    9. One of the interpretive difficulties for those reading Sartre that is a staple of Sartre schol-
arship is that he said almost nothing about who was influencing him (although he did give obvious credit to Husserl, Heidegger, Hegel, and Marx). Hyppolite kept the Hegel-Marx-Heidegger
nexus (already established by Kojève) on the front burner of French philosophy in the 1950s.
Sartre (1992a) makes it clear that he has read both Hyppolite's translation of Hegel's *Phenomenology* and Hyppolite's renowned commentary on it. Sartre also mentions Hyppolite's importance for his knowledge of Hegel in his conversations with John Gerassi (see Gerassi 2009, 254),
but that is not conclusive. I have incorporated some of the evidence about Hyppolite's place
in the postwar generation of French philosophers; see Gutting 2011, Roth 1988, and Rockmore
1995. It would be worth tracing out in much more detail the specific appearance and transformations of Hyppolite's ideas in Sartre's *Critique*, but that is not the task for this book. Stefanos
Geroulanos (2010) discusses Hyppolite's contribution to what he calls a new form of atheist anti-
humanism emerging in France, which would also have had a great impact on Sartre, although

Sartre's appropriation of the later Heidegger's critique of the history of being would have also suggested to Sartre a way of answering Hyppolite's doubts.

10. Sartre 2007; Heidegger 1977, "Letter on Humanism," 213–266.

11. See Birchall 2004; Khilnani 1993; Judt 1986. Birchall on the whole holds Sartre's political efforts in high regard, and he certainly does not disparage Sartre's philosophical work, nor does he see it as the expression of some colossal historical error, as do Khilnani and Judt, but in his book—which clearly situates Sartre in the French debate about Stalinism and upends the myth of Sartre's "Stalinist" period—he expresses the view that the *Critique* is not a particularly coherent book, although it is easily intelligible as a particular move in the particular political climate of the time it was written. Birchall's work contrasts nicely with Lévy's (2004) rather superficial accusation of "totalitarianism" in Sartre's later thought.

12. With regard to Sartre's place in a larger circle of ideas that does not depend on seeing who exactly was reading whom, see the classic study by Jay (1984).

13. There are several very good accounts that go a long way in filling in the historical detail. See Gutting 2001, 2011; Kleinberg 2005; Roth 1988; Russon 2014; Geroulanos 2010; and partially, Howard 1977; Flynn 2014; Rockmore 1995.

14. The conceptual relations between Sartre and Wittgenstein have not been completely ignored, although they have by and large only been seen in terms of Sartre's early work, especially *Being and Nothingness*. See Longuenesse 2017; Narboux 2015, 2018; and Morris 2008, although for the most part Morris restricts himself to comparing some of Wittgenstein's points made in his *Philosophical Investigations* with Sartre's phenomenological approach.

15. Aron 1975, xii. Aron qualifies this by adding that Sartre "owes his experience and his vision of the world only to himself." The relation of Sartre's early ideas to those found in German idealism is very well developed in Gardner 2009, 2017.

16. Sartre had in fact already noted to himself in the notebooks he kept in 1947–48: "No love without deeper recognition and reciprocal comprehension of freedoms (a missing dimension in B[eing and] N[othingness]" (1992a, 414). Thomas Flynn (2014) suggests that Sartre got the idea of reciprocity from Simone de Beauvoir and that it first appears in his writings in the posthumously published *Notebooks for an Ethics* of 1947–48.

17. Sartre 1976a, 65; 1960, 153.

18. Sartre 1976a, 18; 1960, 118. To make this even clearer, Sartre adds: "These formal remarks cannot, of course, claim to add anything at all to the certainty of the synthetic reconstruction which Marx carried out in *Capital*; they are not even intended to be marginal comments on it" (1976a, 216; 1960, 276). It might be tempting to assimilate Sartre's statements in this context to some form of pragmatism, as Thomas Flynn does when he claims that for Sartre "the 'apodictic' is really the "nonnegotiable" in Quine's famous thesis" (2014, 319). Quine's thesis was that there is no difference of any useful sort between synthetic and analytic statements, so in effect all statements more or less have an empirical status, the only real differences among them being those that are more and those that are less central to the "web of belief" (Quine's phrase) than others. Sartre wanted to adhere to a more classical conception of the a priori.

19. The "formality" of Sartre's enterprise is thus like the way in which Hegel saw his dialectic as the "formal" successor to Kant's transcendental logic. Kant says: "In transcendental philosophy we consider not objects, but reason itself. . . . One could therefore also call transcendental philosophy transcendental logic. It is concerned with the sources, the extent, and the bounds of pure reason, and pays no regard to objects. Hence it is wrong to call it ontology. For there we do indeed consider things according to their universal properties. Transcendental logic abstracts

from all that; it is a kind of self-knowledge" (Kant 1997, 116). Like Hegel's first title for the *Phenomenology* ("The Science of the Experience of Consciousness"), Sartre also speaks throughout the *Critique* of the dialectical *expérience* to be investigated. Hegel's investigation is thus formal but in a way that rules out and rules in certain kinds of content, and Sartre follows him on that point.

20. On Sartre's admission of the non-dialectical nature of his early work, see the short account in Gardner 2009, esp. 217.

Chapter One

1. Sartre 1991c, 31–32.

2. Sartre states it thusly: "All reflecting consciousness is, indeed, in itself unreflected, and a new act of the third degree is necessary in order to posit it. Moreover, there is no infinite regress here, since a consciousness has no need at all of a reflecting consciousness in order to be conscious itself. It simply does not posit itself as an object" (1991c, 45).

3. Sartre 1991c, 52.

4. This was one of the objections that Fichte made against Reinhold in the early development of German idealism, which led Fichte to construct a different model of the "I." See Henrich 1967; Pinkard 2002, 2015a.

5. In the 1975 interview in Schilpp 1981, Sartre says of the position he took in *The Transcendence of the Ego*: "I maintained that point of view even in *L'Être et le Néant*; I would still maintain it today; but at the stage it is no longer a subject of my reflections" (10).

6. "It is certain, however, that the *I* does appear on the unreflected level. If someone asks me 'What are you doing?' and I reply, all preoccupied, 'I am trying to hang this picture,' or 'I am repairing the rear tire,' these statements do not transport us to the level of reflection" (Sartre 1991c, 89).

7. This is not to say that for Sartre, we are always perfectly clear about what we are doing. Quite the opposite: as he put it in *Being and Nothingness*, "This is indeed what linguists and psychologists have perceived, and their embarrassment can be of use to us here as a counter-proof; they believed that they discovered a circle in the formulation of speaking, for in order to speak it is necessary to know one's thought. But how can we know this thought as a reality made explicit and fixed in concepts except precisely by speaking it? Thus speech refers to thought and thought to speech . . . This circle . . . is not unique with speech; it is the characteristic of the situation in general" (1956, 518).

8. Sartre notes: "The 'I' would be to the concrete and psycho-physical *me* what a point is to three dimensions: it would be an infinitely contracted me" (1991c, 41).

9. In this way, Sartre's early line of thought somewhat lines up with that of Wittgenstein in the *Tractatus*: "If I wrote a book 'The world as I found it,' I should also have therein to report on my body and say which members obey my will and which do not, etc. This then would be a method of isolating the subject or rather of showing that in an important sense there is no subject"; "The subject does not belong to the world: rather, it is a limit of the world" (Wittgenstein 1963, 5.631–33). This conceptual similarity has not gone unnoticed. Jean-Philippe Narboux (2015) offers an interesting explication of Sartre's early work in light of the conceptual similarities with Wittgenstein's ideas as expressed in the *Tractatus*.

10. Sartre notes: "But this 'I' which is here in question nevertheless is no mere syntactical form. It has a meaning; it is quite simply an empty concept which is destined to remain empty" (1991c, 89). Jean-Philippe Narboux holds this to be intelligible only in terms of the "I" not being

a referring term of any sort, since there is nothing to which it could refer; and that this meta-physical point that there is nothing to which the "I" could refer can itself only be made intel-ligible if there is a deeper sense of negation than that of propositional negation, which is Sartre's point about holding "being" and "nothingness" absolutely apart in *Being and Nothingness*. See the discussion in Narboux 2015. Narboux is also responding there to what he takes to be Béatrice Longuenesse's argument that Sartre has a view of "I" as a referential term. See Longuenesse 2017. That particular disagreement between Longuenesse and Narboux is not at issue in my discus-sion as far as I can tell.

11. Sartre 1991c, 101.

12. Sartre 1991c, 100. Sebastian Gardner notes: "The problem which we found in *The Tran-scendence of the Ego*, namely that Sartre left it unexplained why reflection should create an 'I,' is thus resolved. Pre-reflective and reflective consciousness are referred back to a more basic, unitary teleological ground, which realizes itself originally as pre-reflective consciousness, and then, because this takes it no closer to its projected end, as reflective consciousness. This ground provides the *explanans* of reflexivity in general. The for-itself is in this way an *organic unity*, but only an *aspirant, would-be* organic unity, not an achieved whole" (2009, 99). The for-itself aspires to "totality" (an organic unity) but necessarily fails at this endeavor and ends up as a "detotalized totality," an image of itself as an organic unity that has somehow fallen apart into a dispersed, inorganic unity.

13. Sartre 1992a.

14. See the good discussion in Haase 2016.

15. "But we do not possess these techniques in this abstract and universal form: to know how to speak is not to know how to pronounce and understand words in general; it is to know how to speak a certain language and by it to manifest one's belonging to humanity on the level of the national collectivity . . . in the sense that the reality of speech is language and that the reality of language is dialect, slang, jargon, etc. And conversely the truth of the dialect is the language, the truth of the language is speech. This means that the concrete techniques by which we mani-fest our belonging to the family and to the locality refer us to more abstract and more general structures which constitute its meaning and essence; these refer to others still more general until we arrive at the universal and perfectly simple essence of any technique whatsoever by which any being whatsoever appropriates the world" (Sartre 1956, 512−513).

16. Hegel 2018, 108, ¶177.

17. Sartre accuses Hegel of being both epistemologically and ontologically optimistic. Of Hegel's "epistemological optimism," Sartre says: "Thus Hegel's optimism results in failure: be-tween the Other-as-object and Me-as-subject there is no common measure, no more than be-tween self-consciousness and consciousness of the Other. I can not know myself in the Other if the Other is first an object for me; neither can I apprehend the Other in his true being—that is, in his subjectivity. No universal knowledge can be derived from the relation of consciousnesses. This is what we shall call their ontological separation" (1956, 243). Of Hegel's "ontological opti-mism," he says, "For individual consciousnesses are moments in the whole, moments which by themselves are *unselbständig*, and the whole is a mediator between consciousnesses. Hence is de-rived an ontological optimism parallel to the epistemological optimism: plurality can and must be surpassed toward the totality. But if Hegel can assert the reality of this surpassing, it is because he has already given it to himself at the outset. In fact he has forgotten his own consciousness; he is the Whole, and consequently if he so easily resolves the problem of particular consciousnesses it is because for him there never has been any real problem in this connection" (244)

18. "We must understand by this that each one must be able by starting out from his own

interiority, to rediscover the Other's being as a transcendence which conditions the very being of that interiority. This of necessity implies that the multiplicity of consciousnesses is on principle unsurpassable, for I can undoubtedly transcend myself toward a Whole, but I can not establish myself in this Whole so as to contemplate myself and to contemplate the Other. No logical or epistemological optimism can cover the scandal of the plurality of consciousnesses" (Sartre 1956, 244).

19. For a defense of Sartre's view on the ultimacy of the distinction between being and noth-ingness, see Narboux 2015.

20. There are many passages in the *Critique* that bring this up as part of Sartre's new "ma-terialism." It appears more front and center in the writings immediately following the *Critique*. He discusses this, for example, in places in his notes for his new ethics. See Sartre 1964d, 399, where he notes: "Life is a value we should not understand in terms of the ensemble of physi-ological behaviors of the organism but in terms of the perpetual totalization achieved by this organism which is both the rough shape and the foundation of all valorized behaviors." See also Sartre 1964a, 2015.

21. Sartre 1976a, 92; 1960, 175.

22. Sartre 1976a, 486; 1960, 491.

23. On *praxis*, see Jay 1973, 4.

24. Sartre 1988, 194.

25. Sartre 2016, 10.

26. Sartre 1976a, 93; 1960, 176.

27. Sartre 1964a, 75; 2015, 70.

28. Sartre 1976a, 231; 1960, 288.

29. Sartre sums up this way: "Every *praxis* explains itself in terms of the objective and the object" (1976a, 503; 1960, 505).

30. Sartre 1976a, 734; 1960, 687.

31. This has been the topic of a lot of discussion. One of the foci of the discussion is the lucid presentation in Boyle 2015.

32. In *The Problem of Method*, Sartre replies to Gyorgy Lukács's criticism of him by saying that "we were convinced at one and the same time that historical materialism furnished the only valid interpretation of history and that existentialism remained the only concrete approach to reality. I do not pretend to deny the contradiction in this attitude. I simply assert that Lukács does not even suspect it" (1963, 21).

33. The passage runs: "Let us imagine that moved by jealousy, curiosity, or vice I have just glued my ear to the door and looked through a keyhole. I am alone and on the level of a non-thetic self-consciousness. This means first of all that there is no self to inhabit my consciousness, nothing therefore to which I can refer my acts in order to qualify them. They are in no way known; I am my acts and hence they carry in themselves their whole justification. . . . But all of a sudden I hear footsteps in the hall. Someone is looking at me! What does this mean?" (Sartre 1956, 259–260).

34. Sartre 1956, 273; 1943, 312: "Ceci nous marque assez que ce n'est pas dans le monde qu'il faut d'abord chercher autrui, mais du côté de la conscience, comme une conscience en qui et par qui la conscience se fait être ce qu'elle est" (my underlining).

35. Sartre 1956, 259.

36. Sartre notes: "Recognition by others (as individuals). What gives them the quality of be-ing able to recognize me? My recognition of them. Reciprocal recognition. But since they only have the right that I lend to them and I have no more right than they lend me, the whole is not

recognized and falls into an unjustifiable subjectivity. . . . This reciprocal recognition is a game of mirrors, which finally ends up as a lie. This is what a historical succession of recognitions by the absolute third person who is God is. Recognition must be without reciprocity; an absolute witness, himself the definition of good and evil, must justify me in recognizing me. When this witness is no more, we try to replace him with the interplay of give and take of mutual recognition" (1992a, 70).

37. A representative Kantian view of this is found in Christine Korsgaard's account of the second person: "We might put this by saying that because of the reflective structure of human consciousness, I think that every rational agent stands in what Darwall would call a second-personal relation to herself—she has a second-personal voice within" (2007, 11).

38. "But we have equally recognized that Hegel, although his vision is obstructed by the postulate of absolute idealism, has been able to put the discussion on its true plane" (Sartre 1956, 244). See the lucid interpretation and defense of Sartre's position in Gardner 2017.

39. Sartre 1956, 326.

40. One of the issues in reading Sartre's work has to do with how much continuity there is between his earlier work, culminating in *Being and Nothingness*, and his later work, culminating in the *Critique* and the unpublished works on ethics. David Sherman denies that there is indeed a break in Sartre's thought, and he cites a couple of interviews with Sartre done late in life where Sartre said that there had been not a break but a developmental continuity in his thought. However, the way he treats the second person here is a good example of where a "break" (if that is the right word) should be seen (Sherman 2007, 70–74). (Whether this constitutes an "epistemological break" in Louis Althusser's sense of the term—which is Sherman's main focus—is another issue, which will not be dealt with here.)

41. The term comes into Hegel's vocabulary in his published works after the publication of the *Phenomenology* in 1807. In his *Logic*, Hegel says of the concrete universal that it is "the two moments, that of the objective universal, that is, the species, and that which is separated off from it (*das Vereinzelte*). Here is therefore the universal, which is only itself, the universal, in unity with its opposite [that which is separated off from it], and which continues itself through its opposite" (1969b, 349–350).

42. "The universal that I realize here is always under the form of singularity. This is what I call incarnation" (Sartre 1964a, 137; 2015, 116; and "Incarnation is precisely that: the concrete universal constantly producing itself as the animation and temporalization of individual contingency" (Sartre and Elkaïm-Sartre 1991, 40; 1985, 50).

43. "Indeed, all the concepts forged by history, including that of man, are similarly individualized universals and have no meaning apart from this individual process. . . . Thus the universals of the dialectic—principles and laws of intelligibility—are individualized universals; attempts at abstraction and universalization can only result in schemata which are continually valid for that process" (Sartre 1976a, 49; 1960, 140).

44. This point about generic universality as distinguished from quantificational generality in Hegel's thought is also made in a different way in Stern 2007. Stern holds that this is a point about Hegel's metaphysics in general (for which he provides some powerful textual evidence) and is one of the conceptual links as well as the differences between Hegel and those "British idealists" who were also characterized as "Hegelians." Here I am arguing that the conception of the concrete universal as more or less taken over by Sartre from Hegel has to do with the relation between practices and specific actions that exhibit the practice, so that I leave aside for now the issue about how best to interpret Hegel.

45. Sartre 1964a, 32; 2015, 38.

46. Sartre 1976a, 92–93; 1960, 176.

47. For example, Sartre notes with regard to the set of social relations that he calls "serial-ity" that "there are serial behavior, serial feelings and serial thoughts; in other words a series is a mode of being for individuals both in relation to one another and in relation to their common being and this mode of being transforms all their structures" (1976a, 266; 1960, 316).

48. Thomas Flynn seems to think that Sartre does not keep these as sharply distinguished as Sartre claims they are. For example, Flynn says, "Yet curiously, Sartre seems intent on excluding the moral significance of both expressions, despite his use of each in an obviously pejorative sense. Sartre describes various "ruses of flight," one of which, the rationalist habit of mind, the "passion for the universal," he designates "the royal road of flight" (Flynn 2014, 247). However, Sartre distinguishes between failing to do what one ought (a moral failing) and failing to be or become what one really is (a spontaneously free being). In all these cases, this distinction is perhaps made less distinct by the Hegelian and Sartrean idea that one can fail to be what one is and that matters such as "spontaneous freedom" are items at which a subject can aim and yet still fail to hit.

49. Sartre 1964d, 398. On this idea of appropriation in another context of critical theory, see Jaeggi's (2014b) treatment of *Aneignung*; see also Jaeggi 2014a.

50. As Sartre notes, "In this way, historical action appears as an open ended interiority, that is to say, which can never come to a closure on itself as an integration-in-perpetual-disintegration, or, better, as a detotalized totalization" (1964d, 409).

51. The whole passage runs: "The experience of the We-subject cannot be primary; it can not constitute an original attitude toward others since, on the contrary, it must in order to be real-ized presuppose a twofold preliminary recognition of the existence of others" (Sartre 1956, 426).

52. See Sartre 1956, 424–426.

53. Sartre 1956, 427.

54. See Narboux 2014. See also the treatment of this from a Wittgensteinian point of view in Fisher 2019.

55. Hegel 2018, 108, ¶177 and 389, ¶671.

56. Sartre seemed to pick up the language of *dévoiler*, "unveiling," from Heidegger. One sees its key role in Sartre's 1948 text "Truth and Existence," which he decided against publishing but which was written in light of Heidegger's *Das Wesen der Wahrheit*, which itself appeared in French translation in 1948. This essay was written around the time of Sartre's most Marxist essay, "Materialism and Revolution," and also when he was working on his early but also failed *Notebooks for an Ethics*, in which he had not yet put together how this conception of a practice manifesting itself fit with his emerging social and political philosophy at the time. See Sartre, Elkaïm-Sartre, and Aronson 1992. (Ronald Aronson's introduction to that volume is very help-ful in placing where it fits in the development of Sartre's thought.) The essay "Materialism and Revolution" can be found in Sartre 1955.

57. Sartre 1976a, 99; 1960, 181. Or, as Wittgenstein supposedly quipped, "A language can be taught by Correspondence courses, but language can't" (Wittgenstein and Moore 2016, 109). Sartre adds: "'Human relations' are in fact inter-individual structures whose common bond is language and which actually exist at every moment of History. Isolation is merely a particular aspect of these relations" (99; 181).

58. Sartre 1976a, 109; 1960, 189. Late in the *Critique*, Sartre adds: "Struggle as reciprocity is a function of reciprocity of comprehension. If one of the adversaries should cease to comprehend he would become the object of the Other" (816n133; 753).

59. "The foundation of the human relation as the immediate and perpetual determination of everyone by the Other and by all is neither an a priori communication engineered by a kind of Great Telephone Operator (*Grand Standardiste*), nor the indefinite reiteration of essentially separate patterns of behavior" (Sartre 1976a, 105–106; 1960, 186).

60. Sartre 1976a, 550; 1960, 542.

61. This is perhaps *the* basic point of contention among those who see Sartre's later works as essentially continuous with his earlier writings. Gardner, for example, makes the interesting argument that Sartre in his early work argues that since "individual mindedness consists in consciousness grounded on freedom, which misrepresents itself as sharing in the unfree mode of being of the in-itself" (Gardner 2017, 69), there cannot be any coherent or intelligible sense to be given to the idea of an apperceptive "We" (or at least that any such "We" must be metaphysically incoherent in its self-conception). This is certainly true for the Sartre of *Being and Nothingness*, and Gardner proposes that this denial of an apperceptive "We" structures the whole project of the later *Critique*. As he puts it, the result for the early Sartre is that "the failure of subjects to cohere intelligibly renders human reality ontologically vulnerable: it defines an empty space into which the entities which give the social and historical world its pseudo-substantiality project themselves" (69). Interpreted in Gardner's way, the *Critique* would have to conclude that at best the apperceptive "We" can only appear, and even then more or less in illusory form, in brief moments of violent revolutionary upheaval (in the "group-on-the-way-to fusion"). This way of seeing the *Critique*—as arguing that at best free non-alienated action only appears in passing moments of violent group rebellion—led Alasdair MacIntyre in 1962 to condemn it as "the anarchism and nihilism of the last century, and it is that anarchy and nihilism as portrayed by its harshest critics, by Conrad for example, in *Under Western Eyes*, or by Dostoevsky" (MacIntyre 2009, 206). However, the passages in the main body of the text that I cited from Sartre suggest something different (evidenced in these and other Sartrean quotes: "But language cannot have come to man, since it presupposes itself" and "It is really only the actualization of a relation which is given as having always existed, as the concrete and historical reality of the couple which has just been formed"). The relation between the "totality" and the individual actor is analogous to that between the language and its speakers. The language is not a finished totality which then is instantiated in single speakers. Rather, there is a language only insofar as there are speakers, and there are speakers only insofar as there is a language. Neither is a pole (as Husserlian phenomenology might want to put it) interacting with another pole—say, that of a "totality" interacting with a "totalizing subject"—nor is it a matter of subsumptive judgment (of bringing the singular under the universal kind). The mode of generality is logically different in the cases at issue. In the practice/practitioner case, the "universal" is not instanced in the particular. It *manifests* itself in the activities of the singular agents. Judgments about the relation between universal and singular do not therefore have the logical structure that Gardner claims they have: "Intersubjective relations presuppose that subjects have access if not explicitly or in fact, then implicitly or in principle—to a universal under which they can jointly know themselves to fall . . . all parties must be able to conceive themselves as being in some essential respect, however indefinite, of a single kind" (Gardner 2017, 51). In the relation between agent and universal, the singular agent itself acts universally, as when the dance instructor shows the pupil how to do the move by doing the move herself. The individual action there is not a subsumption under a general rule, and it is not quantificational generality which is at issue, but rather a manifestation of a shared background that has no full reality outside of the ongoing activities of the individual agents. (Its generality is also therefore not a statistical probability, not a "it usually happens

that . . ."). It, like language itself, is always, in Sartre's jargon, a "detotalized totality." This issue of the logic of generality and its normativity is also a theme taken up by interpreters of both Wittgenstein and Hegel. For Wittgenstein's relation to this idea, see, for example, Floyd 2016. On this idea in Hegel, see Kern 2019, Pippin 2018, Ng 2020, and Khurana 2017.

62. Sartre 1976a, 21; 1960, 119. Sartre seems to complicate this when he also says: "Therefore, if there is to be any such thing as totalization, the intelligibility of constituted dialectical Reason (the intelligibility of common actions and of *praxis*-process) must be based on constituting dialectical reason (the abstract and individual *praxis* of man at work)" (67; 154). Although that might seem to move him in the direction of seeing the individual agent with his own projects as the foundational starting point, he quickly qualifies this: "Whether we grasp the individual, within our investigation, as the practical ground of an ensemble and the ensemble as producing the individual in his reality as historical agent, this formal procedure will lead us to a dialectical circularity" (68; 154). The point is that "constituted" dialectical reason as institutionalized norms is itself always upheld and reactualized by the "constituting" activities of the agents within the practice and that the "constituting" activities themselves are intelligible only in terms of the social, "constituted" norms.

63. On this theme in Wittgenstein, the best discussion is to be found in Fisher 2019. See also Sandis 2019.

64. In one place at least, Sartre partially identifies alterity with anonymity. See Sartre 1976a, 746; 1960, 697: "This transitivity necessarily plunges it into anonymity—that is to say, into alterity."

65. "On the contrary, interest arises, as always, out of alterity as the primary human practical relation, but as deformed by the matter which mediates it; and it maintains itself in the milieu of alterity" (Sartre 1976a, 210). Sartre also speaks of "reciprocity as a fundamental human relation, the separation of individual organisms, the practical field with its dimensions of alterity in depth" (1976a, 210; 1960, 272).

66. "The milieu appears immediately to its members as a *homogeneous container* and as a permanent (practico-inert) *linking force* which unites everyone to everyone without distance; from this point of view, every human relation which establishes itself concretely between two or more individuals arises in the milieu as an inessential *actualization* of a practico-inert structure already inscribed in Being" (Sartre 1976a, 279; 1960, 327).

67. Sartre puts it this way: "But specifically, outside the human relation of reciprocity and the relation to the third party, which in themselves are not social (although in a sense they condition all sociality and are conditioned by sociality in their historical content), the structural relation of the individual to other individuals remains in itself completely indeterminate until the ensemble of material circumstances on the basis of which the relation is established has been defined, from the point of view of the historical process of totalization" (1976a, 255; 1960, 308). On the idea of a "form of life," a term common to Hegel and Wittgenstein, see Pinkard 2019.

68. Sartre 1976a, 51; 1960, 142.

69. Sartre places the natural sciences outside the purview of dialectical reason, since the sciences only study matters from the standpoint of "exteriority." He dismisses all attempts to submit the natural sciences to dialectical reason with the brusque judgment that "one cannot set a priori limits to science," since the concatenations of objects discovered by sciences are exterior and do not follow from each other as a matter of logic (1976a, 92; 1960, 175). "Since the law discovered by the scientist, taken in isolation, is neither dialectical nor anti-dialectical (it is only a quantitative determination of a functional relation), the consideration of scientific facts

(that is to say, of established laws) cannot furnish, or even suggest, a proof of the dialectic" (28; 125–126).

70. Sartre writes *exis* instead of the more usual way of transliterating the Greek as *hexis*. The word appears a couple of times in *Being and Nothingness* in the same way, although it plays no real role there. Following the lead of a number of different Sartre scholars, I will always quote and discuss it as *hexis*. Gary Gutting is among those who point out that for some reason or another, in deciding to transliterate it that way, Sartre "ignores the Greek rough-breathing mark" (Gutting 2001, 152).

71. Sartre notes this in the following passage where he speaks of the pledge as an exercise of spontaneity binding agents to each other: "Every organization which has the reciprocity of the pledge is a new beginning, since it is always the victory of man as communal freedom over seriality, whatever it may be" (1976a, 436n24; 1960, 453).

72. Sartre 1974c, 35.

73. Wittgenstein says: "Let us not forget this: when 'I raise my arm', my arm goes up. And the problem arises: what is left over if I subtract the fact that my arm goes up from the fact that I raise my arm?" (1953, ¶621). Wittgenstein uses this example to show how easy it is to think that therefore there "must" be some hidden extra in the distinction between rising and raising and that this "must" be some other, independent mental event (such as a "willing" or a "trying"), which further suggests that the event of an arm raising "must be" the addition of two different events, an inner willing and a bodily movement. James Conant reads this as Wittgenstein's pointing out that this is one of many kinds of a conjuring trick that leads us down the additive path. He makes this point vis-à-vis language, but the point applies to action too: "Hence a fundamental target—a crucial moment in the philosophical conjuring trick that is apt to strike us as perfectly innocent—in these sections is precisely the idea that there is a highest logical common factor across a field of incised marks and squeaked-out noises (marks and noises that are not yet language) and a field of genuine linguistic activity—that there is a highest common factor across the case of the dead sign qua mere sound or shape and the case of the sign qua that which has its life in use" (Conant 2020, 30–31). This is the same mistake as thinking that identifying the movement of an arm apart from its place in the "synthetic," non-additive unity of an action gives us what is the common factor in both instances. One can describe physically the movement of the arm as an element in playing a cello and one can see it as "playing a cello." The two are different cases, and seeing them as sharing the element in exteriority as the common factor leads to the idea that "I" must somehow be breathing life and meaning into what is otherwise a meaningless movement in exteriority. The family of views that rejects such additive conceptions has Sartre's conception of *praxis* as a member.

74. In his study of Sartre's work as a whole, André Guigot draws the plausible conclusion that "alienation is for Sartre in the *Critique of Dialectical Reason* an a priori necessity. Violence is certainly contingent, but it is a contingent necessity" (2007, 227). Yet alienation seems more like an a priori possibility rather than a necessity—at least that is what Sartre says: "This means: the dialectical investigation of alienation as an *a priori possibility* of human praxis on the basis of the *real* alienations to be found in concrete History" (1976a, 66n27; 1960, 154). It is certainly possible to imagine a political order where alienation is not present, that is, where one's powers are not thwarted by the conditions in which they must be exercised. However, under conditions of scarcity, it seems this a priori possibility remains a practical impossibility. Nonetheless, the realization of freedom need not be an all or nothing affair. There can social formations in which spontaneity is more thoroughly thwarted than in others. Chiara Collamati points to a key pas

sage in the *Critique* where Sartre speaks of "necessity as the destiny in exteriority of freedom," which she identifies with "alienation" in Sartre's sense (Collamati 2016, 95n10). However, Sartre himself in the following sentence in the *Critique* asks himself rhetorically, "Should we describe this as alienation? Obviously we should," but he quickly qualifies it: "However, a distinction must be made: alienation in the Marxist sense begins with exploitation" (1976a, 227; 1960, 285). Sartre then goes on in a footnote to say: "Fundamental alienation does not derive, as *Being and Nothingness* might mislead one into supposing, from some prenatal choice: it derives from the univocal relation of interiority which unites man as a practical organism with his environment" (1976a, 228n68; 1960, 286). In other words, alienation is not simply that of interiority as caught up in the realization of aims in the world. There may be realizations in "exteriority" that are not alienated at all, namely, those that do not thwart the realization of full reciprocity in freedom and equality. Alienation in Marx's sense begins with exploitation in that it is one of the main assertions of Sartre's appropriation of Marx that the capitalist system of exploitation is to be identified as necessarily thwarting the constitutive aims of agency. In another essay, Collamati (2017, 146) argues that when Sartre says, "Taking things this way, we note that the colonized has as its unconditional end the realization in his person of the integral man. Simply because he claims, through the system, by the system against him the possibility of reproducing his naked life" (1964a, 80; 2015, 73), Sartre means to stake out a general background of normativity that would permit a new form for thinking about political formations other than the bourgeois-juridical model that functions at the basis of a lot of social contractarian thought, but it remains unclear just how that background is to be conceived and how it is to supplant the juridical model. I think this is all the more complicated by Collamati's view, as she puts it, that "totalizing and temporalizing are one and the same movement" (2019, 45). If that were true, then Sartre would not say things like, for example, "if history is a totalization which temporalizes itself, culture is itself a temporalizing and temporalized totalization" (1976a, 54; 1960, 144). That would also put out of bounds talking about fully alienated totalizations in exteriority, as Sartre does and which happen in social structures such as "Taylorism" (see Sartre 1976a, 559–563; 1960, 549–552).

75. Sartre remarks: "There can be no *hexis*, no *habit* without practical vigilance, that is to say, without a concrete objective to determine them in their essential indetermination, and without a project to actualize them by specifying them" (1976a, 455; 1960, 468).

76. Sartre 1964a, 32; 2015, 38.

77. Sartre 1966, 89.

78. Sartre 1976a, 329; 1960, 367.

79. Sartre says of this that it is "comprehension," which "is nothing other than my real life; it is the totalizing movement which gathers together my neighbor, myself, and the environment in the synthetic unity of an objectification in process (*en cours*)" (1963, 155).

80. For Sartre, it is a social possibility to do so for purposive actions to be decomposed, for example, the way in which workers on the assembly lines had their actions broken down into discrete, measurable units under the conditions of the deskilling of labor in "Taylorism"—the attempt in the late nineteenth century by F. W. Taylor to analyze workers' actions into discrete components so that they could be automated and rationalized—that "no action is a priori incapable of being decomposed into several operations; these operations are passivized and can be grasped by analytical Reason," but nonetheless are fully intelligible only in terms of their place within a set of actions in the social group that themselves show a purpose, such that even though "analytical Reason can conceive a universal combinatory of functions in a given group; it will have the concrete ability to construct it only in so far as it is a special case of dialectical Reason, that is to say, a function produced, directed and controlled by it" (Sartre 1976a, 561; 1960, 551).

81. Sartre 1976a, 325; 1960, 364. Sartre adds later, "But in so far as everyone perceives his own impossibility (that is to say, his inability to change or reorganize anything) through his praxis (which posits itself in its dialectical structure as a permanent possibility of transcending any actual circumstances), this impossibility inside freedom appears to him as temporary and relative" (1976a, 329; 1960, 367).

82. Sartre 1976a, 558; 1960, 549.

83. Sartre introduces the idea of "passive activity" to characterize a certain way of participating in the world that does not look much like activity but requires me to do what I do as the kind of person I am—to be and to carry on as "the average": "From my window, I can see a road-mender on the road and a gardener working in a garden. Between them there is a wall with bits of broken glass on top protecting the bourgeois property where the gardener is working. . . . Meanwhile, I can see them without being seen, and my position and this passive view of them at work situates me in relation to them: I am 'taking a holiday', in a hotel; and in my inertia as witness I realize myself as a petty bourgeois intellectual; my perception is only a moment of an undertaking (such as trying to get some rest after a bout of 'over-working', or some 'solitude' in order to write a book, etc.), and this undertaking refers to possibilities and needs appropriate to my profession and milieu. From this point of view, my presence at the window is a passive activity (I want 'a breath of fresh air' or I find the landscape 'restful', etc.) and my present perception functions as a means in a complex process which expresses the whole of my life" (1976a, 100; 1960, 182).

84. Sartre characterizes active passivity as follows: "We have considered active passivity both as the regulated production of pledged inertia and as a condition for common activity. . . . The important point is that—at least as long as it still has its finality—it can never be entirely assimilated to the practico-inert: its meaning is still that of an action undertaken in the light of a certain objective (regardless of what counter-finalities may have developed); but on the other hand, the presence of alterity in it as suffered separation makes it impossible for it to become identical with the inert (if slight) forms of active passivity which are based simply on the pledged untranscendability of certain possibilities" (1976a, 603; 1960, 583).

85. "The dialectic, if it exists, can only be the totalization of concrete totalizations effected by a multiplicity of totalizing individualities. I shall refer to this as dialectical *nominalism*" (Sartre 1976a, 37; 1960, 132). Klaus Hartmann (1966, 60, 169) takes this to be a deep misunderstanding of the possibilities of dialectic, and he contrasts Sartre's dialectic with Hegel's in this regard. Hegel's dialectic always proceeds from the abstract to the concrete, whereas Sartre's view, Hartmann argues, starts out with something already concrete, namely, an individualizing, totalizing subject, and then develops necessarily one-sided abstractions based on that. On Hartmann's reading, Sartre thus makes much the same mistake as Fichte. Hartmann bases this objection on Sartre's offhanded comment about dialectical nominalism. However, Sartre is not recapitulating Fichte in that Sartre thinks that the individuality of the agent as a "concrete totalization" always involves the generic background of the practices involved in his actions. The "I" cannot be without the "We" to which it belongs. A truly "nominalist" theory of agency would have to build up the "we" out of individual interactions, which Sartre does not do and which he thinks cannot be done. Sartre does qualify his so-called nominalism throughout the book. For example, he says, "It has been obvious from the beginning of our dialectical investigation that the original foundation of unity, of action, and of finality is individual *praxis* as the unifying and reorganizing transcendence of existing circumstances towards the practical field. But we also know that this individual *praxis can no longer be recognized* at the most concrete level of the practico-inert and that it exists there only to *lose itself*, to the advantage of the maleficent actions of worked matter"

(1976a, 310–311n93; 1960, 352). An interpretation similar to that provided by Hartmann is found in Howard 1977. Howard claims that "Sartre's project is to present a transcendental social philosophy . . . Sartre's project is transcendental in that it attempts to articulate a categorial structure based on a principle of which each successive development can be seen as a *principiatum*; each moment must have its intelligibility in a ground of which it is the grounded realization" (1977, 144). However, contrary to Hartmann, Howard also claims that Sartre's "nominalism is in fact a relation" (145). Nonetheless, Howard insists: "Sartre's transcendental-yet-real ground is the immediate, 'abstract' human individual and its praxis" (145). If so, this would put Sartre back into the Fichtean position criticized by Hartmann, where something that is real (the existing individual) is real only in relation to some other, in which case the individual considered apart from the relation is not real. Howard's idea that Sartre's "nominalism is in fact a relation" itself seems to rest on the conception Sartre voiced in *Being and Nothingness*, that the "other" is built into the monadic relation of consciousness to itself and therefore the "other" is only a virtual other, not a real other (Sartre 1956, 273). Like Hartmann and Howard, Raymond Aron (Sartre's youthful friend and later his political opponent in the French debates in the postwar period) in his simultaneously friendly but also harshly critical (and very flawed) interpretation of Sartre also takes Sartre's comment about "nominalism" seriously and, like Hartmann and Howard, thus takes Sartre's project to be transcendental in character, as when he says that "the *transcendental analysis of sociality* constitutes the essential part of the *Critique*" (Aron 1975, 89), and that Sartre's theory thus amounts to a kind of "transcendental deduction of a philosophy of violence" (58) or of "the foundations of political concepts or . . . the authentic meaning in them" (61–62). (See also Aron 1975, 18, 37, 51, 91.) In the last analysis, Aron takes Sartre's position in the *Critique* to be merely an extension of *Being and Nothingness*: "The model of the dialectic in Sartre's eyes is not the dialogue and the relation *between* consciousnesses but solitary consciousness, the totalization, by the gaze of what is presented to it, the unification of a field thanks to the project that brings data together with a view to a future" (107). In a manner similar to Aron, the prominent Sartre interpreter and critic Ronald Aronson faults Sartre for having a "totalization without a totalizer" (1987, 83, 87), although unlike Aron, Aronson does not see Sartre as pursuing a transcendental project. See Aronson 1987, 235–237.

86. Coming out of the Franco-German tradition in philosophy, Sartre takes the kind of neo-Aristotelian account of action as the paradigm form and asks questions of it that have to do with how it is compatible with a certain form of materialism and the like. Thus, one may at least partially impute to Sartre a version of what Michael Thompson (2008) endorses as the "naïve theory" of action. This idea is extended to the concept of a kind of naturalism to which Sartre could at least partially subscribe in Thompson 2013. This goes some way to meeting the proposal by Paul Crittenden that in light of what he takes to be the overall failure of Sartre's ethical thought, "he would have had a better chance at arriving at a working synthesis had he been able to give a greater place to the Aristotelian dimension of his sociality or realist ethics as mediated especially by Hegel's appropriation of Greek ethics" (Crittenden 2009, 139). However, what still separates Sartre's views from most of the various forms of neo-Aristotelianism is that he thinks that what is natural to the human species is its capacity to self-consciously distinguish itself from the natural, to institute new values that are not the satisfaction of prior natural needs but of the various conditions under which freedom can be actualized.

87. Sartre notes: "Negativity and contradiction come to the inert through organic totalization. As soon as need appears, surrounding matter is endowed with a passive unity, in that a developing totalization is reflected in it as a totality: matter revealed as passive totality by an

organic being seeking its being in it—this is Nature in its initial form" (1976a, 81; 1960, 167); "Every negation is a relation of interiority" (101; 183).

88. "But we should not be disturbed by the fact that the relation of scarcity is contingent. It is indeed logically possible to conceive of other organisms on other planets having a relation to their environment other than scarcity. (However we are completely incapable of simply imagining such a relation, and supposing that there is life on other planets, it is most likely that it too would suffer from scarcity.) Above all, although scarcity is universal, at a given historical moment it may vary from one region to another" (Sartre 1976a, 123; 1960, 201).

89. Sartre 1976a, 124; 1960, 201.

90. Sartre 1976a, 129; 1960, 206.

91. Sartre 1976a, 130; 1960, 206. This idea about society creating "superfluous individuals" was also famously taken up by Hannah Arendt (1966), who seemed to think that this was a characteristic feature of modern life, or more likely (as Sartre thinks) an ever present possibility of agency that has only been fully actualized in the ultra-marketized "bourgeois" society of modernity. European imperialism, on Arendt's account, was a response to the existence of surplus capital and superfluous people.

92. Sartre puts it this way: "But in the moment in which our *praxis* experiences its alienation, an internal and external structure of objectification appears, and this is precisely *Necessity*" (1976a, 152; 1960, 224).

93. "The latter [alienation through recurrence], although it appears in the relevant aspect only at a certain technical level, is a permanent type of separation against which men unite, but which attacks them even when united" (Sartre 1976a, 164n42; 1960, 234).

94. This is what Sartre is expressing when he says, "At the level of objectification, worked matter can be seen in all its docility both as a new totalization of society and as its radical negation. At this level the real foundations of alienation appear: matter alienates in itself the action which works it, not because it is itself a force nor even because it is inertia, but because its inertia allows it to absorb the labor power of Others and turn it back against everyone. In the moment of passive negation, its interiorized scarcity makes everyone appear to Others as Other" (1976a, 151; 1960, 224).

95. Sartre characterizes *praxis*-process this way: "We can also observe here, in this elementary form, the Nature of reification. It is not a metamorphosis of the individual into a thing, as is often supposed, but the necessity imposed by the structures of society on members of a social group, that they should live the fact that they belong to the group and, thereby, to society as a whole, as a molecular status. What they experience or do as individuals is still, immediately, real *praxis* or human labor. But a sort of mechanical rigidity haunts them in the concrete undertaking of living and subjects the results of their actions to the alien laws of totalizing addition. Their objectification is modified externally by the inert power of the objectification of others" (1976a, 176; 1960, 243–244).

96. Sartre 1976a, 110; 1960, 190.

97. Sartre 1976a, 103; 1960, 184–185. He also notes: "Subjectivities are enveloped within this moving totality as necessary but elusive significations; but they define themselves as a common relation to a transcendent end rather than as each apprehending its own ends in a reciprocity of separations" (1976a, 118; 1960, 196).

98. "Reciprocal ternary relations are the basis of all relations between men, whatever form they may subsequently take. Though reciprocity is often concealed by the relations which are established and supported by it (and which may, for example, be oppressive, reified, etc.), it

becomes evident whenever it manifests itself that each of the two terms is modified in its very existence by the existence of the Other. In other words, men are bound together by relations of interiority" (Sartre 1976a, 111; 1960, 191).

99. See Sartre 1976a, 113; 1960, 192: "The origin of struggle always lies, in fact, in some concrete antagonism whose material condition is scarcity. . . . Hegel, in other words, ignored matter as a mediation between individuals."

100. Sartre 1976a, 111; 1960, 191.

101. Sartre 1976a, 111; 1960, 191.

102. Sartre 1976a, 394–395; 1960, 420. In a *Zusatz* (an editor's addition) to the *Philosophy of Right* Hegel himself is quoted as saying about the "concrete concept of freedom" that we "already possess [the concrete concept of freedom] in the form of feeling, for example in friendship and love. Here, we are not one-sidedly within ourselves, but willingly limit ourselves (*beschränkt sich*) with reference to an other, even knowing ourselves in this limitation (*Beschränkung*) as ourselves" (1991, 42; 1969a, §7 Zusatz, p. 57). In putting it this way, Hegel is drawing attention that in one's own singular concept of oneself as "friend" or "citizen," one is necessarily thinking of oneself non-monadically. One is a friend only of a determinate "other" person and a citizen only of a political ordering with actual others in it. He is said to repeat this in Hegel, Brinkmann, and Dahlstrom 2010, §24, p. 60: "Thus spirit relates purely to itself and is therefore free, for freedom is precisely this: to be at one with oneself in one's other, to be dependent upon oneself, to be the determining factor for oneself" (translation of *bei sich selbst* as "at home with oneself" altered).

Chapter Two

1. Sartre himself sometimes uses the phrase *mode de vie*, which I have taken to be something very much like the phrase "form of life" as it came to be used in those circles influenced by Wittgenstein and Hegel. For example, Sartre speaks of clashes between forms of life: "The clash of mores is linked to that of the way of life (of the reproduction of life): for example, on the frontiers of ancient China, the nomadic life, as work, is opposed to the agricultural work of the settled population" (2005, 308). He also characterizes a *mode de vie* as "a mixture of abilities and inertia, or rather an ensemble of abilities based on the inertia these had gradually produced" (Sartre and Elkaïm-Sartre 1991, 136; 1985, 148).

2. All actions can have unintended consequences—there's no real debate about that, and there would hardly be anything novel on Sartre's part to point that out, nor any need to develop a new term of art for it. There is also a lot to be said about what role unintended consequences play in the moral evaluation of action, such as whether culpability should be negligence— whether it was a faulty part of the action (such as recklessness) that led to some harm—or strict liability—whether the actor is responsible for the consequences independently of whether he acted negligently. Important as those considerations are, they are not Sartre's focus. Not everyone agrees. Thomas Flynn seems to identify counter-finality with unintended consequences in his discussion of the *Critique*. He notes that "the experience of dialectical necessity, where the exigencies and counter-finalities of the practico-inert reveal their positive force, might be taken to support the claim that some larger logic is directing the unintended results of individual actions" (Flynn 1997, 228). He states later that "the intention is foiled by the very achievement of the end," which is a form "of Nietzschean 'inversion' where cause and effect exchange roles" (Flynn 2014, 30). G. Rae thinks much the same way, that counter-finality is a term for the way in

which the consequences of one's actions can alter future actions and that they emerge as additive characteristics of individual actions. Rae says: "Whenever the individual acts to overcome a counter-finality, he reorganizes the dynamics of the social field. New relations arise which produce alternative counter-finalities that impact upon the individual. But while he is acting so is every other individual. . . . The combination of these practico-inert structures produces a dynamic tightly integrated web of counter-finalities" (2011, 94–95). Joseph Catalano thinks— wrongly to my mind—that matter actually comes to have purposes within itself (or, as he puts it, "totalized matter then has finalities *of its own*," which has to do with what he calls "Sartre's unique materialism"). He also seems to think that this counter-finality is not a result of any kind of "dialectical reason," somehow conflating Sartre's senses of dialectical and analytical reason, as when he says, "In the abstract, there is no reason why our alteration of the environment should have resulted in a counter-finality" (Catalano 1986, 121). "No reason" in that sentence could only be "no analytical reason." William McBride likewise thinks of counter-finalities in terms of unintended consequences that have effects on later actions; he says, for example, "Sartre shows how, often enough, human beings' need-satisfying intentions have unanticipated and radically self-destructive outcomes; in short, they become counter-finalized" (McBride 1991, 132). All of these conflations of unintended consequences with counter-finality would, as Sartre says, confuse the necessity of practical action—he who wills the end wills the means—with constraint by the facts and by matter. Sartre notes: "But necessity must not be confused with constraint. We are subjected to constraint as to an exterior force, with the contingent opacity of a fact" (1976a, 222–223). Besides those who equate (wrongly, I think) counter-finality with unintended consequences, Christopher Turner equates it (wrongly, I think) with the way in which the material world sometimes makes it impossible to get what we have willed, when in fact counter-finality has to do with discovering that we had willed something else entirely. See Christopher Turner, who speaks of "the finality of human praxis, our capacity to actually obtain our ends" (2014, 42). Mark Poster identifies counter-finality with the idea that "the original intention . . . was alienated (made other)" (1982, 59). However, it is not that the intention is ascribed to somebody or something else. It is that my (or our) action has become something other than what I (or we) originally took it to be, not that things did not turn out as we had originally intended. Sartre explicitly says that counter-finality is characterized by lack of an author: " a *praxis without an author* . . . whose hidden meaning is counter-finality" (1976a, 166; 1960, 235); and "thus there is no difference between the comprehension of a finality and that of a counter-finality, except for one crucial point: the second has to include the negation of every *author*" (697; 658).

3. Sartre 1976a, 164; 1960, 234.

4. Sartre 1976a, 337; 1960, 373.

5. Sartre 1976a, 166; 1960, 235.

6. Sartre 1976a, 518; 1960, 516.

7. Sartre 1976a, 311; 1960, 352. It is worth noting in passing that this conception is in some ways a transposition of Sartre's earlier conception of the for-itself as linked to its own facticity.

8. Sartre himself says of tragedy as an art form: "The chief source of great tragedy—the tragedies of Aeschylus and Sophocles, of Corneille—is human freedom. Oedipus is free; Antigone and Prometheus are free. The fate we think we find in ancient drama is only the other side of freedom. Passions themselves are freedoms caught in their own trap" (1976b, 3).

9. On this idea of tragedy, although from more of a Hegelian perspective, see Pinkard 2015b.

10. This is brought out by Sartre when he notes: "But, above all, we must return to this notion of 'class struggle': if it is a practico-inert structure (a passive contradictory reciprocity of

conditioning), or if it is *hexis*, the human order is strictly comparable to the molecular order, and the only historical Reason is positivist Reason, which posits the unintelligibility of History as a definite fact. But, on the other hand, if it is praxis through and through, the entire human universe vanishes into a Hegelian idealism" (1976a, 734; 1960, 688). This is also part of Sartre's answer to Merleau-Ponty's (1973, 95–201) charge of "ultra-Bolshevism" against Sartre.

11. Sartre notes that counter-finalities "are grasped not as transformation and alienation of an action in the milieu of mediating exteriority, but as obscure and wholly immanent limits that freedom itself seems to give itself. . . . And this limit, which at first appears negatively although it is necessarily tied to the sworn limit, seems *suffered by freedom* precisely in so far as it is *produced by it*" (Sartre and Elkaïm-Sartre 1991, 58; 1985, 68). Merely unintended results (such as somebody's finding something you said to be funny, even though you had not intended it as humorous) would be cases of "alienation of an action in the milieu of mediating exteriority."

12. "In fact, counter-finalities have practically the same structure as teleological practices: so even if they are not produced by any human intention, they may have the structure of a project and of intentional transcendence. . . . Thus there is no difference between the comprehension of a finality and that of a counter-finality, except for one crucial point: the second has to include the negation of every author" (Sartre 1976a, 697; 1960, 658).

13. Sartre 1976a, 176; 1960, 244.

14. In his later book on Flaubert, Sartre discusses in these terms Flaubert and one of Flaubert's characters: "If it is perfectly intolerable to him to have killed his father by accident, it is because he knows in his heart that he is not innocent; the crime has all the *appearances* of an accident, a matter of mistaken identity. But wasn't he afraid all his life of *wanting* to commit it? Did he not flee the paternal residence because he was not sufficiently certain of vanquishing his bad thoughts? He chose to make it physically impossible to realize the stag's prophecy himself because he hadn't the necessary love and virtue to create in himself the *moral impossibility* of accomplishing it" (1991b, 131).

15. The analysis of shame takes up a large part of *Being and Nothingness*, but the point is that shame is inadequacy or even pollution in the eyes of the other (and thus a negation of freedom). Sartre notes: "It is a shameful apprehension of something and this something is me. I am ashamed of what I am. Shame therefore realizes an intimate relation of myself to myself. Through shame I have discovered an aspect of my being" (1956, 221).

16. Sartre 1976a, 261, 262; 1960, 313. Iris Marion Young (1994) had suggested at one point that certain things such as gender identity (for example, "woman") might be best understood in terms of Sartrean seriality, since that would be a crucial way to sidestep the danger of "essentialism" in gender relations (reprinted in Murphy 1999).

17. It is thus a bit misleading to equate, as William McBride does, seriality with atomization. McBride speaks of "'seriality,' Sartre's carefully chosen word for atomization in daily life" (2005, 315). Gary Gutting also tends to see "seriality" as atomization, since he thinks that seriality necessarily leads to competition, where what unites people is that they both want the same thing, and where one having it rules out the other's having it (2001, 153). Sartre's own example of people waiting for the bus illustrates the way in which the end can be common without being shared but which need not be competitive unless scarcity enters the picture. People listening to a radio program in common are also not competing with each other, but they are in a serial relationship. Alasdair MacIntyre seems to make the same mistake when he says in his 1962 review of the *Critique* that "where 'bad faith' was once omnipresent, the fate of man is now 'serialization'. We lose our individuality and our capacity for action by being turned into merely one term in a se-

ries which could equally well be replaced by any other term" ("Sartre as a Social Critic," in Mac-Intyre 2009, 205). Because he thinks Sartre is making some sweeping claim about serialization as a "necessary feature of the human condition" (205), MacIntyre thinks that Sartre also holds that "there is a kind of political group, . . . the disciplined revolutionary, activist group whose mode of life exempts them from serialization. We gain an identity through such a group in which we renounce our (presumably spurious) individuality" (205). This makes Sartre's views not into the "ultra-Bolshevism" of which Merleau-Ponty accused him, but into a form of "Leninism without Marxism," according to MacIntyre, which itself is really just the "the anarchism and nihilism of the last century" (206). This misinterpretation rests on MacIntyre's shortsighted interpretation of Sartre (early and late) along psychological lines and his view that Sartre's work is only another version, as he puts it, of the kind of Marxism advocated by Gyorgy Lukács.

18. "In modern representative democracies, the individual voter typically waits in line, goes into a booth, fills out her ballot, deposits it in a box and leaves (thus ensuring the secret ballot, a keystone of contemporary bureaucratic democracy). This too would be seriality and might even be positive in that context" (Rosanvallon 2013, 37).

19. The example is given in Sartre 1976a, 270; 1960, 320.

20. Sartre 1976a, 259; 1960, 311.

21. Sartre 1976a, 259; 1960, 311.

22. Sartre 1976a, 247; 1960, 302.

23. Sartre 1976a, 267; 1960, 317.

24. In this monograph, I render *l'individu commun* as "communal individual" rather than the translator Alan Sheridan-Smith's equally valid choice of "common individual," since I wish to emphasize that it is the "communal," shared self-identity aspect in which Sartre is interested and not merely the "common" aspect as any kind of statistical average or lowest common denominator.

25. Sartre 1976a, 233; 1960, 290.

26. In keeping with this conception, Sartre argues that we must adopt a certain type of realist and not "subjectivist" conception of motivation: "This is precisely what characterizes free individual *praxis*: when it develops as an undertaking which temporalizes itself in the course of a life, motivations are never 'psychical' or 'subjective': they are things and real structures in so far as these are revealed by the project through its concrete ends and on the basis of them. Thus there is normally no act of consciousness: the situation is known through the act which it motivates and which already negates it" (1976a, 327; 1960, 365). What motivates people to act are not their mental states but the features of the situation that give them reasons to form, complete, or abandon a project. It is the practical field that motivates the actors, and it is their subjectivity, their interiority, that moves them as taking up themselves in the practical field and acting in terms of that. One might put Sartre's point as being that desire itself (as a mental state) does not motivate, but rather that desire just is the state of being motivated by the real elements of the practical field.

27. Sartre 1976a, 237; 1960, 293.

28. Nagel 1986. This may be the only thing that Sartre and Nagel share. Sartre comes closest to the Nagelian conception when he says, speaking of Comte and the later Marxist materialists, "From the point of view of man, and for man, it is true that science succeeds. They took good care not to ask themselves whether the universe in itself supported and guaranteed scientific rationalism, for the very good reason that they would have had to depart from themselves and from mankind in order to compare the universe as it is with the picture of it we get from science,

and to assume God's point of view on man and the world. The materialist, however, is not so shy. He leaves behind him science and subjectivity and the human and substitutes himself for God, Whom he denies, in order to contemplate the spectacle of the universe" ("Materialism and Revolution," in Sartre 1955, 201).

29. Sartre 1964c, 274.

30. Sartre 1976a, 238; 1960, 294.

31. Marx's influence on Sartre becomes evident when Sartre takes up the question of whether his theory of practical ensembles implicates a conception of a unitary working class—the Marxian proletariat—as a matter of intelligibility. Sartre rejects the idea to the effect that there was (or at least no longer is) a single "working class" and that instead that there "are only individuals threatened by a single destiny, victims of the same exigencies, possessing the same general interest" rather than a class destiny. As he puts the same point in different terms (but a bit more densely), "It is precisely the ensemble of structures of the practico-inert field that necessarily conditions the substantial unity of the being-outside-oneself of individuals, and conversely, this being-outside-oneself as a substantial and negative unity on the terrain of the Other conditions the structures of this field in its turn" (1976a, 251; 1960, 304). But as for whether there is a "deeper unity" of the working class that underlies all the contemporary divisions within it, Sartre says that "everyone's experience testifies" to that, that "there can be no doubt" about the unity of the working class, that "no one would dream of arguing" otherwise, and that "it cannot be argued that this substance does not really exist" (251; 304). Now, the idea that some substantial commitments "simply cannot be argued" is about as un-Sartrean as a statement can get, but Sartre says it anyway. In mitigation of that, it should be noted that he also explicitly notes that although he does indeed think that the classical Marxist conception of class antagonisms holds true, "we will not immediately attempt a definition of the practico-inert sociality of class" in the book (252; 305). Instead, he will presuppose the conception and use his theory to cast light on how one would comprehend the class divisions of bourgeoisie and proletariat within the terms of his theory, which in turn should help to show how the terms of the "pure intelligibility" of *praxis* are to be more concretely understood.

32. Sartre 1976a, 348; 1960, 383. Sartre also overdramatizes his case when he says, "It would be quite wrong to interpret me as saying that man is free in all situations, as the Stoics claimed. I mean the exact opposite: all men are slaves in so far as their life unfolds in the practico-inert field and in so far as this field is always conditioned by scarcity. . . . The practico-inert field is the field of our servitude, which means not ideal servitude, but real subservience to 'natural' forces, to 'mechanical' forces and to 'anti-social' apparatuses" (332; 369).

33. Sartre 1976a, 348; 1960, 383. Of such "gatherings," Sartre says: "I define gatherings by the co-presence of their members, not in the sense that there must be relations of reciprocity between them, or a common, organized practice, but in the sense that the possibility of this common *praxis*, and of the relations of reciprocity on which it is based, is immediately given" (270; 320).

34. Sartre 1976a, 345; 1960, 381.

35. Here is how Sartre puts it: "However, the action is *one* as individual action, the objective is *one*, and the temporalization and the rule it gives itself are one; so everything is as it would be if a hyper-organism had temporalized and objectified itself in a practical end, by unifying and unified labor of which every common individual with his constituent mediation would be a completely inessential moment" (1976a, 506–507; 1960, 507). In a couple of places he also refers to the "organicist illusion" of there being some kind of entity such as *Geist* that is driving the

various "organs" to do what they have to do, as if this is a kind of tendency of thought to create a conceptual problem where there isn't one. See Sartre 1976a, 345, 386; 1960, 381, 413. In any event, Sartre is clear on the "organicist" point: "Organicism has to be absolutely rejected" (82n2; 168).

36. Sartre notes in this regard: "This double exclusion is perfectly conveyed by language with the first person plural, when it expresses the interiorization of the multiple: in the we, in fact, the multiple is not so much eliminated as disqualified; it is preserved in the form of ubiquity" (1976a, 535; 1960, 530).

37. "Since each is sovereign over the sovereignty of all, at the same time as being the organized object of each practical synthesis in interiority, he ought to be described as quasi-sovereign and quasi-object; and the group itself, in so far as it is totalized by the practice of a given common individual, is an objective quasi-totality and, as a negated multiplicity of quasi-sovereignties, it is in a state of perpetual *detotalization*" (Sartre 1976a, 579; 1960, 564).

38. "The members of the group are *third parties*, which means that each of them totalizes the reciprocities of others. And the relation of one third party to another has nothing to do with alterity: since the group is the practical milieu of this relation, it must be a human relation (with crucial importance for the differentiations of the group), which we shall call mediated reciprocity. And, as we shall see, this mediation is dual, in that it is both the mediation of the group between third parties and the mediation of each third party between the group and the other third parties" (Sartre 1976a, 392; 1960, 404).

39. Sartre 1976a, 350n2; 1960, 385n.

40. "For each of the adversaries, this struggle is intelligible; or rather, at this level, it is intelligibility itself. Otherwise, reciprocal *praxis* would in itself have no meaning or goal" (Sartre 1976a, 816; 1960, 753).

41. See Tackett 2015, 98: "Within days after the fall of the Bastille a first group of dissident nobles began trooping across the frontiers. Many of them followed the king's youngest brother, the count of Artois, to the kingdom of Piedmont-Sardinia in northwestern Italy, ruled at the time by the count's father-in-law. By September the young prince had established the first counterrevolutionary committee with the explicit intention of overthrowing the Revolutionary government. For the next fifteen months the group attempted to foment a variety of insurrections."

42. See Tackett 2015; "Historical Events as Transformations of Structures: Inventing Revolution at the Bastille," in Sewell 2005, 225–270; Edelstein 2012.

43. This conception of freedom has been articulated and defended as a Hegelian conception notably by Neuhouser 2000 and Honneth 2014.

44. See Sartre 1976a, 357; 1960, 391.

45. Sartre's somewhat romanticized expression of this is the following: "In reciprocity, my partner's *praxis* is, as it were, at root my *praxis*, which has broken in two by accident, and whose two pieces, each of which is now a complete *praxis* on its own, both retain from their original unity a profound affinity and an immediate understanding" (1976a, 131; 1960, 206). I call this "romanticized" because in Sartre's account, there is no original, undivided unity at the heart of dialectical reason. As with Hegel's dialectic, Sartre's version of dialectical reason begins with a fissure within itself at the outset.

46. The trope about constituting and constituted is of course Spinozistic in origin (*natura naturans* versus *natura naturata*, the distinction, roughly, between nature "naturing" and nature as having structured itself), although Sartre is surely also relying on the Abbé Sieyès's use of it to distinguish the constituting power that establishes the bodies of the constitution and the constituted powers that the constitution establishes. Sieyès identified the "nation" as the constituting

power, and the delegated bodies as the constituted power. Such delegated bodies, Sieyès insisted, cannot alter the conditions of its delegation. Béatrice Longuenesse used the trope to good effect to bring out the specific way the Hegelian dialectic structures itself by distinguishing in it the *pensée pensée* and the *pensée pensant* (1981, 33), which was rendered accurately although less elegantly in the English translation as "thinking thought and thought that is thought" (2007, 26). Sartre sums it up this way: "The difference between constituting Reason and constituted Reason can be concentrated into two words: the former is the basis of the intelligibility of a practical organism, while the latter is the basis of the intelligibility of an organization" (1976a, 411; 1960, 433). (I have changed the translator's term "constituent" into "constituting.")

47. In an interview in 1969, Sartre clarified the point about spontaneity in the group-infusion: "The thought of a fused group—by virtue of the fact that it is born in the stress of a particular situation and not because of some kind of 'spontaneity'—has a stronger, fresher, more critical charge than that of a structured group" (1974b, 121).

48. "Thus my *praxis* appears to me not only as myself, here, now, but also as myself approaching me through my neighbor, and as sustained by its own totalized effect on my neighbor and myself. (By acting in the same way and by making myself the same as him, I encounter him in the group as a totalizing increase of its strength, which by totalization determines me through the group itself: his individual action which is mine gives me, through the expansion of the whole, a greater security)" (Sartre 1976a, 392–93; 1960, 418).

49. "The intelligibility of this new . . . structure, that is to say, of unity as ubiquity within each and every synthesis, depends entirely on the two following characteristics: this ubiquity is practical: it is not that of a being or of a state, but that of a developing action; and it can be conceived only as the ubiquity of freedom positing itself as such" (Sartre 1976a, 401; 1960, 425).

50. Sartre 1964a, 137; 2015, 116.

51. As Sartre notes to himself in his drafts for his later attempt at an ethics, "Freedom: giving a practical sense (instrumentality) that *was not there* previously on the basis of an objective that does not exist" (Liberté: donner un sens pratique (ustensilité) qui *n'était* pas auparavant à partir d'un objectif qui n'est pas) (1964b, 162).

52. This idea of reasons as anchored in the nature of the kind of organic life in question is discussed in Pinkard 2017a and very differently in Larmore 2012. Larmore's realism about practical reasons comports well with Sartre's later "materialism" about reasons.

53. See the discussion of this in relation to German idealism in Pinkard 2002 and Khurana 2017. See also the collection Khurana 2011.

54. Sartre 1976a, 418; 1960, 438.

55. Sartre notes the contradiction in Sieyès's views (1976a, 382–383; 1960, 410).

56. Sartre 1976a, 474; 1960, 483.

57. Sartre 1976a, 435–436; 1960, 452.

58. Sartre 1976a, 436; 1960, 453: "C'est le commencement de l'humanité."

59. Sartre puts it this way: "Here again, it does not matter whether this right is conceived as a duty towards the group (that is to say, concretely as an imperative negation of a possibility: this obviously has nothing to do with morals or even with codes) or whether it is conceived as a power of the group, consented to by me, of taking my life if I do not act in accordance with a given directive" (1976a, 433; 1960, 450).

60. In a passing aside, Sartre mentions love and friendship as immediate relations of reciprocity but still insists that they occur within the larger sphere of a structured group of mediated reciprocity: "What is later called comradeship, friendship, love—and even fraternity, using the

term in a vaguely affective sense—arises on the basis of particular circumstances and within a particular perspective" (1976a, 438; 1960, 454).

61. "This reciprocity is mediated: I give my pledge to all the third parties, as forming the group of which I am a member, and it is the group which enables everyone to guarantee the status of permanence to everyone. A given third party can pledge the permanence of the group against alterity only in so far as this permanence depends on him, that is to say, in so far as the other third parties have assured him, on their account, of future *unchangingness*" (Sartre 1976a, 433; 1960, 441).

62. Sartre 1976a, 441; 1960, 456.

63. Sartre is thus more "Hegelian" here than he recognizes, at least in the terms argued in Barba-Kay 2016. Antón Barba-Kay helpfully notes: "Rational cares and practices do not arise from or by force (because force could not itself count as a reason), but they do arise with the enforcement of reasons (in the sense that force can serve to direct attention, to show what it means for reasons to be transgressed, to demonstrate a reason where the context of reason is not yet fully in place, and so forth). . . . Hegel is pointing to the underlying relation between obeying and commanding: they are two sides of the same activity of giving oneself the law for the sake of being able to share the world with others. . . . Meaning what we say requires backing what we say through other practical means, whether through an appeal to another authority or through all out conflict" (2016, 53).

64. Sartre elaborates on this point in this way: "The errors of the classical economists . . . assumed that man is what he is at the outset and that scarcity conditions him externally. . . . Nor is it a feature of Nature or a hidden potentiality. It is the constant non-humanity of human conduct as interiorized scarcity; it is, in short, what makes people see each other as the Other and as the principle of Evil" (1976a, 148–149; 1960, 221). He also notes that the concept of free agency on its own does not contain a concept of violence within itself: "Freedom as the sovereignty of individual *praxis* is not violence: it is simply the dialectical reorganization of the environment" (406; 429; and "It is precisely this that we have called violence, for the only conceivable violence is that of freedom against freedom through the mediation of inorganic matter" (736; 689).

65. Sartre 1976a, 133; 1960, 209.

66. Sartre 1976a, 149; 1960, 221.

67. Sartre notes: "There is no Platonic Idea of Terror, but only different Terrors and if the historian wishes to identify characteristics which are common to them, he will have to do it a posteriori, on the basis of careful comparisons. . . . I am not attempting to set out the essential relations, even reduced to the utmost simplicity, which might constitute an essence of Terror: there is no such essence. I only wish to describe certain conditions—the dialectical chain of abstract determinations (infinitely indeterminate except at a particular point)—which is necessarily realized by the being-in-the-group of a communal individual when Terror occurs as a historical development in specific circumstances" (1976a, 597n73; 1960, 578). It is perhaps also worth noting that Sartre dates the Terror from 1789–94, giving it a wider berth than many other historians of the Revolution.

68. Sartre 1964a, 10; 2015, 19; he makes this point again: "There comes a time when one 'puts one's life on the table' in order to make oneself into a subject of interiority" (2005, 389).

69. Sartre 1964a, 10; 2015, 19. It would be a mistake, I think, to interpret what Sartre means by this in terms of the rather implausible claim that moral action only has to do with those instances in which one is significantly risking one's life. He means that only when life itself as a whole is the issue—as, to take one example, Aristotle did when he spoke of the flourishing

person in terms of a whole life—does the appearance of the ethical and not merely that of the socially relative "mores" of a group come into play. The point is also related to Hegel's observation in the *Phenomenology* (in the section on self-consciousness in the struggle over mastery and servitude) that "this consciousness [that of servitude] was not driven with anxiety about just this or that matter, nor did it have anxiety about just this or that moment; rather, it had anxiety about its entire essence. It felt the fear of death, the absolute master" (Hegel 2018, 114–115, ¶194). This same mistake, I think, about interpreting the way in which death gives rise to the idea of "the unconditioned" about risking one's life also colors the otherwise very helpful account given of the Gramsci lecture in Arthur 2010.

70. Sartre 1976a, 433; 1960, 450.

71. "But here again it would be quite wrong to think that the aim is the annihilation of the adversary or, to use Hegel's idealist language, that each consciousness seeks the death of the Other. The origin of struggle always lies, in fact, in some concrete antagonism whose material condition is scarcity, in a particular form, and the real aim is objective conquest or even creation, in relation to which the destruction of the adversary is only the means. . . . Hegel, in other words, ignored matter as a mediation between individuals. Even if one uses his terminology, one has to say that while each consciousness is the counterpart of the Other, this reciprocity can take an infinity of different forms, positive or negative, and that it is the mediation of matter which determines these forms in every concrete case" (Sartre 1976a, 113; 1960, 192). See also Sartre's argument against Hegel's conception of servitude (158n37; 229).

72. "But this is precisely what a pledge is: namely the common production, through mediated reciprocity, of a status of violence; once the pledge has been made, in fact, the group has to guarantee everyone's freedom against necessity, even at the cost of his life and in the name of freely sworn faith. Everyone's freedom demands the violence of all against it and against that of any third party as its defense against itself (as a free power of secession and alienation). To swear is to say, as a common individual: you must kill me if I secede" (Sartre 1976a, 431; 1960, 448–449).

73. As is often the case, the real qualifications Sartre puts on his overdramatized characterizations are to be found in the footnotes: "Let there be no misunderstanding: I am not talking about those few great revolutionary moments in which contemporaries actually have the feeling of producing, and being subjected to, man as a new reality. Every organization which has the reciprocity of the pledge is a new beginning, since it is always the victory of man as common freedom over seriality, whatever it may be" (Sartre 1976a, 436n24; 1960, 453).

Chapter Three

1. Sartre puts it in his terms this way: "But, by introducing this specification under the pressure of circumstances, the group being organized has to pass from fluid homogeneity (everyone being *the same*, here and everywhere) to a regulated heterogeneity. Alterity reappears explicitly in the community" (1976a, 463; 1960, 474).

2. Sartre 1976a, 500; 1960, 503.

3. Sartre 1964a, 7; 2015, 16.

4. Philippa Foot used the term "fact-stating evaluations" for descriptions of some form of life (plant or animal) in terms of facts about it that are also evaluative of how that life flourishes or does best. If it is a fact that camellia bushes grow best in partial shade and especially require shelter from hot afternoon sun and do not grow well in alkaline soil, then stating such facts is also stating an evaluation of how and under what conditions camellias flourish. Likewise, it is

just as true of humans that there are facts about them that are also evaluative of how their lives go best, and that involves facts about their social ensembles. See Foot 2001. Of course, Sartre does not confine such fact-stating evaluations about human agents to natural features. There are also social and historically variable features.

5. Sartre 1976a, 456; 1960, 469.

6. Sartre 1976a, 458; 1960, 470.

7. Sartre 1976a, 460; 1960, 471.

8. Sartre 1964a, 12; 2015, 20.

9. Sartre 1964a, 58, 59.

10. Sartre 1964d, 377.

11. Sartre 1976a, 247–248n75; 1960, 301.

12. Sartre 1976a, 249; 1960, 302.

13. Sartre says that the "ontological character of the norm" is this, that "the end does not impose itself *as an obligation*, and yet it imposes itself *on each* as his unique possible end, as nontranscendable (*indépassable*) and the real sense of all final senses" (1964a, 50; 2015, 51). Nonetheless, as we have already seen, Sartre holds that the very idea of a pure *praxis* unencumbered by facticity is to be rejected: "But, on the other hand, if it is praxis through and through, the entire human universe vanishes into a Hegelian idealism" (1976a, 734; 1960, 688).

14. Sartre 1964d, 399.

15. This is a point that has come to prominence in various places but especially in Thompson 2013. For an extended discussion, see also Fisher 2019, Ng 2020, and Pippin 2018.

16. "The sole aspect common to all the ethical norms is that they are presented as unconditional possibilities" (Sartre 1964d, 404).

17. Sartre speaks of a kind of self-understanding on the part of some nineteenth-century syndicalist workers as "a limit which could not be transcended, since it was themselves, or in other words, the theoretical and practical expression of their practico-inert relations with other workers" (1976a, 244; 1960, 299). He also describes such limits as "invisible walls" (245; 300). (I take it that what Sartre is calling "limits" here are really just "limitations" in the senses at work in this monograph.) Sartre says at one point with regard to the "inability" of being-for-itself to serve as its own foundation that is a limit of being-for-itself, not just a contingent limitation. He says it is "not a question of a limit which freedom trips over," since "it would be equally useless to speak of a constraint on the mind of a mathematician because he, being able to conceive of a circle or a square, cannot conceive of a square circle" (1992a, 559–60). Sartre thus draws a distinction between limits—beyond which there is nothing, no sense to be made at all—which have no "beyond" or "other side" to them, and limitations, which may be real but which always have an "other side" to them. (It is a limitation on our part that we cannot, for example, count up to two trillion because we do not have enough time.) The sharp distinction between limits and limitations is central to the work of A. W. Moore. See especially Moore 2002, 2012. (That distinction runs throughout Sartre's works, although Sartre does not draw it as clearly as Moore. Moore takes it from Wittgenstein.) In his account of Sartre's and Hegel's conceptions of the infinite in their dialectical theories, Pierre Verstraeten, I think, exactly conflates limitation with limit in a way that undermines what Sartre is after in the *Critique*. Verstraeten says that "any limit is in fact a limit for anyone for whom it has a meaning, that is to say, for anyone who could equally well not take it into account, namely for a free being, for only a free being can be alienated and can measure the obstacles and prohibitions it encounters" ("Appendix: Hegel and Sartre," in Howells 1992, 354–355).

18. See the discussion in Fisher 2019.

19. A friendly and very sympathetic commentator, Ronald Aronson, gives a sharp criticism of Sartre's *Critique* on this point—that it fails to show how we could have "a totalization without a totalizer." As Aronson puts the question, "Can we really expect to add individuals to individuals and somehow *arrive at* a larger totality? Does the totality not have to be given in advance, at least in the form of a totalizing force, in order for it to appear at the end?" His answer is that with "Sartre's starting point of individual *praxis*" there can be no solution to that problem—that "a totalization without a totalizer is inaccessible to Sartre's thought *on principle*" (Aronson 1987, 235–237). Mark Hulliung, in his very helpful study of Sartre's relation to history and historicism (2013), himself accepts Aronson's criticism as valid, which leads him to speculate on whether Sartre in his heart of hearts was thus really some kind of "social contract" thinker. Likewise, Hadi Rizk, in his study of the *Critique* (2014), looks to a comparison with Spinoza's social contract theory to throw light on Sartre's conception of "the group" in fusion. Since Sartre puts the stress on avoiding any kind of "hyper-organism" to serve as the group—for Sartre, the idea of the "hyper-organism" is really *the* basic Hegelian mistake—friendly commentators such as Aronson, Hulliung, and Rizk think that the "nominalism" that Sartre mentions must entail that there can really be no genuine first-person plural apperception in his view. Rizk is emphatic on this point: "All the originality of the group in fusion, for which Sartre intends to theorize, is born from the fact that the unification is designed there to be folding into an impossible unity" (2014, 168). This idea of looking to social contract theory or being irremediably individualistic goes astray in ignoring Sartre's mature "reciprocity" conception of subjectivity. Aronson's own suggestion for how to get out of this is to locate *praxis* in "larger" contexts of a "larger *praxis*" or a "larger collectivity" (1987, 238). However, adding larger things to get out of the problem will surely not solve it, since the same problem will only appear with each of the larger ones. On the view presented here, the problem Aronson finds in Sartre and which he thinks needs to be solved is not really a problem at all but only the illusion of a problem brought on by thinking in terms of the active/passive dichotomy or of "producing and produced." It fails to see Sartre's commitments to the medium in which any action makes sense and to the role that the "singularized universal" plays in Sartre's thought (very analogous to the role it plays in Hegel's thought about the concrete universal). As for the question "What produces the background medium of meaning?" Sartre's answer is that it is a philosophical mistake to look for some "being" to produce in some deeply metaphysical way other beings as a final account of meaning itself. This is not to deny that there could be a scientific naturalistic account of how some beings produce other beings, nor to deny a scientific account of how humans came to possess language and practices of the type Sartre supposes, but that would not affect the status of the medium of meaning in our comprehension of what "thinking, meaning, understanding" consist. The medium is "that which one cannot get further behind" in the analysis of meaning. This is also one of the basic reasons why, for example, Hegel thought that the medium had therefore to be self-explicating, and put such enormous effort into showing this in his *Science of Logic*. See the recent discussion of this rather thorny issue having to do with Hegel in Pippin 2018. See my account in Pinkard 2017b.

20. Around 1948 Sartre wrote an essay titled "Truth and Existence" (apparently prompted by reading a translation of Heidegger's *The Essence of Truth*). He decided against publishing it, and it only appeared after his death (Sartre, Elkaïm-Sartre, and Aronson 1992). He was thus familiar with the "turn" in Heidegger's thought. On Sartre's early reception of Heidegger, and on the new reading of Heidegger prompted at the time by Jean Beaufret, see the discussion in Kleinberg 2005. On Kleinberg's account, Sartre's early philosophy shows the influence of Henri

Corbin's translation of Heidegger's *Dasein* as *réalité-humaine*, a translation apparently endorsed (at least at first) by Heidegger himself in 1936, and of *Vorhandenheit* as *réalité-des-choses*, of *Zuhandenheit* as *réalité-ustensiles*, and of *Geworfenheit* as *sa dérélicton* (abandonment), also endorsed at first by Heidegger. Corbin's translation seemed to bring Heidegger much closer to Alexandre Kojève's more "anthropological" interpretation of Hegel and, importantly for people such as Sartre, even closer to Jean Wahl's early "existentialist" interpretation of Hegel's "unhappy consciousness." See Kleinberg 2005, 70–71. Gary Gutting (2011) gives a slightly different reading of Beaufret's introduction of the later Heidegger to the French audience, and he (rightly, I think) stresses the importance of Jean Hyppolite in the reception. I myself think that the influence of Merleau-Ponty's interpretation of the later Heidegger is also at work in Sartre's *Critique*. There is good evidence that Sartre took seriously Merleau-Ponty's criticism of his earlier philosophical stances, for example, where Merleau-Ponty characterized Sartre's political philosophy as a form of "ultra-bolshevism." Merleau-Ponty (1973) had seemed to think that the "mediating third" in Sartre's theory logically had to be the singular Leninist party that was serving as the point of unity for the social and political world, and that this singular party would be sovereign in itself, having no normative bounds outside of itself. In his conversations with John Gerassi, at a point in the conversation where Gerassi seemed to endorse a version of Merleau-Ponty's critique of Sartre as ultra-voluntarist, ultra-Bolshevist in his understanding of social action, Sartre says: "Did you read Merleau's *Adventures of the Dialectic*? You should. He attacks me precisely along those lines. He says that I am an ultra-Bolshevik voluntarist. I think you're both wrong" (Gerassi 2009, 134). In his reply to Gerassi, Sartre is referencing his change of mind in his move in the *Critique* to a "reciprocity" view of subjectivity so that, in his newer reformed version, Merleau-Ponty's critique would have no bite. Simone de Beauvoir also penned a reply to Merleau-Ponty in which she noted that in Sartre's new version of his philosophy (i.e., the not-yet fully worked-out *Critique*) his position would not be subject to those criticisms, and she published her reply in *Les temps modernes* in July 1955.

21. Heidegger extends the use of this term, *Gelassenheit*, to indicate a more fundamental orientation to what he had called the "meaning of being" in *Being and Time*, such that scholars dispute using the ordinary term to translate it. Getting straight on Heidegger's use of *Gelassenheit* is, however, not the issue for this book.

22. Heidegger suggested in *Being and Time* that the more revelatory way of seeing the relation between being and beings would employ what has been called the "middle voice" (somewhat contestably said to be a tense in ancient Greek). The "middle voice" represents something which requires our participation (such as the way a practice requires participation by practitioners to be a practice) but which does not fully depend upon any particular actor participating, and, more crucially, where the subject is neither fully initiating the process nor is the subject merely being acted upon by the process. See especially Fisher 2019; also Han-Pile 2009; Narboux 2014. Fisher and Narboux differ, correctly I think, from Han-Pile on what she calls the "eventive" character of the middle voice. The middle voice involves a unity of being and doing—a kind of semi-Aristotelian idea that what you are is what you do, and that what you do depends on what you are—not a kind of Heideggerian "propriative event," *das Ereignis*. The "middle voice" locates where the subject is in the process. Sartre himself does not use the term "middle voice," but he seems to be attempting to use something like that to conceptualize tragic counterfinality, which involves a transformation of "human *praxis* into *anti-praxis*, that is to say, into a *praxis without an author*, transcending the given towards rigid ends, whose hidden meaning is counter-finality" (1976a, 166; 1960, 235). He would certainly have read of the middle voice in

Heidegger's explicit use of it in characterizing the "phenomenon" as showing itself (Heidegger 1962, 51). Although Hegel also does not use the term "middle voice," it is not far-fetched to see him speaking of *Geist* or "the Idea" in this middle voice, and this is, I would think, what Sartre, perhaps also under the influence of Hegel, is doing. Wittgenstein too can be said often to be speaking in this way when he speaks of how the form of reality "shows itself." See Floyd 2016; Fisher 2019; Narboux 2014. Sartre also rejects at least one sense of what he takes to be Heidegger's focus on "being": "So there is no question of seeking some deep origin, an existence under the opening to being, as in Heidegger. There is nothing of the sort. This is just man, and simply man. The manner in which he is present to himself, at first, excludes knowledge" (2016, 40). I take Sartre not to be saying that the later Heidegger is looking for an "origin" (and that would in any event badly mischaracterize Heidegger's view). "Being" is the medium in which both sides appear, and neither is privileged against the other, and "Being" is not some separate third realm that mediates the practice and practitioner. It is this part of Heidegger's view that Sartre seems to have appropriated for himself and put to his own later use. More likely, he is saying something to the effect that Corbin's use of *réalité-humaine* really was in fact the best way to take Heidegger's conception of *Dasein*, even if there were reasons to doubt that it adequately translated what Heidegger himself was trying to convey in the period of *Being and Time*. For the later Sartre, the form of agency is the form of the human. Agency is not a separate form that just happens to be instanced in one animal form of life on planet Earth. In this, his views match up with those of Hegel, although he does not speak of Hegel in this context. Recent work on Hegel has brought to light this view of the way in which he tries to offer a different alternative to the fractured view of self-consciousness as a "form" that has particular instances in human life (but might in principle appear in other forms of life). How Hegel conceives of the human form not as the instancing of a more general form of agency in a particular organic shape but as the form of "mindedness" itself is well summarized by Andrea Kern in her claim that "the human species has a formally distinctive form with the claim that a human child does not yet manifest those activities in terms of which we understand what it means to be rational, such as speaking a language or judging, giving reasons or keeping promises. The acquisition of any particular capacity is, indeed, a matter of practice and education in the sense specified above. But self-consciousness, conceived as the consciousness of the form of life one manifests, is not the result of practice and education. It is the form of one's form of life" (2020, 288). Her more detailed reconstruction of Hegel's way of taking this—in terms of the contrasting views of John McDowell and Michael Thompson on the issue of how the form of self-consciousness relates to the concrete instances of self-consciousness in human life—is to be found in Kern 2019. See also Ng 2020. A very similar point is made by Thomas Khurana, who notes that the issue of continuity versus discontinuity of self-consciousness with life (or, roughly, that having to do with the dispute over "first nature" and "second nature" between Michael Thompson and John McDowell) is finessed by Hegel into the claim that the "continuity/discontinuity" issue is really about how the human form is "also inwardly not at one with itself" (2017, 403). Robert Pippin (2018) discusses this in terms of the "life of concepts" as having to do with Hegel's *Logic*. I discuss this in Pinkard 2017a, where I take a line that fundamentally agrees with Khurana's point. See also the discussion in Ng 2020.

23. Sartre and Elkaïm-Sartre 1991, 315; 1985, 325.

24. Sartre notes: "The point is, therefore, that the critical investigation should bear on the nature of bonds of interiority (if they exist), on the basis of the human relations which define the investigator. If he is to be totalized by history, the important thing is that he should re-live

his membership of human ensembles with different structures and determine the reality of these ensembles through the bonds which constitute them and the practices which define them. . . . But it will never be sufficient to show the production of ensembles by individuals or by one another, nor, conversely, to show how individuals are produced by the ensembles which they compose. It will be necessary to show the dialectical intelligibility of these transformations in every case" (1976a, 52, 65; 1960, 142, 153).

25. To see it as "co-production" would be, to put it in the terms of Hegel's *Logic*, to see it as belonging to the "logic of essence" in which appearances are seen as the displays or products of some underlying entity or substructure. Such a logic inevitably ends up seeking the "ground" of appearance in something that produces it, and Hegel took himself to have shown that such a view is itself manifested in a kind of conceptual movement that goes back and forth between seeing what was formerly taken to be the productive factor instead into the produced factor, ad infinitum. Viewing the "substance of the world" in that way, so Hegel says, makes it into something like the early modern *lumen naturale*, the light of nature: it illuminates everything else, but it can only "manifest" itself or "show itself" in its capacity to illuminate the things of the world and cannot itself be "said" in any way. The "substance" thus becomes the "form of the world" that cannot be said but can only be shown (which is the position that Schelling in his Jena phase ended up adopting). It does not and cannot illuminate itself. As such, it remains apart from all discursive form and is thus discursively empty. Hegel says it is a "manifestation" of the world, which is a manifestation of "absolute form" (1969b, 201). As such, it is only the "absolute" that can only show itself (*sich selbst zeigt*)" (218). It is this "showing, not saying" that Hegel derisively called the night in which all cows are black and to which Schelling took a lifelong offense.

26. A highly influential interpretation of Hegel's idealism as involving the idea that it relies on the conception of consciousness as producing its object and is therefore deeply flawed is to be found in some of the writing of Jürgen Habermas, for example, Habermas 1973. His critique of Hegel as falling under the "productive" model of consciousness is also modified and carried forward in Honneth 1995 and Benhabib 1986. On their view, Hegel had something like a workable materialist conception of social interaction until about 1803, when he suddenly shifted into the "philosophy of consciousness" that informed the *Phenomenology*. On the view being expressed here, this is a misguided interpretation of Hegel, but this is not the place to stake out that claim. The view articulated by Habermas in rejecting what he takes to be Hegel's big mistake about "consciousness" is to make the move to what Habermas calls "communicative freedom." That view of communicative freedom, however, belongs to the family of views here being attributed to Sartre. One could profitably, I think, reread and maybe refashion Habermas's later writings in light of this—especially Habermas's later full statement of his political theory in Habermas and Rehg 1996, but that would be something for another time. The suggestion of rereading Habermas in light of Sartre is also made in Howard 1977, in which Howard fleshes the idea out more. The idea of linking Habermasian communicative freedom to the Hegelian-Sartrean conception might seem novel, but the very idea that Hegel's logic of the concept and the Habermasian concept of communicative freedom might be more closely related was explicated much earlier and forcefully in the Hegel literature in Theunissen 1978.

27. This is according to Flynn (2014, ix).

28. Several of the books already mentioned go into this debate over humanism in great and helpful detail. See especially Geroulanos 2010; Kleinberg 2005; Rockmore 1995; Gutting 2001.

29. See the discussion of Malraux's crucial place in this debate in Geroulanos 2010.

30. Heidegger was no fan of Sartre's work. The American philosopher Hubert Dreyfus,

himself a great interpreter of Heidegger, reported the following encounter: "When I went to visit Heidegger he had *Being and Nothingness* on his desk, in German translation, and I said, 'So you're reading Sartre?', and he responded, 'How can I even begin to read this muck?' (His word was 'Dreck'.)" The story is recounted in the interview with Dreyfus in Magee 1988, 275. However, apparently in his quest for rehabilitation after the war, Heidegger even wrote Sartre a letter praising his work and Sartre's use of Heidegger's concepts (according to Geroulanos 2010, 376n37).

31. Sartre 2007, 25.

32. Sartre 2007, 45–46.

33. Sartre 2007, 45.

34. Although the text might suggest that Sartre might have been trying to incorporate Kant's own conception of aesthetic judgment into the moral realm, Sartre does not mention Kant's *Critique of Judgment*, nor does he discuss it anywhere else in his ethical writings. In fact, he seems more or less to be ignorant of it, although the text at least suggests some awareness of Kant's conception of aesthetic judgment.

35. Sartre 1956, 615.

36. "This is humanism because we remind man that there is no legislator other than himself and that he must, in his abandoned state, make his own choices, and also because we show that it is not by turning inward, but by constantly seeking a goal outside of himself in the form of liberation, or of some special achievement, that man will realize himself as truly human" (Sartre 2007, 53).

37. Sartre 1956, 412.

38. Sartre 2007, 24.

39. Sartre 2007, 45.

40. Sartre 2007, 50.

41. This is to be found in Sartre 1992a.

42. See Sartre 1976a, 247n75; 1960, 301–303.

43. In an often-cited passage in *Being and Nothingness*, Sartre says, "This does not mean that I am free to get up or to sit down, to enter or to go out, to flee or to face danger—if one means by freedom here a pure capricious, unlawful, gratuitous, and incomprehensible contingency. To be sure, each one of my acts, even the most trivial, is entirely free in the sense which we have just defined; but this does not mean that my act can be anything whatsoever or even that it is unforeseeable" (1956, 453). Freedom is always freedom "in" a situation, which always is limited and which always includes the facts about the agent's own embodiment, education, imagination, etc. None of those facts, however, imply what the agent is to do independently of his orientation toward them.

44. Sartre 2007, 48.

45. Sartre 1956, 25.

46. Sartre notes: "At least we assert this in order to remain faithful to the principle of inertia which constitutes all nature as exteriority" (1956, 313).

47. Sartre says: "These are ideal conditions for the interiorization of an enterprise as [falling] under the form of reciprocity. At this level, the movement of the reciprocal worker gives birth to the union as his interior flight (he passes me a brick and I hold out my hands), and this is understood as well as my gesture coming towards me from elsewhere (elsewhere the brick is freely given to my expectation) as well as the movement of the reciprocal worker and being continued through me. There is no ego in that affair" (1964b, 6).

NOTES TO PAGES 68−71

48. Sartre 1964b, 1.

49. Sartre puts it this way: "Thus the intersubjectivity of the reciprocal is no more binding . . . than my particular subjectivity. Provided that matter (*matière*) does not intervene between us as a way of carrying on the enterprise. To the extent, in fact, that a will is inscribed in it and recognized (instructions or order), this will that comes to me in the enterprise is always mine; I mean to the extent that I participate in the enterprise. . . . But this will of mine is metamorphosed by its inscription in matter: it is born there as an inert will—that is, incapable of being modified by my own will, which breaks reciprocity. It is not the will of another nor the will of others . . . but rather another will. Totalization is impossible (radical heterogeneity of the practico-inert and praxis) and yet the inertia of the task as it appears in matter determines me inwardly. In this way, determined in interiority by another will, my own will becomes an other" (1964b, 6).

50. Sartre 1974d, 153. Sartre adds to that to underscore the way in which the singularity of individual existence is not something to be conceived as instantiating a universal: "Man, irremediable singularity, is the being through whom the universal comes into the world; once fundamental chance starts to be lived, it assumes the form of necessity" (158); "The origin of singularity is the random at its most radical: if I had had a different father . . . if my father had not blasphemed, etc." (157).

51. Sartre 1976a, 666; 1960, 633.

52. This is why Sartre says that "value" in that usage is the "practico-inert imposing itself on a freedom" (1964b, 209). This contrasts with what he takes to be a more fundamental sense of value.

53. Sartre 2005, 310.

54. Sartre 2005, 310.

55. Sartre 1964b, 10. Sartre also says: "Duty, for example, as it manifests itself in morals, has the structure of command which, in principle, is an order given by an other and which conserves for the agent its character of alterity" (1964a, 14; 2015, 22).

56. Sartre thus notes: "We will see later that life—insofar as it is given by the need so as to be reproduced—is also the absolute foundation of the ethical norm" (1964d, 399). He qualifies that with "the foundation of the ethical norm is neither the choice of life nor the choice of death, but the restructuring of the practical field in the light of our radical possibility of living or dying" (342).

57. See Sartre 1964a, 6; 2015, 15.

58. See Sartre 1964b, 25.

59. "Axiology" was part of the background in European and British philosophy in the 1930s and 1940s from which Sartre's own thought emerged. For Sartre in his time, the real choices in ethical theory have to do with whether Kantian universalization provides any determinate content (Sartre thinks it cannot), whether the ends justify the means (Sartre thinks this is not much of a theory at all), or whether an axiological theory can provide the determinate values that Kantian universalization needs but cannot offer. Sartre opts for the third, axiology, and speaks of it in several places, for example, "It is on the intuitive apprehension of the value that the axiological judgements are formed" (1964d, 399; and 1964a, 6; 2015, 15). In particular, Sartre manifests his awareness of Max Scheler's axiological philosophy in his references to Scheler in his 1947–48 *Notebooks*. He seems to have been particularly influenced by Scheler's idea that ultimate values are disclosed to us by emotions that have a particular "intentional" directedness— they have an "aboutness" to them that is not the same as the causal effect such objects may have

on us; but he seems to have fully jettisoned many of Scheler's other views, such as Scheler's dismissal of needs as the basis of value. On the importance of Scheler to French thought of the 1930s, see the very brief discussion in Geroulanos 2010 and Rockmore 1995. On the brief history of "axiology" in the twentieth century, see Findlay 1970. Because Sartre occupies himself with "value" as that which is ultimately worthwhile, he does not concern himself in any serious way with much of what contemporary "value theory" does in terms of marking out and clarifying issues about "good for," "intrinsic goodness," "better than . . . ," etc. Nor does Sartre ever take anything like anglophone utilitarianism seriously at all.

60. Sartre 1964b, 209.

61. Sartre 1964a, 7; 2015, 16.

62. Sartre 1964a, 15; 2015, 23.

63. Sartre 1964b, 132.

64. Sartre 1974c, 39.

65. See the very helpful discussion of this in Boyle 2009, from which I draw some of these points.

66. Sartre 1976a, 100; 1960, 182.

67. Sartre's notes for his new ethics show that even in 1964, he was still working within certain frames of mind from the 1930s, some of which he ended up disavowing shortly thereafter. For example, like many after the war, Sartre was a bit obsessed with the theme of "heroism" in the Resistance, more specifically, about who could resist torture and who would break and reveal information. His notes go into this theme in great detail, and the discussion reappears in the projected but never given lectures at Cornell in 1965. He later said as much: "However, I understood all this only much later. What the drama of the war gave me, as it did everyone who participated in it, was the experience of heroism. Not my own, of course—all I did was a few errands. But the militant in the Resistance who was caught and tortured became a myth for us. Such militants existed, of course, but they represented a sort of personal myth as well. Would we be able to hold out against torture too? The problem then was solely that of physical endurance—it was not the ruses of history or the paths of alienation. A man is tortured: what will he do? He either speaks or refuses to speak. This is what I mean by the experience of heroism, which is a false experience. After the war came the true experience, that of society. But I think it was necessary for me to pass via the myth of heroism first" (1974a, 34). Even a cursory reading of the notes for his new ethics shows that he was still obsessing with the "heroism-Resistance figure" when he began them. The heroism theme had also been underwritten by Malraux in a 1946 UNESCO lecture, discussed in Geroulanos 2010, 37–38, 108–109. Geroulanos notes that "Malraux warned that the death of man could now be averted only through a recognition of the heroism of the *résistance* and a turn to the 'human creativity' to be found in art" (37) and "Malraux's readers interpreted this heroism by way of their own engagements: for Jacques Maritain, Malraux pointed to a spirit of self-sacrifice that was Christian by default; for Paul Nizan, this heroism confirmed the superior ethics of Communism" (108). Sartre was obviously for many years still a bit obsessed with the theme, especially as it concerned the various and conflicting treatment of "humanism" in that period.

68. Sartre 1964d, 399.

69. Sartre 1964d, 399.

70. Sartre puts it this way: "The ethical paradox comes from the fact that the moral agent actualizes what he is in the moment where he tears himself away from 'being' (*à la être*) in order to produce himself in freedom" (2005, 295). Seeing the ethical paradox this way departs from the more usual way of seeing it as it has been developed by most notably Thomas Flynn, who claims

that it "is the old question of relating 'is' to 'ought,' fact to moral value, that Hume revived in modern thought," which is part of "any ethics that claims to be both moral and concrete" (2014, 359–360). The paradox is not the distinction of "is/ought" (which is not a paradox), nor that of abstract and concrete (which is also not a paradox). It is, however, not entirely clear if Sartre is entitled to speak of this as a "paradox" rather than a deep conceptual conundrum.

71. Sartre also makes it clear that this spontaneity is a feature of the individual agent—a carryover from *Being and Nothingness*—and not a feature, for example, of certain forms of "we," for example, serialized peoples (such as a class). Sartre makes that distinction in his 1969 interview: "This is why it does not seem to me that one can speak of class spontaneity; it is only appropriate to speak of groups, produced by circumstances, and which create themselves in the course of particular situations; in thus creating themselves, they do not rediscover some kind of underlying spontaneity, bur rather experience a specific condition on the basis of specific situations of exploitation and of particular demands; and it is in the course of their experience that they achieve a more or less accurate consciousness of themselves" (1974b, 120).

72. This theme of appropriation and owning oneself is notably drawn in Jaeggi 2014a, although without much reference to Sartre. Jaeggi discusses Sartre's conception of bad faith in *Being and Nothingness*, and in a footnote (234n37) notes that she thinks that her critique of Sartre's conception of freedom as overly negative—that Sartre can see no positive features to "role playing" but only a distancing that masks the positive way in which one can appropriate a role for oneself—also extends to the *Critique*. I think that, whatever justice there is to that interpretation of "bad faith" in *Being and Nothingness*, the objection does not apply to the *Critique* and the especially to the later ethics. Sartre's discussion of "ethos" shows that. In this context, see the discussion of what Heidegger would mean by "owning emotions" in Withy 2015. There the discussion is not about Sartre's theory but about some themes in Heidegger's work that also make their appearance in Sartre's later thought.

73. Sartre 2005, 277.

74. Sartre 1964b, 39.

75. Sartre puts it this way: "It must be said that we are frankly addressing the ethical paradox which means that the *ethos* (the ensemble of praxis and its object) would be at the same time a) a historical fact and, as such, observable and accessible to all instruments of sociological investigation (statistics, etc.); b) and a radical surpassing (*dépassement*) of the fact" (1964c, 301).

76. It is another matter altogether, but it is not clear that Hegel's other uses of *Sittlichkeit*—such as in his 1807 *Phenomenology of Spirit*—match up with the 1820 usage. In the *Phenomenology*, *Sittlichkeit* as harmony is the great ancient Greek achievement, and the suggestion is that although this harmony vanished with the appearance of the Roman Empire and feudal Europe, Europe after the French Revolution is poised to recreate a modern *Sittlichkeit*. However, in many other works—particularly in the lectures on the philosophy of history—Hegel seems to use *Sittlichkeit* simply to denote the moral ethos (harmonious or not) of any of the major shapes of the history of *Geist* (spirit). Sartre's conception of ethos has more to do with that latter use of *Sittlichkeit* in Hegel.

77. Piketty 2020, 2.

78. Sartre illustrates this by this example: "All of 'human engineering' is based on the idea that the employer must behave towards his subordinate as if the latter was his equal, because— this is implicit—no man can renounce this right to equality. And the worker who falls into the trap of the 'human relations' of paternalism becomes its victim, to the very degree that he wants effective equality" (1974b, 129).

79. Sartre 1964b, 13.

80. Sartre 1964b, 15.

81. As the historian Keith Thomas puts it in his study of the changing shapes of what was taken to count as human fulfillment in early modern England, "Contemporary prescriptions were repeatedly flouted or ignored; and the search by men and women for personal fulfilment is abundantly evident in the decisions and choices they made in their daily lives. Most people may have lacked autonomy, in the sense that they did not choose for themselves their values or their plan of life. But they had agency, that is to say the ability to make the best of the position in which they found themselves. They were able to maneuver within the structures which enclosed them and they often succeeded in manipulating them to their individual advantage" (2009, 29).

82. Sartre 1964d, 445. Likewise, he says in his notes for the Gramsci lectures, "The normative as the sense of 'history to be made' manifests itself in terms of the struggle of the historical man against the man of repetition" (1964a, 41; 2015, 45).

83. Rubel's work was well known and well received at the time, and he also edited the French edition of Marx and Engels's collected works. In *Karl Marx: Essai de biographie intellectuelle*, Rubel (1957) in fact titles one of the chapters "From Alienation to the Integral Individual" (*De l'aliénation a l'individu intégral*), and it is likely that Sartre was partly inspired by this.

84. Maritain 1936. See Maritain's précis (1939) of his position for the American audience.

85. This seems to be the way in which Sartre took up his earlier suggestion that the philosophy in *Being and Nothingness* could serve as a basis for constructing a secular form of "salvation." Sebastian Gardner's short discussion of this is insightful. Gardner notes: "The religious terminology is used by Sartre without irony, to signal his claim that the philosophy of B&N has implications which lie on the same plane as religious doctrine, and furthermore that it entails at least the possibility of man's realizing his good"; he adds that "Sartre's thinking seems to be that the metaphysically correct and complete way to relate to the Good is to be the Good, to incarnate Value, and that this is something which only God can do; we can relate to the Good only in the inferior mode of positing values. (If God existed, then his freedom would be the Good; there would be no need for him to affirm his freedom, as we need to do.) . . . Sartre's tragic view contains an inverted theological residue" (2009, 199).

86. Maritain stakes his claim as based on the "concrete logic of the events of history," which he characterizes as "a concrete development determined on the one hand by the internal logic of ideas and doctrines, and on the other hand by the human milieu within which these ideas operate and by the contingencies of history as well as by the acts of liberty produced in history. Necessity and contingency are quite remarkably adjusted in the concrete logic, and to designate this logic we may use the world 'dialectic' in the sense I have just expressed, a sense neither Hegelian nor Marxist" (1939, 2). Maritain also goes on to condemn racism along with the banalities of modern bourgeois society—the overtones there in Sartre's work are obvious.

87. Sartre 1964a, 38; 2015, 43.

88. It seems to take a wrong turn therefore to conclude, as Thomas Anderson does, that Sartre substitutes "the satisfaction of needs" in his "second ethics" for the freedom he was seeking in his first ethics. In effect, Anderson makes Sartre into a kind of axiological philosopher in a lightly naturalistic neo-Aristotelian or Thomist vein who would be claiming to have found people's true needs as opposed to their inauthentic or false needs. This involves substituting for what Sartre says is "inconceivable" (integral humanity) a whole set of perfectly "conceivable" ends. Anderson notes: "Nevertheless, inasmuch as Sartre sharply distinguishes there between norms that are grounded in the needs of human beings as members of the human species, called true norms or norms of true morality, and norms whose source is a particular society, class, or

culture, he has provided the basis for claiming that some norms, namely 'true' ones, are universal. Norms that are rooted in needs present in all members of the human species extend, of course, to all human beings." Anderson concludes from that: "As we saw, the Sartre of the sixties and seventies often speaks as if freedom is our most fundamental human need, but at the same time he recognizes that human reality also has many other needs. He insists on the importance of the body and its needs (for example, for protein, for vitamins, for life). He emphasizes our need for others, in particular for their love and valuation. He refers to our need for knowledge, for a meaningful life, and for culture, and insists that without the latter we would not become human. . . . Still, the goal of integral humanity, the fulfillment of the human organism in all its dimensions, has far more content than the abstract freedom of the first ethics. As a result, the second ethics is able to be more specific than the first about what concrete acts or practices or policies are morally desirable" (1993, 148–149, 154–155). Whatever that position may be, it is not dialectical in Sartre's sense, nor could it live up to the demands for a pure intelligibility that Sartre states as the aim of the *Critique of Dialectical Reason*. See also Anderson's brief statement of his view (2013).

89. Sartre says of such values (or "ends"): "The ends—what I will call normative maxims— are diverse in space and time; they change, at the interior of the same society according to the situation of the agent in the social ensemble; it is clear that they are *conditioned* by historical structures. However, they give themselves to ethical experience as *unconditional*, and the praxis to which they give rise—at the fundamental level of their radicalism—remains the same, whatever they may be: whether one defends one's feudal honor, one's right to property, or one affirms one's right not to starve, there comes a moment when one 'puts one's life on the table' to become a subject of interiority. In that way, historically variable ends are reached from one end of history to the other by the same type of action" (2005, 388–389).

90. Sartre 1964d, 377.

91. This position is staked out a bit more in Sartre's final work on Flaubert. See Sartre 1991b, 195: "In literature this means that one has nothing to tell but the tragic, grandiose emptiness of a Godless universe, but it must be told through a particular adventure, localized and dated" (193); "Thus, neither is annihilation in the all carried to its conclusion, nor does the all as such appear to Gustave in its poverty: there is this suspended sliding in which the invisible transfinite derealizes the qualities of Being and in which Being lends to the Transfinite the infinite iridescence of its multiple details. The real causes itself to be *dreamed* as the inexhaustible and singular concretization of the absolute, and the transfinite—imagined as the meaning of all reality—gives to all visible objects a tragic temporality by presenting itself as their meaning and by producing itself behind them in order to be annulled as it leads them away into Nothingness."

92. Sartre notes that "psychological theater—the theater of Euripides, Voltaire, and Crébillon *fils*—announces the decline of tragic forms. A conflict of characters, whatever turns you may give it, is never anything but a composition of forces whose results are predictable. Everything is settled in advance. The man who is led inevitably to his downfall by a combination of circumstances is not likely to move us. There is greatness in his fall only if he falls through his own fault" (1976b, 3–4).

93. Sartre 1964a, 32; 2015, 38.

94. Schilpp 1981, 20.

95. Schilpp 1981, 20.

96. Sartre 1963, 30. (The references to "going beyond it" refer to the way Marxism is *indépassable*, not to be overtaken or transcended.)

97. In his 1969 interview with Rossana Rossanda, Sartre makes this even more clear in saying that "advanced capitalism . . . manages to satisfy the elementary needs of the majority of the working class. . . . It is this situation which has caused me to revise my 'theory of needs' since these needs are no longer, in a situation of advanced capitalism, in systematic opposition to the system. . . . The consciousness of the intolerable character of the system must therefore no longer be sought in the impossibility of satisfying elementary needs but, above all else, in the consciousness of alienation—in other words, in the fact that this life is not worth living and has no meaning, that this mechanism is a deceptive mechanism, that these needs are artificially created, that they are false, that they are exhausting and only serve profit" (1974b, 124–125).

98. Sartre 1963, 179; 1960, 110: "Il ne peut se penser qu'en termes marxistes et se comprendre que comme existence aliénée, que comme réalité-humaine chosifiée."

99. Sartre also clearly thinks that this adequately characterizes Marx's own thought, even though Marx himself did not actually employ the term "reification." At the time of the writing of the *Critique*, Sartre apparently thought that one could fairly infer the concept of reification from what Marx said. He says, "Marx clearly indicated that he distinguished human relations from their reification or, in general, from their alienation within a particular social system. He says, in effect, that in feudal society, based on different institutions and tools, a society which presented different questions, its own questions, to its members, the exploitation of man by man did exist, together with the fiercest oppression, but that everything happened differently and, in particular, human relations were neither reified nor destroyed" (1976a, 96; 1960, 179).

100. Sartre notes: "Thus man freely becomes a commodity: he sells himself. And this freedom is absolutely necessary: not on the superficial plane of law or civil society, but at a deeper level, because this freedom governs output" (1976a, 741; 1960, 693). The idea of the worker selling himself and not just his labor power appears in Marx's *Economic and Philosophical Manuscripts of 1844*, which is probably where Sartre picked up the phrase.

101. What Sartre calls "active passivity" is a self-conscious purposiveness in carrying out some merely given, "practico-inert" activity as the activity it is. He says of active passivity that it is "the regulated production of pledged inertia and as a condition for communal activity," and that "there can be numerous intermediaries between active passivity and passive activity, and it is impossible to know the status of a given institution a priori: this can only be determined by its entire concrete history" (1976a, 603; 1960, 583). "Passive activity" is the counterpart to that, which Sartre illustrates by an example of his looking out of the window from his vacation room and seeing two workers each laboring on opposite sides of a wall: "From this point of view, my presence at the window is a passive activity (I want 'a breath of fresh air' or I find the landscape 'restful', etc.) and my present perception functions as a means in a complex process which expresses the whole of my life" (1976a, 100; 1960, 182).

102. See Sartre 1964a, 136; 2015, 116: "Communism is the suppression of all systems. The practico-inert makes its appearance only to be dissolved. But socialism is once again a system. The practico-inert exists in a socialist society."

103. Sartre 1976a, 661; 1960, 629.

104. Sartre says: "And the reason why the dictatorship of the proletariat (as a real exercise of power through the totalization of the working class) never occurred is that the very idea is absurd, being a bastard compromise between the active, sovereign group and passive seriality. . . . From our point of view, the impossibility of the proletariat exercising a dictatorship is formally proved by the fact that it is impossible for any form of group to constitute itself as a hyper-organism" (1976a, 662; 1960, 630).

105. Sartre 1964d, 460: "The Marxist myth of the universal man (apt for all tasks) [which] means that I would not be a *writer* but only a person who (in this moment) writes or has written. It is not as a product of *my* product that I am humanely alienated but as a product of others."

106. Sartre 1964a, 137; 2015, 116.

107. Sartre and Elkaïm-Sartre 1991, 116; 1985, 128.

108. Sartre's own admission in 1975 that his position was not really Marxist is underwritten by Betschart, who argues that "Sartre's existentialism derives from a philosophy in opposition to Hegel and Marx . . . Sartre's understanding of ontological freedom is incompatible with the understanding shared by both Hegel and Marx that freedom is insight into necessity" (2019, 85). He helpfully shows how Sartre kept to certain key political ideas throughout his career, even as he changed his view on other political ideas. Betschart notes: "Sartre's political core values can be defined by four primary refusals: no to militarism, no to colonialism, no to discrimination (against women, Jews, blacks, gays), and no to bourgeois morality with its values regarding authority and honor, family and money. Most of these values date back to his time at the ENS" (82). (Ronald Aronson, the object of Betschart's critique, replies by noting that although much of Sartre's philosophy may be incompatible with orthodox Marxism, his "existential Marxism" remains a live option; see Aronson 2019.)

109. Translating *classes défavorisées* as "least favored" is suggested by Paige Arthur (2010, 143n17) as the best way of rendering Sartre's concern with justice as oriented to the worst-off in the world. Sartre also speaks, as Arthur notes, of *classes exploitées* and *opprimées* as well as *défavorisée.*

110. See Sartre 1964a, 31; 2015, 38. He says there that "history itself, as a future beyond the system, remains borne by the defavorized classes." In contrast to this idea, Mark Poster claims that Sartre's *Critique* lacks the means to deal with any form of oppression that is not Marxist-style class oppression (Poster 1982, 112). In the interpretation given here, that is far too narrow and conflates the frequency of Sartre's focus on class oppression in the *Critique* with the resources of the theory in the book, some more of which are drawn out in the manuscripts for the late ethics.

111. As Sartre overdramatically puts it in his notes for the Gramsci lecture, we are "to identify history with the dramatic development of morality" (1964a, 137; 2015, 117).

112. Sartre 1964a, 59; 2015, 57.

113. Sartre 1964a, 58; 2015, 57.

114. Sartre 1976a, 300–301n 88; 1960, 344.

115. "If by 'race' is understood that indefinable complex into which are tossed pell-mell both somatic characteristics and intellectual and moral traits, I believe in it no more than I do in ouija boards" (Sartre 1995, 61).

116. Sartre 1995.

117. Sartre 1995, 38.

118. Sartre 1995, 12, 38.

119. Sartre's point appears paradigmatically in his statement "This is why racism is not a mere 'psychological defense' of the colonialist, created for the needs of the cause, to justify colonization to the metropolitan power and to himself; it is in fact Other-Thought (*Pensée-Autre*) produced objectively by the colonial system and by super-exploitation" (1976a, 714; 1960, 671). See the good discussion of how this fits into Sartre's development and his mature views in Arthur 2010.

120. The point about superfluous people and superfluous capital is also part of Hannah Arendt's well-known thesis (1966). It is one of several points where Arendt—who did not seem

to hold Sartre's work in high regard—and Sartre overlap. She marked little of her copy of the *Critique* (in French), but she seemed to focus on the points about superfluous people and scarcity, the points where she and Sartre had some convergence. See https://www.bard.edu/library/arendt/pdfs/Sartre-Critique.pdf.

121. Paige Arthur (2010) lays out the ways in which Sartre's fierce anti-colonialism, otherwise so evident in his political writings in the postwar period and front and center in the examples used in the *Critique* (and thus, Arthur argues, forms one of the central concerns of the book), was, curiously enough, virtually ignored by almost all of the early reviews of the book. In her view, this was in turn linked to the way in which Sartre's defense of human dignity was transformed within the anti-colonial debates into the more recent stereotype of Sartre as endorsing totalitarianism and turning a blind eye to post-colonial denials of human rights. Along with the account in Birchall 2004 and 1996, Arthur's book goes a long way toward correcting that misrepresentation.

122. See my discussion of the early Romantics in Pinkard 2002.

123. Sartre 2005, 319.

124. Sartre 2005, 319.

125. Sartre 2005, 319.

126. Sartre 1964d, 400–401.

127. Sartre 2005, 321.

128. Sartre 1964d, 404.

129. Sartre 1964d, 411. In the 1965 lectures originally intended to be given at Cornell University (but canceled nominally because of Sartre's opposition to the Vietnam War), he says: "Thus, we wish to condemn it unconditionally—apart from the content of the imperative—in order to deny destiny: By speaking the truth, we both claim to escape history (insofar as it is the conditioning of the interior by the exteriority on the basis of a transcendence [*dépassement*] of the exterior by the practical interiorization) and to produce on the basis of history and against it, the model of historical action as it is posited at the moment of heuristic freedom, that is to say, of the closed action, non-deviated, the mistress of its practical field" (2005, 360).

130. Sartre 1964a, 2; 2015, 13: "Cette conception correspond à la mise en vacance de la morale." At another point, Sartre somewhat sarcastically says of life in the atomic age that in it "politics is putting morals on holiday in the name of necessities that render *a single* action possible" (1964b, 82).

131. Sartre 1964a, 3; 2015, 14.

132. Sartre 1976a, 635; 1960, 608.

133. Sartre 1964c, 284.

134. Bernard Williams saw the "basic legitimation demand" as a feature of all political life, forming what he called the "first political question" ("Moralism and Realism," in Williams and Hawthorn 2005, 3–4).

135. The idea of Sartre's using the French Revolution as a "laboratory" is put forth by a French historian of the Revolution (and political theorist), Sophie Wahnich. See Wahnich 2017. Wahnich by and large defends Sartre's approach (especially against the later dominant "discourse-based" analyses of the Revolution that were so prominent in France from the 1970s until the early 2000s.). In particular, it helped to situate her own work on the Revolution: "It opened the way to a Marxist work on the sacred and the emotions, a work on the materiality of the conditions of the sacred, a work on what animates the passage from seriality to fusion, and finally it called for work on this edge of death when the institution of the oath comes to congeal

a group in fusion" (Wahnich 2017, Kindle edition, location 6226). She also has good discussion of the context in the late 1950s and early 1960s in terms of the debate about the nature of the Revolution. Sartre's texts (mostly just citations from other books and some thoughts of his own) on the subject of the Revolution were from 1951–53, but in 1954 famously the British historian Alfred Cobban staked out his claim that, taken in the terms that the Marxists had given it, the French Revolution was a myth. On his account, there was no grand overthrow of the aristocracy by the bourgeoisie, and French society actually changed very little in terms of distribution of wealth. What did change was the setup of political power and new sense of equality. The reign of Louis XVI had, he argued, already been a period of fundamental reforms, and the Revolution more or less simply continued them. In fact, by the time of the Revolution, so Cobban argued, the feudal system no longer in fact really existed, except for some odd remnants. This view was challenged by the Marxist George Lefebvre in 1956. It was into this controversy that Sartre stepped in writing about the Revolution in the *Critique*.

136. Sartre 2008a, b. Wahnich (2017) discusses the notes extensively. The two sets of notes display less of the minor provincialism of the *Critique*, as they take in more than the limited French examples that populate the *Critique* (which, given Sartre's attachment to Marxist history, is explicable in terms of the way in which the French and Russian revolutions were supposedly the paradigm events of the bourgeois and then the proletarian revolutions). It is also clear from the drafts of the second volume of the *Critique* that Sartre was thinking seriously of extending his analyses even further than the French examples, but time ran out on him.

137. Sartre 2008a, 168.

138. Sartre 2008a, 165–166.

139. Sartre 2008a, 220. He says: "Hegel admirably saw: The claim of equality is the claim of equality in slavery in relation to a transcendence. (Today again: Stalin)." In this observation, Sartre is clearly drawing on Jean Wahl's book on the "unhappy consciousness" in Hegel's thought, a book we know Sartre read.

140. Sartre 2008a, 176. According to the editor of these notes (Vincent de Coorebyter), Sartre is apparently modeling this way of putting Sieyès's point from one of his sources for the notes, Paul Bastid, *Sieyès et sa pensée* Paris: Hachette, 1939). Sartre also draws some unflattering comparisons between Sieyès's conception of the nation and the ideas found in Gnosticism, Plotinus, and various mystics, and notes in addition the rather Spinozistic cast of the whole idea: "There is God as undifferentiated power [and] then God the object to himself in the creation. . . . It is noesis and noema" (Sartre 2008a, 176).

141. Sartre 2008a, 177.

142. Sartre 2008a, 177.

143. The contingency of the nation is shown in the way that the class differences in the Revolution of 1789 had to create and forge the nation. There was not originally any basis for any kind of "national solidarity." As Sartre points out with regard to the (largely) German alliance that tried to invade and stop the Revolution, "In 1793, given that the first invasion had taken place, that several towns had precipitously surrendered to the enemy, and that the enemy occupation of border areas resulted in fraternizations in various places, and given that the idea of a nation was new whereas that of international solidarities between aristocracies was very old, the frontiers did not in any way make Frenchmen into a multiplicity contained in one place" (1976a, 597n73; 1960, 579).

144. Sartre describes it in this way: "The State belongs to the category of institutionalized groups with a specified sovereignty . . . whose objectification demands the manipulation of inert

serialities" (1976a, 640; 1960, 612). He adds, "In another sense, the State really does produce itself as a national institution."

145. Sartre 1964a, 59; 2015, 57.

Dénouement

1. See the account of this development in Forrester 2019.

2. It should be noted, however, that although Sartre has little in common with the disputes about distributive models that followed in the wake of Rawls, he and Rawls nonetheless share a common conception of the role of political philosophy in general. Both are concerned to show that it is really in fact possible (and not just desirable as an ideal) for there to be a social and political order in which the members cooperate as free and equal.

3. In his 1964 notes for his ethics, Sartre takes up Betty Friedan's 1963 discussion of moving women out of the confines of the household and into workplace equality (in the process, unfortunately, misspelling her name). He is mildly critical in pointing out that although women's liberation from the inequality forced on them by masculine authority is certainly to be supported, it has obvious limits in that in achieving workplace equality women would simply take up slots in the otherwise inegalitarian social order of capitalism. In the vein of similar Marxist critiques of some forms of feminism, Sartre thinks Friedan's program simply overlooks the element of class struggle, however much he supports liberation from being confined to the role of *la femme au foyer*," as he calls it (1964c, 296).

4. One statement of that project comes in a footnote: "The abstract point of view of critique can obviously never be that of the sociologist or the ethnographer. It is not that we are denying or ignoring the concrete distinctions (the only real ones) which they establish: it is simply that we are at a level of abstraction at which they have no place. In order to connect with them, one would need the set of mediations which transform a *critique* into a *logic* and which, by specification and dialectical concretization, redescend from logic to the real problems, that is to say, to the level at which real History, through the inversion which is to be expected of this abstract quest, becomes the developing totalization which carries, occasions, and justifies the partial totalization of critical intellectuals" (Sartre 1976a, 482n41; 1960, 488).

5. Sartre does not mention Berlin specifically, but Sophie Wahnich has made the case that the Berlin distinction between positive and negative liberty was well known and discussed in French intellectual circles at the time. See Wahnich 2017.

6. Sartre 1976a, 329; 1960, 367.

7. Sartre 1956, 412.

8. The interest in the idea of an alternative humanist "salvation" also runs throughout the notebooks Sartre (1992a) made for his proposed ethics in 1947–48 but which he abandoned, most likely because he came to see that his original project for such a salvation had misfired. In the notebooks, he seems to at least toy with the idea that freedom affirming itself is not merely a "second best" for agents but is salvation itself. In discussing freedom and the impossibility of being one's own foundation, he says (starting with a reprise of his views on inauthenticity): "His project is inauthentic when man's project is to rejoin an In-itself-for-itself and to identify it with himself; in short, to be God and his own foundation, and when at the same time he posits the Good as preestablished" (559). But, as he notes in a passage already mentioned, this is "not a question of a limit which freedom trips over," since "it would be equally useless to speak of a constraint on the mind of a mathematician because he, being able to conceive of a circle or a

square, cannot conceive of a square circle." Salvation, he says, would finally be "the constitution of a freedom that takes itself as its end," however difficult that may be from psychological point of view (559–60). Sebastian Gardner argues for the "second-best" view. He says that when Sartre claims his philosophy offers an alternative salvation for what is otherwise a tragic picture of the human condition, Sartre's language embeds a "theological residue" within itself. Simone de Beauvoir, so Gardner argues, gives a novel twist to this in her interpretation of Sartrean freedom's "self-affirmation [as] one of rational enlightenment," the correction of a commonsense mistake about freedom and values. On de Beauvoir's account, the only possible value is the one we already have, namely, our own autonomy in representing ourselves as valuable. Although this is a possible reading of Sartre's text, Gardner argues that Sartre instead most likely understands the self-affirmation of freedom as only a second-best value. What we really hope for, on the earlier Sartre's view, is the metaphysically impossible realization of being an in-itself-for-itself, that is, to be our own foundation, to be God. Since God is metaphysically impossible, we have to settle for the second best, exercising an autonomy without ever being our own foundation and thus never really being autonomous (Gardner 2009, 197–199).

9. Schilpp 1981, 20.

10. André Guigot (2007) suggests that the failure to achieve the full philosophy of history in the two volumes of the *Critique* thus mirrors the open-endedness of the dialectic that Sartre uncovers.

11. Sartre 1966, 95.

12. The idea of "libertarian socialism" seems to have originated with Daniel Guérin, with whom Sartre had, to say the least, a complicated relationship. See the discussion of it in Birchall 1996, as well as in Birchall 2004. Thomas Flynn claims that "libertarian socialism" was just the ordinary French shorthand at the time for some form of political anarchism (2005, 6). Alfred Betschart claims that anarchists describing themselves as libertarian socialists dates all the way back to the *lois scélérates* of 1893–94, which sought to make even the advocacy of anarchism a crime (2019, 84). The very idea of a "libertarian socialism" was, moreover, more widespread than just in France. Noam Chomsky discussed it in 1970, also drawing on Daniel Guérin's works for the idea. Chomsky concluded approvingly that "libertarian socialism . . . preserved and extended the radical humanist message of the Enlightenment and the classical liberal ideas that were perverted into an ideology to sustain the emerging social order. In fact, on the very same assumptions that led classical liberalism to oppose the intervention of the state in social life, capitalist social relations are also intolerable" (Chomsky and Pateman 2005, 122). Sartre, however, would likely have taken umbrage at Chomsky's linking of Enlightenment thought and libertarian socialism. For large stretches of his career, Sartre was sensitive to and prickly about the charge that he was only carrying forward the older eighteenth-century ideals of French "republicanism." Some, such as Alfred Betschart, claim that this shows that in his heart of hearts Sartre had more or less always been an anarchist: "This first political philosophy that Sartre ever developed was emphatically not a Marxist, but an anarchist one. Nothing proves this better than the fact that state power worried him more than its economic counterpart. The term 'existentialist Marxism' would definitely not have found favor with Sartre in the years before his death" (2019, 84). Michel Contat, interviewing Sartre after Sartre had turned seventy, reminded Sartre that Sartre had once told him he had always been an anarchist, to which Sartre replied, "That is very true," and Sartre added, "I have never accepted any power over me, and I have always thought that anarchy, which is to say a society without powers, must be brought about" (Sartre and Contat 1975). In that exchange, Sartre probably meant "hierarchy" and not "powers" per

se, and even if Sartre was right in realizing that maybe he had always been an anarchist at heart, "anarchism" nonetheless did not appear as any kind of explicit theme in his thought, and he never really developed the idea, as Contat pointed out. At one point, he did speak of "anarchist individualism" (*individualisme anarchiste*), although not in an entirely approving way (Sartre 2005, 133). In one of his later short pieces, "Elections: A Trap for Fools," in 1973, Sartre did seem to indicate somewhat more clearly that he was advocating for some sort of anarchism-as-direct-democracy. He indicates there that he accepts something like Rousseau's conception of the inadmissibility of representation in democratic politics. In good Rousseauian fashion, Sartre says that "indirect democracy is a hoax. Ostensibly the elected Assembly is the one which reflects public opinion most faithfully. But there is only one sort of public opinion, and it is serial," whereas direct democracy is "the democracy of people fighting against the system, of individual men fighting against the seriality that transforms them into things. . . . Indirect democracy . . . reduces us all to powerlessness." He concludes: "We must try, each according to his own re-sources, to organize the vast anti-hierarchic movement which fights institutions everywhere" (1977, 209–210). However, he did not think that this had to be purely negative, mere "revolt" and nothing constructive. In 1969, he noted: "Without a moment of unification of the struggle, without a cultural mediation and a positive response, it is impossible to go beyond revolt; and revolt is always defeated politically" (1974b, 131). However, on his own terms he sees institutions as rationally necessary developments of *praxis*, and thus the "fight" against them would have to be perpetual. Whatever Sartre's own personal inclinations toward such anarchism might have been late in his life, he never worked out what it might look like except to note that it involved a reciprocal commitment to the freedom of all as a condition of the freedom of each. In that same interview, he said of the term "libertarian socialism": "It is an anarchist term, and I keep it because I like to recall the somewhat anarchist origins of my thought. I have always been in agreement with the anarchists, who are the only ones to have conceived of a whole man to be developed through social action and whose chief characteristic is freedom. On the other hand, obviously, as political figures the anarchists are somewhat simple" (Schilpp 1981, 21).

13. The term "anarchistic core" comes from Jürgen Habermas's brief aside that his own theory of communicative freedom draws on such a core. Habermas says, "Of course, the poten-tial of unleashed *communicative* freedoms does contain an anarchistic core. The institutions of any democratic government must live off this core if they are to be effective guaranteeing equal liberties for all" (Habermas and Rehg 1996, xl).

14. Sartre 1974b, 121.

15. Sartre 1974b, 132.

16. Sartre and Elkaïm-Sartre 1991, 162; 1985, 175.

17. "Elections: A Trap for Fools," in Sartre 1977, 210.

18. To appropriate one of Hannah Arendt's distinctions, Sartre implicitly distinguishes be-tween liberation from oppression or injustice (as rebellion) and founding a new form of life that is not subject to those conditions (revolution). Arendt (1963) draws this distinction in the following ways: "Liberation and freedom are not the same; that liberation may be the condition of freedom but by no means leads automatically to it" (22); "The end of rebellion is liberation, while the end of revolution is the foundation of freedom" (140); "The act of founding the new body politic, of devising the new form of government involves the grave concern with the sta-bility and durability of the new structure; the experience, on the other hand, which those who are engaged in this grave business are bound to have is the exhilarating awareness of the human capacity of beginning" (225).

19. Two major texts in which this is worked out are Habermas 1984 and Habermas and Rehg 1996.

20. This is an ongoing theme in Honneth's work, but it emerges front and center in Honneth 2014. T. Storm Heter (2006) says that he wants to do for Sartre what Honneth did for Hegel vis-à-vis recognition, namely, to provide him with a proper concept of recognition to put to use in political philosophy. Heter points out very helpfully some of the more Hegelian moments of Sartre's late work. However, he seems to want to force Sartre's philosophy into a shape that he would rather it have had than the one it actually does. Sartre uses the term "recognition," rather sparingly in the two *Critiques* and not much at all in the later ethics. He recognizes the importance of recognition, but it is not the "master concept" at work there. Heter only discusses the first volume of the *Critique* and none of the later ethics (no part of which was, however, available when his book was published).

21. Wittgenstein himself never uses the term *Lebenswelt*, and uses the term *Lebensform* only sparingly. On the difference between the uses to which "lifeworld" and "form of life" can be put, see the discussion of Wittgenstein's conception of *Lebensform* in Floyd 2021. On the difficulties in putting the concept of the "lifeworld" into use in critical theory, see the discussion in Fraser and Jaeggi 2018.

22. Sartre 1974b, 124.

23. See Sartre 1976a, 326; 1960, 364.

24. Young 1990.

25. Sartre makes this point in a few places. In one of them, he says, "It goes without saying that, although the real existence of organic totalities and totalizing processes reveals a dialectical movement, the existence of organic bodies can in no way be derived from the dialectic. However biology may develop in [the] future, organic bodies can never be regarded as any more than de facto realities; we have no means of establishing their existence by reason alone. The theory that they originate from unorganized matter is a reasonable and economical hypothesis, on which even Christians can agree. But this hypothesis is no more than a belief. Thus neither analytical Reason, which applies to relations in exteriority, nor dialectical Reason, which derives its intelligibility from totalities, and which governs the relations of wholes to their parts and of totalities to one another in a process of increasing integration, can establish a statute of intelligibility for organized bodies. If they emerged from inorganic matter, there was a passage not only from the inanimate to life, but also from one rationality to the other" (1976a, 91–92; 1960, 175).

26. The conceptual affinity for Sartre's thought for that of pragmatism was already noted at the time by an Italian philosopher, Giuseppe Semirari, who said, "It seems to me that here Marxism opens up, and decidedly so, to pragmatism in its most noble and classic form, namely Dewey's form of concrete existentialism, which I don't think we can define as a bourgeois philosophy in this regard" (Sartre 2016, 65).

27. In his much earlier work (1995), Sartre proposed replacing what he called an "abstract liberalism" not with anything like "anarchism," but with what he called a "concrete liberalism," which he characterized in this way: "By that we mean that all persons who through their work collaborate toward the greatness of a country have the full rights of citizens of that country. What gives them this right is not the possession of a problematical and abstract 'human nature,' but their active participation in the life of the society. This means, then, that the Jews— and likewise the Arabs and Negroes—from the moment that they are participants in the national enterprise, have a right in that enterprise; they are citizens. But they have these rights as Jews, Negroes, or Arabs— that is, as concrete persons" (146). Whereas Sartre held onto the

commitment to multiculturalism, he abandoned the idea that this should be described as "liberalism" at all.

28. Beauvoir and Sartre 1984, 369.

29. Sartre notes that "this dialectical transcendence, which shows the becoming-*praxis* (*le devenir-praxis*) of need is itself the foundation of all rights" (1976a, 610; 1960, 588).

30. Sartre 1974e, 267.

Bibliography

Anderson, Thomas C. 1993. *Sartre's Two Ethics: From Authenticity to Integral Humanity*. Chicago: Open Court.

———. 2013. "Sartre's Second or Dialectical Ethics." In *Jean-Paul Sartre: Key Concepts*, edited by Steven Churchill and Jack Reynolds, 195–205. London and New York: Routledge.

Arendt, Hannah. 1963. *On Revolution*. New York: Viking Press.

———. 1966. *The Origins of Totalitarianism*. New York: Harcourt.

Aron, Raymond. 1975. *History and the Dialectic of Violence: An Analysis of Sartre's "Critique de la raison dialectique."* Oxford: Blackwell.

———. 1987. *Sartre's Second Critique*. Chicago: University of Chicago Press.

———. 2010. "Celebrating the *Critique*'s Fiftieth Anniversary." *Sartre Studies International* 16 (2):1–16.

———. 2019. "Revisiting Existential Marxism: A Reply to Alfred Betschart." *Sartre Studies International* 25 (2):92–98.

Arthur, Paige. 2010. *Unfinished Projects: Decolonization and the Philosophy of Jean-Paul Sartre*. London: Verso.

Barba-Kay, Antón. 2016. "Locating Hegel's Struggle for Recognition." *Hegel-Studien* 50:33–61.

Beauvoir, Simone de, and Jean-Paul Sartre. 1984. *Adieux: A Farewell to Sartre*. New York: Pantheon Books.

Benhabib, Seyla. 1986. *Critique, Norm, and Utopia: A Study of the Foundations of Critical Theory*. New York: Columbia University Press.

Betschart, Alfred. 2019. "Sartre Was Not a Marxist." *Sartre Studies International* 25 (2):77–91.

Birchall, Ian H. 1996. "Sartre's Encounter with Daniel Guérin." *Sartre Studies International* 2 (1):41–56.

———. 2004. *Sartre against Stalinism*. New York: Berghahn Books.

Boyle, Matthew. 2009. "Two Kinds of Self-Knowledge." *Philosophy and Phenomenological Research* 78 (1):133–164.

———. 2016. "Additive Theories of Rationality: A Critique." *European Journal of Philosophy* 24 (3):527–555.

Catalano, Joseph S. 1986. *A Commentary on Jean-Paul Sartre's Critique of Dialectical Reason, Volume 1, Theory of Practical Ensembles*. Chicago: University of Chicago Press.

Chomsky, Noam, and Barry Pateman. 2005. *Chomsky on Anarchism*. Oakland: AK Press.

Cohen-Solal, Annie, and Norman MacAfee. 1987. *Sartre: A Life*. New York: Pantheon Books.

Collamati, Chiara. 2016. "Alienation between the 'Critique of Dialectical Reason' and the 'Critique of Economic Reason': Sketch of a Materialist Ethics." *Sartre Studies International* 22 (1):83–98.

———. 2017. "Pour une philosophie politique sartrienne: Réflexions à partir d'un ouvrage récent." *Études sartriennes* 21:131–147.

———. 2019. "'Du cercle à la spirale': Totalité ouverte et structures du temps historique." *Études sartriennes* 23:41–62.

Conant, James. 2020. "Wittgenstein's Critique of the Additive Conception of Language." *Nordic Wittgenstein Review* 9.

Crittenden, Paul. 2009. *Sartre in Search of an Ethics*. Newcastle upon Tyne: Cambridge Scholars.

Edelstein, Dan. 2012. "Do We Want a Revolution without Revolution? Reflections on Political Authority." *French Historical Studies* 35 (2):269–289.

Findlay, J. N. 1970. *Axiological Ethics: New Studies in Ethics*. London: Macmillan.

Fisher, Quentin. 2019. "Being Together: An Essay on the First-Person Plural." PhD diss., Georgetown University.

Floyd, Juliet. 2016. "Chains of Life: Turing, *Lebensform*, and the Emergence of Wittgenstein's Later Style." *Nordic Wittgenstein Review* 5 (2):7–89.

———. 2021. "*Lebensformen*: Living Logic." In *Language, Form(s) of Life, and Logic: Investigations after Wittgenstein*, edited by Christian Martin. Berlin: de Gruyter.

Flynn, Thomas R. 1997. *Sartre, Foucault, and Historical Reason*. 2 vols. Chicago: University of Chicago Press.

———. 2005. "Sartre at One Hundred—a Man of the Nineteenth Century Addressing the Twenty-First?" *Sartre Studies International* 11 (1–2):1–14.

———. 2014. *Sartre: A Philosophical Biography*. Cambridge: Cambridge University Press.

Foot, Philippa. 2001. *Natural Goodness*. Oxford: Clarendon.

Forrester, Katrina. 2019. *In the Shadow of Justice: Postwar Liberalism and the Remaking of Political Philosophy*. Princeton: Princeton University Press.

Fraser, Nancy, and Rahel Jaeggi. 2018. *Capitalism: A Conversation in Critical Theory*. Medford, MA: Polity.

Gardner, Sebastian. 2009. *Sartre's "Being and Nothingness": A Reader's Guide*. London and New York: Continuum.

———. 2017. "Sartre's Original Insight." *Metodo* 5 (1):45–71.

Gerassi, John. 2009. *Talking with Sartre: Conversations and Debates*. New Haven: Yale University Press.

Geroulanos, Stefanos. 2010. *An Atheism That Is Not Humanist Emerges in French Thought*. Stanford: Stanford University Press.

Guigot, André. 2007. *Sartre: Liberté et histoire*. Paris: J. Vrin.

Gutting, Gary. 2001. *French Philosophy in the Twentieth Century*. Cambridge: Cambridge University Press.

———. 2011. *Thinking the Impossible: French Philosophy since 1960*. Oxford: Oxford University Press.

Haase, Matthias. 2016. "Three Forms of the First Person Plural." In *Rethinking Epistemology*, edited by Günter Abel and James Conant, 1:229–256. Berlin: De Gruyter.

Habermas, Jürgen. 1973. *Theory and Practice*. Boston: Beacon Press.

———. 1984. *The Theory of Communicative Action*. 2 vols. Boston: Beacon Press.

Habermas, Jürgen, and William Rehg. 1996. *Between Facts and Norms: Contributions to a Discourse Theory of Law and Democracy*. Cambridge: Polity.

Han-Pile, Béatrice. 2009. "Nietzsche and *Amor Fati.*" *European Journal of Philosophy* 19 (2):224–261.

Hartmann, Klaus. 1966. *Sartres Sozialphilosophie: Eine Untersuchung zur "Critique de la raison dialectique I."* Berlin: De Gruyter.

Hegel, Georg Wilhelm Friedrich. 1969a. *Grundlinien der Philosophie des Rechts*. Edited by Eva Moldenhauer and Karl Markus Michel. Vol. 7 of *Theorie-Werkausgabe*. Frankfurt a. M.: Suhrkamp.

———. 1969b. *Wissenschaft der Logik II*. Edited by Eva Moldenhauer and Karl Markus Michel. Vol. 6 of *Theorie-Werkausgabe*. Frankfurt a. M.: Suhrkamp.

———. 1991. *Elements of the Philosophy of Right*. Translated by Hugh Barr Nisbet. Edited by Allen W. Wood. Cambridge: Cambridge University Press.

———. 2010. *Encyclopedia of the Philosophical Sciences in Basic Outline, Part 1, Science of Logic*. Edited and translated by Klaus Brinkmann and Daniel O. Dahlstrom. Cambridge and New York: Cambridge University Press.

———. 2018. *The Phenomenology of Spirit*. Translated by Terry P. Pinkard. New York: Cambridge University Press.

Heidegger, Martin. 1962. *Being and Time*. New York: Harper.

———. 1977. *Basic Writings: From "Being and Time" (1927) to "The Task of Thinking" (1964)*. New York: Harper & Row.

Henrich, Dieter. 1967. *Fichtes ursprüngliche Einsicht, Wissenschaft und Gegenwart*. Frankfurt a. M.,: Klostermann.

Heter, T. Storm. 2006. *Sartre's Ethics of Engagement: Authenticity and Civic Virtue*. London and New York: Continuum.

Honneth, Axel. 1995. *The Struggle for Recognition: The Moral Grammar of Social Conflicts*. Cambridge: Polity Press.

———. 2014. *Freedom's Right: The Social Foundations of Democratic Life*. New York: Columbia University Press.

Howard, Dick. 1977. *The Marxian Legacy*. London: Macmillan.

Howells, Christina. 1992. *The Cambridge Companion to Sartre*. Cambridge: Cambridge University Press.

Hulliung, Mark. 2013. *Sartre and Clio: Encounters with History*. Boulder, CO: Paradigm Publishers.

Jaeggi, Rahel. 2014a. *Alienation*. New York: Columbia University Press.

———. 2014b. *Kritik von Lebensformen*. Berlin: Suhrkamp.

Jay, Martin. 1973. *The Dialectical Imagination: A History of the Frankfurt School and the Institute of Social Research, 1923–1950*. Boston: Little, Brown.

———. 1984. *Marxism and Totality: The Adventures of a Concept from Lukács to Habermas*. Berkeley: University of California Press.

Judt, Tony. 1986. *Marxism and the French Left: Studies in Labour and Politics in France, 1830–1981*. Oxford: Clarendon.

Kant, Immanuel, 1997. *Lectures on Metaphysics*. Translated and edited by Karl Ameriks and Steve Naragon. Cambridge: Cambridge University Press.

Kern, Andrea. 2019. "Life and Mind: Varieties of Neo-Aristotelianism; Naive, Sophisticated, Hegelian." *Hegel Bulletin of the Hegel Society of Great Britain* 41 (1):40–60.

———. 2020. "Human Life, Rationality, and Education." *Journal of Philosophy of Education* 54 (2):268–289.

Khilnani, Sunil. 1993. *Arguing Revolution: The Intellectual Left in Postwar France*. New Haven: Yale University Press.

Khurana, Thomas. 2017. *Das Leben der Freiheit: Form und Wirklichkeit der Autonomie*. Frankfurt: Suhrkamp.

Khurana, Thomas, and Christoph Menke, eds. 2011. *Paradoxien der Autonomie*. Berlin: August Verlag.

Kleinberg, Ethan. 2005. *Generation Existential: Heidegger's Philosophy in France, 1927–1961*. Ithaca: Cornell University Press.

Korsgaard, Christine M. 2007. "Autonomy and the Second Person Within: A Commentary on Stephen Darwall's 'The Second-Person Standpoint'." *Ethics* 118 (1):8–23.

Larmore, Charles E. 2012. *Vernunft und Subjektivität: Frankfurter Vorlesungen*. Suhrkamp Taschenbuch Wissenschaft. Berlin: Suhrkamp.

Lévy, Bernard Henri. 2004. *Sartre: The Philosopher of the Twentieth Century*. Malden, MA: Polity Press.

Longuenesse, Béatrice. 1981. *Hegel et la critique de la métaphysique: Étude sur la doctrine de l'essence*. Paris: Vrin.

———. 2007. *Hegel's Critique of Metaphysics*. Cambridge: Cambridge University Press.

———. 2017. "Self-Consciousness and Self-Reference: Sartre and Wittgenstein." In *I, Me, Mine: Back to Kant, and Back Again*, edited by Béatrice Longuenesse, 44–70. Oxford: Oxford University Press.

MacIntyre, Alasdair. 2009. "Sartre as Social Critic (1962)." In *Alasdair MacIntyre's Engagement with Marxism: Selected Writings, 1953–1974*, edited by Paul Blackledge and Neil Davidson, 201–208. Chicago: Haymarket Books.

Magee, Bryan. 1988. *The Great Philosophers: An Introduction to Western Philosophy*. Oxford: Oxford University Press.

Maritain, Jacques. 1936. *Humanisme intégral: Problèmes temporels et spirituels d'une nouvelle chrétienté*. Paris: F. Aubier.

———. 1939. "Integral Humanism and the Crisis of Modern Times." *Review of Politics* 1 (1):1–17.

McBride, William Leon. 1991. *Sartre's Political Theory*. Bloomington: Indiana University Press.

———. 2005. "Sartre at the Twilight of Liberal Democracy as We Have Known It." *Sartre Studies International* 11 (1–2):311–318.

Merleau-Ponty, Maurice. 1973. *Adventures of the Dialectic*. Evanston: Northwestern University Press.

Moore, A. W. 2002. *The Infinite*. 2nd ed. London and New York: Routledge.

———. 2012. *The Evolution of Modern Metaphysics: Making Sense of Things*. Cambridge: Cambridge University Press.

Morris, Katherine J. 2008. *Sartre*. Malden, MA: Blackwell.

Murphy, Julien S. 1999. *Feminist Interpretations of Jean-Paul Sartre: Re-reading the Canon*. University Park: Pennsylvania State University Press.

Nagel, Thomas. 1986. *The View from Nowhere*. New York: Oxford University Press.

Narboux, Jean-Philippe. 2014. "Showing, the Medium Voice, and the Unity of the Tractatus." *Philosophical Topics* 42 (2):201–262.

———. 2015. "Intentionnalité et négation dans *L'Être et le néant*." In *Sartre, L'être et le néant: Nouvelles lectures*, edited by Jean-Marc Mouillie and Jean-Philippe Narboux, 57–91. Paris: Les Belles Lettres.

———. 2018. "Is Self-Consciousness Consciousness of One's Self?" In *Wittgenstein and Phe-*

nomenology, edited by Mihai Ometita, Oskari Kuusela, and Timur Uçan, 197–248. New York: Routledge.

Neuhouser, Frederick. 2000. *Foundations of Hegel's Social Theory: Actualizing Freedom.* Cambridge, MA: Harvard University Press.

Ng, Karen. 2020. *Hegel's Concept of Life: Self-Consciousness, Freedom, Logic.* New York: Oxford University Press.

Piketty, Thomas. 2020. *Capital and Ideology.* Translated by Arthur Goldhammer. Cambridge: Harvard University Press.

Pinkard, Terry. 2002. *German Philosophy, 1760–1860: The Legacy of Idealism.* Cambridge: Cambridge University Press.

———. 2015a. "Idealism in Nineteenth Century Philosophy." In *The Oxford Handbook to Nineteenth-Century Philosophy*, edited by Kristin Gjesdal and Michael N. Forster, 231–257. Oxford: Oxford University Press.

———. 2015b. "Tragedy with and without Religion: Hegelian Thoughts." In *Tragedy and the Idea of Modernity*, edited by Joshua Billings and Miriam Leonard, 137–158. Oxford: Oxford University Press.

———. 2017a. *Does History Make Sense? Hegel on the Historical Shapes of Justice.* Cambridge, MA: Harvard University Press.

———. 2017b. "Hegel's *Phenomenology* and *Logic*: An Overview." In *The Cambridge Companion to German Idealism*, edited by Karl Ameriks, 227–247. Cambridge: Cambridge University Press.

———. 2019. "Forms of Thought, Forms of Life." In *Wittgenstein and Hegel: Reevaluation of Difference*, edited by Jakub Mácha and Alexander Berg, 181–198. Berlin: DeGruyter.

Pippin, Robert B. 2018. *Hegel's Realm of Shadows: Logic as Metaphysics in "The Science of Logic."* Chicago: University of Chicago Press.

Poster, Mark. 1982. *Sartre's Marxism.* Cambridge: Cambridge University Press.

Rae, Gavin. 2011. *Realizing Freedom: Hegel, Sartre, and the Alienation of Human Being.* Basingstoke: Palgrave Macmillan.

Rizk, Hadi. 2014. *Individus et multiplicités: Essai sur les ensembles pratiques dans la "Critique de la raison dialectique."* Paris: Éd. Kimé.

Rockmore, Tom. 1995. *Heidegger and French Philosophy: Humanism, Antihumanism, and Being.* London and New York: Routledge.

Rosanvallon, Pierre. 2013. *The Society of Equals.* Cambridge, MA: Harvard University Press.

Roth, Michael S. 1988. *Knowing and History: Appropriations of Hegel in Twentieth-Century France.* Ithaca: Cornell University Press.

Rubel, Maximilien. 1957. *Karl Marx: Essai de biographie intellectuelle.* Paris: Librairie M. Rivière et Cie.

Russon, John. 2014. "Dialectic, Difference, and the Other: The Hegelianizing of French Phenomenology." In *Phenomenology: Responses and Developments*, edited by Leonard Lawlor, 17–42. London and New York: Routledge.

Sandis, Constantine. 2019. "Who Are 'We' for Wittgenstein?" In *Wittgenstein and the Limits of Language*, edited by Hanne Appelqvist, 172–196. London and New York: Routledge.

Sartre, Jean-Paul. 1943. *L'être et le néant. Essai d'ontologie phénoménologique.* Paris: Gallimard.

———. 1955. *Literary and Philosophical Essays.* Translated by Annette Michelson. New York: Criterion Books.

———. 1956. *Being and Nothingness: An Essay on Phenomenological Ontology.* Translated by Hazel E. Barnes. New York: Philosophical Library.

————. 1960. *Critique de la raison dialectique, précédé de Questions de méthode.* Paris: Librairie Gallimard.

————. 1963. *Search for a Method.* Translated by Hazel E. Barnes. New York: Knopf.

————. 1964a. "Sartre typed ms (corrected by him). Notes for Gramsci Lecture, Rome 1964." John Gerassi Collection of Jean-Paul Sartre. General Collection, Beinecke Rare Book and Manuscript Library, Yale University.

————. 1964b. "Sartre: Morale 1964 typed GEN MSS 441 Box 4 f. 56 complete, binder I." John Gerassi Collection of Jean-Paul Sartre. General Collection, Beinecke Rare Book and Manuscript Library, Yale University.

————. 1964c. "Sartre: Morale 1964 typed GEN MSS 441 Box 4 f. 57 complete, binder II." John Gerassi Collection of Jean-Paul Sartre. General Collection, Beinecke Rare Book and Manuscript Library, Yale University.

————. 1964d. "Sartre: Morale 1964 typed GEN MSS 441 Box 5 f. 58 complete, binder III." John Gerassi Collection of Jean-Paul Sartre. General Collection, Beinecke Rare Book and Manuscript Library, Yale University.

————. 1966. "Jean-Paul Sartre Répond." *L'Arc,* 87–96.

————. 1974a. *Between Existentialism and Marxism.* Translated by John Matthews. London: NLB.

————. 1974b. "France: Masses, Spontaneity, Party." In *Between Existentialism and Marxism,* 118–137. London: NLB.

————. 1974c. "Itinerary of a Thought." In *Between Existentialism and Marxism,* 33–64. London: NLB.

————. 1974d. "Kierkegaard: The Singular Universal." In *Between Existentialism and Marxism,* 141–169. London: NLB.

————. 1974e. "A Plea for Intellectuals." In *Between Existentialism and Marxism,* 228–285. London: NLB.

————. 1976a. *Critique of Dialectical Reason. Theory of Practical Ensembles.* Translated by Alan Sheridan-Smith. Atlantic Highlands, NJ: Humanities Press.

————. 1976b. *Sartre on Theater.* Assembled, edited, introduced, and annotated by Michel Contat and Michel Rybalka. Translated by Frank Jellinek. New York: Pantheon Books.

————. 1977. *Life/Situations: Essays Written and Spoken.* Translated by Paul Auster and Lydia Davis. New York: Pantheon Books.

————. 1985. *Critique de la raison dialectique.* Vol. 2, *L'intelligibilité de l'histoire.* Edited by Arlette Elkaïm-Sartre. Paris: Gallimard.

————. 1988. *"What Is Literature?" and Other Essays.* Cambridge, MA: Harvard University Press.

————. 1991a. *Critique of Dialectical Reason.* Vol. 2, *The Intelligibility of History.* Translated by Quintin Hoare. London: Verso.

————. 1991b. *The Family Idiot: Gustave Flaubert, 1821–1857.* Translated by Carol Cosman. Vol. 4. Chicago: University of Chicago Press.

————. 1991c. *The Transcendence of the Ego: An Existentialist Theory of Consciousness.* Translated and annotated with an introduction by Forrest Williams and Robert Kirkpatrick. New York: Hill and Wang.

————. 1992a. *Notebooks for an Ethics.* Translated by David Pellauer. Chicago: University of Chicago Press.

————. 1992b. *Truth and Existence.* Edited by Arlette Elkaïm-Sartre. Translated by Adrian van den Hoven. Introduction by Ronald Aronson. Chicago: University of Chicago Press.

———. 1995. *Anti-Semite and Jew*. Translated by George J. Becker. New York: Schocken Books.

———. 2005. "Morale et histoire." *Les temps modernes* 632–633–634 (4):268–414.

———. 2007. *Existentialism Is a Humanism (L'Existentialisme est un humanisme), Including a Commentary on "The Stranger" ("Explication de L'Étranger")*. Translated by Carol Macomber. Edited by John Kulka. New Haven: Yale University Press.

———. 2008a. "Liberté—Égalité: Manuscrit sur la genèse de l'idéologie bourgeoise." *Études sartriennes* 12:165–256.

———. 2008b. "Mai-juin 1789: Manuscrit sur la naissance de l'Assemblée nationale." *Études sartriennes* 12:19–154.

———. 2015. "Les racines de l'éthique: Conférence à l'Institut Gramsci, mai 1964." *Études sartriennes* 19:11–118.

———. 2016. *What Is Subjectivity?* Translated by David Broder and Trista Selous. London and New York: Verso.

Sartre, Jean Paul, and Michel Contat. 1975. "Sartre at Seventy: An Interview." *New York Review of Books* (August 7, 1975). https://www.nybooks.com/articles/1975/08/07/sartre-at-seventy-an-interview/.

Schilpp, Paul Arthur, ed. 1981. *The Philosophy of Jean-Paul Sartre*. La Salle, IL: Open Court.

Sewell, William Hamilton, Jr. 2005. *Logics of History: Social Theory and Social Transformation*. Chicago: University of Chicago Press.

Sherman, David. 2007. *Sartre and Adorno: The Dialectics of Subjectivity*. Albany: State University of New York Press.

Stern, Robert. 2007. "Hegel, British Idealism, and the Curious Case of the Concrete Universal." *British Journal for the History of Philosophy* 15 (1):115–153.

Tackett, Timothy. 2015. *The Coming of the Terror in the French Revolution*. Cambridge, MA: The Belknap Press of Harvard University Press.

Theunissen, Michael. 1978. *Sein und Schein: Die kritische Funktion der Hegelschen Logik*. Frankfurt am Main: Suhrkamp.

Thomas, Keith. 2009. *The Ends of Life: Roads to Fulfilment in Early Modern England*. Oxford: Oxford University Press.

Thompson, Michael. 2008. *Life and Action: Elementary Structures of Practice and Practical Thought*. Cambridge, MA: Harvard University Press.

———. 2013. "Forms of Nature: 'First', 'Second', 'Living', 'Rational' and 'Phronetic'." In *Freiheit: Stuttgarter Hegel-Kongress 2011*, edited by Gunnar Hindrichs and Axel Honneth, 701–735. Frankfurt am Main: Vittorio Klostermann.

Turner, Christopher. 2014. "The Return of Stolen Praxis: Counter-Finality in Sartre's *Critique of Dialectical Reason*." *Sartre Studies International* 20 (1):36–44.

Wahnich, Sophie. 2017. *La Révolution française n'est pas un mythe*. Paris: Klincksieck.

Williams, Bernard. 2005. *In the Beginning Was the Deed: Realism and Moralism in Political Argument*. Princeton: Princeton University Press.

Williams, Bernard, and Geoffrey Hawthorn. 2005. *In the Beginning Was the Deed: Realism and Moralism in Political Argument*. Princeton: Princeton University Press.

Withy, Katherine. 2015. "Owned Emotions: Affective Excellence in Heidegger on Aristotle." In *Heidegger, Authenticity, and the Self: Themes from Division Two of "Being and Time,"* edited by Denis McManus, 21–36. London and New York: Routledge.

Wittgenstein, Ludwig. 1953. *Philosophical Investigations*. New York: Macmillan.

———. 1963. *Tractatus logico-philosophicus: The German Text of Logisch-philosophische Abhandlung*. London: Routledge & Kegan Paul.

———. 2016. *Wittgenstein: Lectures, Cambridge, 1930–1933; From the Notes of G. E. Moore.* Cambridge: Cambridge University Press.

Young, Iris Marion. 1990. *Justice and the Politics of Difference.* Princeton: Princeton University Press.

———. 1994. "Gender as Seriality: Thinking about Women as a Social Collective." *Signs: Journal of Women in Culture and Society* 19 (3):713–738.

Index